THE REMINISCENCES OF
Vice Admiral Bernhard H. Bieri
U.S. Navy (Retired)

INTERVIEWED BY
John T. Mason, Jr.

U.S. Naval Institute • Annapolis, Maryland

Copyright © 1970/1997

Preface--1970

This manuscript is the result of a series of tape-recorded interviews with Vice Admiral Bernhard H. Bieri, U. S. Navy, Retired, in Bethesda, Maryland during 1969 and 1970. These interviews were conducted by John T. Mason, Jr. for the Oral History Office in the U. S. Naval Institute.

Only minor emendations and corrections have been made. The reader is asked therefore to bear in mind that he is reading a transcript of the spoken, rather than the written, word.

Preface--1997

The oral history transcript of Vice Admiral Bieri was among the first to be published by the Naval Institute. As a result, some of the refinements that have later become standard parts of the format were not yet incorporated. This revised transcript has been annotated with footnotes to provide additional information, and the volume has been indexed in the comprehensive format now standard for Naval Institute oral history. In addition to the corrections made originally by Admiral Bieri, some slight editing has been done in the interest of clarity and smoothness. The original version of the transcript is still on file at the Naval Institute.

Paul Stillwell

VICE ADMIRAL BERNHARD HENRY BIERI
UNITED STATES NAVY (RETIRED)

Bernhard Henry Bieri, born in Walnut Lake, Faribault County, Minnesota, attended high school in Wells, Minnesota, before his appointment to the U.S. Naval Academy from his native state in 1907. Graduated in June 1911, he served at sea as then required by law before he was commissioned ensign in March 1912. He subsequently progressed in grade until his promotion to vice admiral, 11 December 1945.

After graduation in 1911, Bieri served in the battleship Delaware (BB-28), the gunboat Nashville (PG-7), and the armored cruiser Montana (ACR-13) until September 1913, when he joined the battleship Virginia (BB-13), in which he served during the occupation of Vera Cruz, Mexico, in April 1914. Detached from the Virginia in April 1916, he joined the battleship Texas (BB-35), serving in that ship while she later operated with the British Grand Fleet during World War I and until June 1919. Assigned duty as aide on the staff of the Commandant, Fifth Naval District, Norfolk, Virginia, he served until January 1922 under Rear Admiral Augustus F. Fechteler, USN, and Rear Admiral Hugh Rodman, USN. In July 1921 he was assigned additional duty as personal aide to Admiral Rodman, who was a member of the Commission to the Centennial of Peruvian Independence in Lima.

Bieri commanded the destroyer Bailey (DD-269) from January to June 1922, when he was transferred to command of the destroyer Corry (DD-334), serving in that command until March 1925. From May of that year until December 1927 he had duty in the Communication Office, Office of the Chief of Naval Operations, Navy Department, Washington, D.C. Returning to sea, he served as navigator of the battleship Utah (BB-31) from December 1927 until August 1928, when he rejoined the Texas, serving as navigator of that battleship until April 1931. He then had duty as head of the Detail Section, Enlisted Personnel Division, Bureau of Navigation, Navy Department, Washington, D.C., until July 1933. In August of that year he joined the destroyer tender Altair (AD-11), serving as her executive officer until June 1935.

After completing the senior course at the Naval War College, Newport, Rhode Island, in May 1936, Bieri served on the staff of that institution until January 1938. Reporting for duty as operations officer on the staff of Vice Admiral John W. Greenslade, USN, Commander Battleships, Battle Force, USS West Virginia (BB-48), flagship, he served in that assignment until June 1939, when he was transferred to like duty on the staff of Admiral James O. Richardson, USN, Commander Battle Force, U.S. Fleet, of which the battleship California (BB-44) was flagship. He continued that duty on Admiral Richardson's staff when the latter in January 1940 hoisted his flag in the USS Pennsylvania (BB-38) as Commander in Chief U.S. Fleet. In February he had duty on the staff of Richardson's relief, Admiral Husband E. Kimmel, USN, Commander in Chief Pacific Fleet.

Bieri commanded the heavy cruiser Chicago (CA-29) from 1 March 1941 until 17 January 1942. That cruiser, under his command when the Japanese struck Pearl Harbor on

7 December 1941, was en route to Midway with a task force built around the aircraft carrier Lexington (CV-2). Upon receipt of the news of the attack, that force began a high-speed offensive sweep to the southeastward on the Oahu-Johnston-Palmyra triangle in an effort to intercept the enemy.

Following detachment from command of the Chicago in January 1942, he reported the following month for duty on the staff of the Commander in Chief, U.S. Fleet, and in August of that year was transferred to duty as deputy chief of staff to the Commander in Chief Atlantic Fleet, in which capacity he served with Allied Force Headquarters during the preparation for, and the invasion of North Africa. In January 1943 he was assigned duty on the staff of the Commander in Chief, U.S. Fleet, and in October of that year became assistant chief of staff (plans) to the Commander in Chief, U.S. Fleet. In May 1944 he was assigned duty with the U.S. Naval Forces in Europe for duty at the Supreme Headquarters, Allied Expeditionary Forces, prior to and during the invasion of Normandy.

After his return to the United States, Bieri reported in September 1944 for duty as deputy chief of staff to the Commander in Chief, U.S. Fleet, and on 10 October 1945 was designated Deputy Chief of Naval Operations (Administration and Service). On 1 March 1946 he assumed duty as Commander Tenth Fleet, Atlantic Fleet. Upon dissolution of this fleet in June 1946, he became Commander U.S. Naval Forces in the Mediterranean, a position he held until February 1948. In May 1948 he became Commandant of the 11th Naval District, with headquarters at San Diego, California, and from February 1949 to May 1951 was senior naval member of the Military and Naval Staff Committee of the Security Council of the United Nations in New York.

Bieri retired from active naval service in May 1951 and subsequently served as a consultant to the Central Intelligence Agency. He died at the National Naval Medical Center, Bethesda, Maryland, on 10 April 1971. His awards included the following: Legion of Merit; Mexican Service Medal; the World War I Victory Medal, Grand Fleet Clasp; American Defense Service Medal, Fleet Clasp; Asiatic-Pacific Area Campaign Medal; European-African-Middle Eastern Area Campaign Medal; American Area Campaign Medal; and the World War II Victory Medal. For services to the Allied cause he was made an Honorary Commander of the Order of the British Empire by the British Government. In 1946 he was decorated by the Greek Government with the Grand Order of the Phoenix with Crossed Swords.

Bieri married Miss Elsie Gunther of Camden, New Jersey, at Camden in June 1913. Their five sons served in the armed forces during World War II: Bernhard H. Bieri, Jr.; John B. Bieri, Robert Bieri, James Bieri, and David Bieri. The oldest son, Bernhard, Jr., graduated from the naval Academy in the class of 1937 and eventually retired as rear admiral in 1970.

CHRONOLOGY COMPILED BY ADMIRAL BIERI

January 1906--Received an appointment to the U.S. Naval Academy as principal from the Honorable J. T. McCleary, member of Congress from the Second Congressional District of Minnesota.

June 1906--Went to Annapolis and took the entrance examinations, failed, and returned home.

June 17, 1907--Admitted to the Naval Academy as midshipman, having been reappointed by Mr. McCleary. Took the examinations this time under the aegis of the Civil Service in Mankato, Minnesota.

June 2, 1911--Graduated from Naval Academy as passed midshipman and proceeded to home, now in Knapp, Wisconsin, to await orders.

July 10, 1911--Reported for duty on the USS Delaware at Boston, Massachusetts.

April 11, 1912--Promoted to the rank of ensign by act of Congress.

October 12, 1912--Detached from Delaware to duty on the USS Nashville in New York.

June 1913--Detached Nashville to temporary duty on the Montana.

September 16, 1913--Reported to USS Virginia for duty.

March 7, 1915--Promoted to rank of lieutenant (junior grade)

April 20, 1916--Detached Virginia to Texas for duty.

July 1, 1917--Given temporary appointment as lieutenant.

August 1917--14-inch turret which I commanded won Navy E for highest score in class in short-range target practice.

September 1917--Given letter of commendation by SecNav as being one of three officers who contributed most to the excellence in gunnery of the ship which stood number one in the fleet.

July 1, 1918--Temporary promotion to lieutenant commander. At the time ship was with the British Grand Fleet in the North Sea. Serving as fire control officer.

January 6, 1919--Assumed duties of first lieutenant of the USS Texas.

June 19, 1919--Reported as aide to Rear Admiral Augustus Fechteler, Commandant Fifth Naval District, Norfolk, Virginia. Detached Texas.

July 7, 1921--Accompanied Rear Admiral Hugh Rodman, Commandant, to Lima, Peru, where he was U.S. naval representative at the Centennial of Peruvian Independence. Returned Norfolk at end of three weeks.

January 4, 1922--Detached Fifth Naval District.

January 5-28, 1922--En route on USS Argonne to duty in Destroyer Squadrons Pacific.

January 28, 1922--Assumed command of Destroyer Division 19 and USS Bailey. Later decommissioned same.

June 26, 1922--Assumed command of the USS Corry, destroyer.

1922--Received permanent appointment as lieutenant commander.

April 1923--Completed first sonic survey of West Coast with USS Hull.

July 1923--USS Corry won trophy for excellence in engineering.

March 1924--In company USS Corry and Hull made survey for the new Alaskan cable from Seattle to Seward. During this period participated in rescuing downed Army aviator who was on round-the-world trip.

March 20, 1925--Detached Corry.

May 1, 1925--Reported for duty as communication officer, Navy Department.

January 1926--Completed war college correspondence course.

December 27, 1927--Detached Navy Department, reported USS Utah as navigating officer.

August 6, 1928--Detached Utah and reported Texas, fleet flag, as navigating officer.

April 16, 1931--Reported Navy Department for duty in the Bureau of Navigation as enlisted detail officer.

June 4, 1931--Promoted to commander.

July 28, 1933--Detached Navy Department to USS Altair as executive, reporting August 31.

June 29, 1935--Reported to U.S. Naval War College, Newport, Rhode Island.

January 28, 1938--Reported as battleships operations officer, San Pedro, USS Maryland.

June 23, 1938--Promoted to captain.

June 24, 1939--Reported as operations officer to Commander Battle Force on California.

February 1, 1941--Special duty with new Commander in Chief Pacific Fleet.

March 2, 1941--Assumed command of the USS Chicago.

January 17, 1942--Ordered to duty CNO; reported Washington February 19, staff of Commander in Chief U.S. Fleet.

August 1, 1942--Ordered as deputy chief of staff, U.S. Atlantic Fleet.

August 9, 1942--Arrived London for this duty and remained with Allied headquarters until December 26 when invasion operations in North Africa completed.

December 26, 1942--Ordered to duty as plans officer, U.S. Fleet, Washington.

October 4, 1943--To duty as Assistant Chief of Staff, U.S. Fleet.

November 4, 1943--Attended Cairo Conference--USS Iowa

November 6, 1943--Promoted upper half, rear admirals.

January 27, 1944--St. Paul, Minnesota, to present Navy Department award to Brown and Bigelow.

May 12, 1944--To Allied Headquarters London as representative of the CinC.

August 28, 1944--Detached, returned to duty as Assistant Chief of Staff, U.S. Fleet.

June 4, 1945--Addressed Naval War College class, Newport, graduation exercises, vice CinC.

July 23, 1945--Served on selection board for flag officers.

October 10, 1945--Reported as Deputy Chief of Naval Operations (Administration and Service).

December 11, 1945--Appointed temporary vice admiral.

January 1946--Received from British Government decoration as Honorary Commander of the Military Division of the Most Excellent Order of the British Empire.

March 1, 1946--Reported to duty as Commander Tenth Fleet.

March 19, 1946--Hoisted flag on USS Fargo, Philadelphia Naval Shipyard. Sailed to Bermuda and South America.

March 1946--Received Legion of Merit for wartime services.

June 16, 1946--Detached command of Tenth Fleet to go with Fargo to report to Admiral H. Kent Hewitt, Commander 12th Fleet, for relief of Rear Admiral Jules James as Commander Naval Forces Mediterranean. Assumed command on arrival Naples.

June 30, 1947--Received from French Government French Legion of Honor Rank of Officer.

September 11, 1947--Appointed permanent rear admiral.

February 7, 1948--Relieved of command of U.S. Naval Forces Mediterranean by Vice Admiral Forrest Sherman. Returned to United States as passenger with wife on USS Sperry.

April 6, 1948--Reverted to the rank of rear admiral.

May 12, 1948--Assumed command of the 11th Naval District, San Diego, California.

January 18, 1949--Detached 11th Naval District, reported to the Chief of Naval Operations.

February 23, 1948--Designated Senior Naval Member of the Military and Naval Staff Committee of the Security Council of the United Nations in New York, with rank of vice admiral.

June 21, 1950--Served as president of a selection board for flag officers.

May 22, 1951--Detached United Nations duty and reported to the Chief of Naval Operations for duty prior to retirement.

May 31, 1951--Transferred to the retired list of the U.S. Navy as a vice admiral.

DECLARATION OF TRUST

The undersigned does hereby appoint and designate as his (her) Trustee herein, the Secretary-Treasurer and Publisher of the United States Naval Institute to perform and discharge the following duties, powers, and privileges in connection with the possession and use of a certain taped interview between the undersigned and the Oral History Department of the United States Naval Institute.

1. Classification of Transcript.

   (✓)a. If classified OPEN, the transcript(s) may be read or the recording(s) audited by the qualified personnel upon presentation of proper credentials, as determined by the Secretary-Treasurer of the U. S. Naval Institute.

   ( )b. If classified PERMISSION REQUIRED TO CITE OR QUOTE, the user will be required to obtain permission in writing from the interviewee prior to quoting or citing from either the transcript(s) or the recording(s).

   ( )c. If classified PERMISSION REQUIRED, permission must be obtained in writing from the interviewee before the transcribed interview(s) can be examined or the tape recording(s) audited.

   ( )d. If classified CLOSED, the transcribed interview(s) and the tape recording(s) will be sealed until a time specified by the interviewee. This may be until the death of the interviewee or for any specified number of years.

2. It is expressly understood that in giving this authorization, I am in no way precluded from placing such restrictions as I may desire upon use of the interview at any time during my lifetime, nor does this authorization in any way affect my rights to the copyright of my literary expressions that may be contained in the interview.

Witness my hand and seal this 18th day of August 1970.

B. H. Bieri

I hereby accept and consent to the foregoing Declaration of Trust and the powers therein conferred upon me as Trustee:

R. E. Bowker J

Vice Admiral Bieri also gave permission for a copy of his memoir to be filed with the Naval History Office.

Bernhard H. Bieri #1 - 1

Interview Number 1 with Vice Admiral Bernhard H. Bieri, U.S. Navy (Retired)

Place: Bethesda, Maryland

Date: Thursday, 17 July 1969

Interviewer: John T. Mason, Jr.

Q: Admiral, it's certainly good of you to consent to do this series in the nature of a biography of your very illustrious career. We'd like to begin by having you tell me something about your family background, something about your early education, maybe a little about your parents.

Admiral Bieri: I was born in southern Minnesota in a township called Walnut Lake. I was born June 24, 1889. I was the fifth child in what eventually was a family of nine. At that time my father was a farmer. We lived on farms a good deal of the time.

Q: What was that, grain farming?

Admiral Bieri: It was varied farming. We'd grow grain, raise cattle, produce milk, poultry, and all that sort of thing. That sort of farming continued in that area right up to about the end of the First World War. Now it's single-crop country: corn and beans.

My childhood was spent mostly in a small town, to which my parents moved when I was about six years old, the town of Wells in Minnesota. I went through the grade school and high school there. We had very good schools in those days. When I finished, I was able to pass the examination for entrance to the Naval Academy, from high school.

Q: Was this a long-standing ambition?

Admiral Bieri: As a boy going to high school, I had given occasional thought to studying law or something like that. About the third year in high school, the superintendent of schools was informed by the congressman of the district that he'd like to have a boy from that area go to the Naval Academy. He had never appointed anybody from that area. It was decided that I was about the only one in the bunch that could pass the examination.

Q: You were a bright boy.

Admiral Bieri: It was offered to me, and my father and I talked it over. Neither of us knew much about the Navy, but we realized that there was a great promise in going to such a school and preparing for a career in the service. So I accepted.

I tried the examination during my third year in school and didn't quite make it. So I came back the next year and tried it again, and I was prepared for it. That was my schooling; we had fairly good schools. We had the usual curriculum that they had in high school at that time--mathematics; we studied Latin and one of the other languages; and history. Then we had electives such as woodwork and whatnot.

I was rather a small fellow, but due to the lack of material in high school, they had to use everybody for athletic teams.

Q: What did you go out for?

Admiral Bieri: I played football. That was the old days of bucking-the-line football, pushing and that sort of stuff. About the only thing I was good for was quarterback, so I played quarterback. I graduated from high school when I was not quite 18 and went immediately to the Naval Academy.

Q: How did your mother feel about this development?

Admiral Bieri: She was very philosophical about it. I had an older sister who had just graduated from Carleton College. I had an older brother who was at that time studying engineering in the University of Minnesota. Another sister, older than myself, was going to the normal school at Mankato, Minnesota.* So this put quite a financial strain on the family, and having another to go off to college would have been quite a burden.

Q: But they obviously believed in higher education.

Admiral Bieri: Yes. As to my parents, they were both born in Switzerland. My father migrated to America in 1880. My mother came the next year, and they were married. In Switzerland my father was the oldest of a large family. In those days in Switzerland--and I think to a certain extent now--they practiced ultimogeniture instead of primogeniture as far as property is concerned. Eventually, the youngest member of the family took over the family business, and the older children went out in the world for themselves.

Q: That's a curious law, isn't it?

Admiral Bieri: It was brought about by the fact that they married comparatively young and had their families young. The fathers were never ready to give up their businesses when their oldest children matured.

My father went to the secondary schools in the village of Brienz, down in the Bernese Oberland. From there he studied at the University of Berne and at the University of Freiburg. He was qualified at the end of that to teach in the secondary schools. He was qualified to teach mathematics, French, German, fencing, and gymnastics. Apparently he wasn't too keen about the teaching field at that time, so he packed up and came to America. My mother's education was limited to the secondary schools that were available at that time in the smaller villages.

My father first went to Wisconsin, where he joined the gathering of other Swiss that came over ahead of him. He was a lumberjack. For a couple of years he ran lumber rafts from Wisconsin down the St. Croix and Mississippi rivers to St. Louis. That sort of a life

---

*A normal school was a preparatory college for elementary school teachers; it was usually two years in duration.

didn't appeal to him either. It was pretty rough on my mother. At the end of about three years they had two children.

So he picked up stakes and moved to southern Minnesota, where he rented a farm. After three or four years there, he bought a farm of his own. Until the oldest children had outgrown the small country school which they had there, we lived at this place. Then we moved up to Wells, Minnesota, where we acquired another farm.

Q: He must have been quite a manager.

Admiral Bieri: He must have been, looking back on it. Both of them must have been good managers.

From his background, he was always very much interested in having his children educated. He took a great interest in civil affairs and particularly school affairs. All during my time at home, he was either secretary or president of the local school board. He was instrumental in improving the schools, getting good teachers, and that sort of thing. He was instrumental in getting the people to build a new schoolhouse in this town. This always amazed me, because it was a 12-room brick building, well built and well equipped. It had everything from kindergarten through high school, including manual training and the domestic science training for the women. He was also instrumental in getting them to build a gymnasium, which was rather unheard of in those parts.

Q: That was the German-Swiss background, wasn't it?

Admiral Bieri: The teachers which they got were pretty well picked. I had very high regard for all the teachers that I had when I went to school and high school.

That about brings you up on the family.

Q: That's a very interesting background, with a heavy emphasis on education.

Admiral Bieri: I went to the Naval Academy in the middle of June 1907.

Q: Did you go to any one of the prep schools in advance?

Admiral Bieri: No, I went directly from high school. I passed my examinations and went directly from there. I did my own studying for the examinations, in addition to doing my work in high school the last two years I was there.

Q: You must have been a very able student.

Admiral Bieri: I was a hard-working student. I must say that our parents taking an interest in our education--and with the background my father had--we were always able to get help when we needed it. I did stand number one in my class when I graduated from high school. It wasn't a very big class, I guess; I can't remember.

Going to the Naval Academy, of course, was quite a strange experience for a small-town country boy.

Q: Did your father come out with you?

Admiral Bieri: No, I came by myself.

Q: And you probably hadn't been very far from home up to that point, had you?

Admiral Bieri: No, until I started Annapolis I don't think that I'd ever been more than 45 miles from home. Mankato, Minnesota, was the nearest fairly large city. Of course, in those days all distant travel was done by train. No one had cars; the roads weren't ready for automobiles. Very few people ever got more than a few miles from home, outside their own county or maybe the next one or two. Occasionally we'd have some boy who went and spent four years in the Army or four years in the Navy. They were world travelers.

When I went to the Naval Academy, I was a dry-land sailor. I didn't know how to swim. We never had any swimming facilities.

Q: In a state with 10,000 lakes?

Admiral Bieri: Yes, but not in our part. We lived on the prairie.

I was taken in hand down there and taught a certain amount of swimming in the old swimming pool at Fort Severn by Matthew Strom, a fellow who was rather famous at the time with a bunch of naval officers and midshipmen.[*] He was the head of the gymnastics teachers, and he was about as wide as he was high. He taught us swimming by standing on the edge of this small tank which was not over 35 or 40 feet square, built up in the middle of this old fort to a depth of maybe six feet. He'd put a belt on us and throw us in the water and teach us the breast stroke. And that's about all we learned in order to swim.

Although going to the Naval Academy and being subjected to the routine and regulations there was a strange experience, it didn't bother me too much because I was used to living in a large family. We all had work to do. We worked hard on the farm, and we worked hard in school. Studying at fixed hours didn't bother me at all. I got along quite well at the Naval Academy with studies and all the people I knew.

The fact that I had a little "velvet up my sleeve," I was able to help some of the less fortunate ones who weren't able to learn quite as fast. I made a great many friends amongst my own class that way.

Q: There's an advantage in having an intellect.

Admiral Bieri: Eventually I graduated in the usual time--four years. I stood pretty well up in the class. I think we graduated pretty close to 200, and I was about 25.[†]

Q: Excellent record.

---

[*] The Naval Academy was built on the site of old Fort Severn, formerly an Army post.
[†] The Naval Academy class of 1911 had 193 graduates; Bieri stood number 26.

Admiral Bieri: I had no trouble with the mathematics and languages that they taught at that time. As a matter of fact, I never worried about my subjects.

The midshipman cruises were very interesting experiences to me. In the first place, when we entered the Naval Academy we were still having drills on the old sailing ships--square riggers. About two weeks after I entered, we were put on board the old Severn, as it was known then. It used to be called the Chesapeake.* It was later stripped down and used as a submarine tender, which they towed around from port to port.

We were put on this Severn, and we went down the Chesapeake Bay on a cruise. The extent of our cruise was down to Solomons Island and around the bay, and then we came back.

We had only sail, of course. The captain was one of the lieutenant commanders at the Naval Academy who was apparently a very good sailor. He had a small crew of enlisted men and a group of about six or eight second classmen who stood officer of the deck watch. He had one or two lieutenants, executive officer, and sailing master. Then he had about 15 or 20 youngsters, who were there to see that the plebes were properly indoctrinated.† The rest of the work on the ship was done by the plebes.

The ship, of course, was a pretty crude sort of a ship compared to the ships nowadays. We had no adequate ice machines or cold water. We drank warm water and slept in hammocks. We made sail and did all the work around the ship.

My first station aloft was on the end of the main yard--main yard man. I was out on the very end of this yard, about 40 feet above the water, and I couldn't swim a stroke. It was a pretty frightening place to be for a fellow my size. The man that was next to me was a classmate of mine named Shorty Merring; he just recently passed away.‡ He was a big

---

* The Chesapeake was first commissioned in 1900; she was a three-masted, sheathed, wooden bark. She was renamed Severn in June 1905 and refitted as a submarine tender in 1910. After being in and out of commission several times, she was decommissioned for the final time in 1916.
† A midshipman in his first year is a plebe; second year, youngster; third year, second classman; fourth year, first classman.
‡ Midshipman Harry L. Merring, USN, stood number 15 among the graduates in the class. He eventually retired as a rear admiral and died in December 1965.

fellow--a little over six feet tall, I guess. He was a football player and crew man at the Naval Academy. When he stepped on the foot rope, he almost catapulted me over the top of the yardarm. Then when he reached around to get a bit of the sail to help furl it, he'd take his weight off the foot rope. I'd be hanging by my fingers, trying to find the foot rope with my feet. After about a week they took me off that detail, and they put me up on the topgallant yard.

Q: It must have been an incentive to hurry up and learn to swim.

Admiral Bieri: Yes, I did that as soon as I got back to the Naval Academy. That was a little less strenuous. I must say that I was never crazy about square-rigged sailing ships.

Our other cruises were made on rather antiquated ships. My youngster cruise, fortunately, was made on the Tonopah, a post-Spanish-American War monitor, which was in those days quite a modern ship.* The other two cruises were made on the Chicago, which was also an old ship, and the other on the old battleship Iowa.† All our cruises were coastal cruises in the United States, except the last one, in which they scraped together enough old battleships to put us all aboard, and they took us to Europe. That, of course, was quite an experience too.

Q: What year was that?

Admiral Bieri: That was 1910. We went to Plymouth, England, and were given several days to go to London. I think first we stopped at Gibraltar and stayed there for several days. Then we went to Marseilles. Then we came back by Funchal in Madeira. Then to the Azores and then home.

Q: Just like Columbus.

---

* Commissioned in 1903 as the Nevada, she was renamed Tonopah in 1909 to release the name for a new battleship.
† The protected cruiser Chicago was commissioned in 1889, the battleship Iowa in 1897.

Admiral Bieri: Yes. Then I graduated in June 1911.

Q: You had some illustrious classmates too.

Admiral Bieri: Yes, we went in the Naval Academy with something around 300 in the class.* With those we acquired from upper classes that were turned back, we finally graduated about 192. We had all kinds, but the majority of them turned out well. The weak ones dropped out early in their careers. We had quite a number of admirals in the class.

We were in the Navy at the time when you spent approximately seven years in each grade, from the time you graduated. In other words, you were an ensign and a junior lieutenant for seven years. Then you were a lieutenant for seven years, and you were lieutenant commander for seven years. Then you were a commander for seven years, if you were promoted. You got to be a captain at about 50 years of age. Maybe at 57, if you were lucky, you got to be an admiral.

Of course, it speeded up a little on account of the wars. My class didn't spend too long as lieutenants. We were given temporary appointments in the First World War as lieutenant commanders. I was a lieutenant commander from 1918 to '32--about 14 years. Then I became a commander. I was a captain when I was 49.

We had Bob Griffin; Roger Paine; O. M. Read; Harry Merring; Robert English; Harry Hill; myself; a civil engineer named Bruns; Oscar Badger; Edward Hanson; Daniel Callaghan and Norman Scott, who were killed down in the Southwest Pacific; and Frank

---

* The class started with 268, of whom 75 did not graduate.

Lowry.[*] We had two officers who resigned and went in the reserve who later became admirals. One was George Lowry, and the other was Paul Foster.[†]

Q: Paul Foster--I know him.[‡]

Admiral Bieri: Ralph Wood was an admiral.[§] John Reeves was an admiral; he was a naval aviator, as was George Murray.[**] Kingman was an admiral; he's dead now.[††] He was down near the bottom of the class. Calvin Cobb was an admiral; he's dead.[‡‡] Morton Deyo lives up in Portsmouth.[§§] Then we had a group of officers who were commodores. We also had several classmates who attained general rank in the other services: Lieutenant General Brereton, Air Force; Major General Jonathan Anderson and Brigadier General Vincent Meyer, USA.[***]

My class didn't get to the flag-rank position until the Second World War started. Only two or three of us had been selected at that time for promotion. The rest of them were captains. They thought that too many of them were too old to go to sea as captains. About the only ones that got to go to sea as captains were the ones that went in command of amphibious outfits, groups of amphibious ships. And they were subsequently made

---

[*] Vice Admiral Robert M. Griffin, USN (Ret.); Rear Admiral Roger W. Paine, USN (Ret.); Vice Admiral Oliver M. Read, USN (Ret.); Rear Admiral Harry L. Merring, USN (Ret.); Rear Admiral Robert H. English, USN, died in plane crash; Admiral Harry W. Hill, USN (Ret.); Rear Admiral Henry F. Bruns, USN (Ret.); Admiral Oscar C. Badger, USN (Ret.); Vice Admiral Edward W. Hanson, USN (Ret.); Rear Admiral Daniel J. Callaghan, USN, killed in action; Rear Admiral Norman Scott, USN, killed in action; Vice Admiral Frank J. Lowry, USN (Ret.).
[†] Rear Admiral George M. Lowry, USNR (Ret.); Vice Admiral Paul F. Foster, USNR (Ret.).
[‡] John Mason had done Foster's oral history for the Columbia University collection.
[§] Rear Admiral Ralph F. Wood, USN (Ret.).
[**] Admiral John W. Reeves, Jr., USN (Ret.); Admiral George D. Murray, USN (Ret.).
[††] Vice Admiral Howard F. Kingman, USN (Ret.).
[‡‡] Vice Admiral Calvin H. Cobb, USN (Ret.).
[§§] Vice Admiral Morton L. Deyo, USN (Ret.).
[***] Lieutenant General Lewis H. Brereton, USAF (Ret.).

commodores in those positions. So we had a half dozen or so commodores in the class. All were able officers.

We were at that age grade where we were considered a little bit too old, those of us that made the flag rank at that time, so the younger classes came up. We lost several people during the war. Callaghan and Scott were two of the best known ones. They were killed down in the fighting at Guadalcanal.[*]

How far are we now?

Q: You have graduated from the academy. Why don't we turn to your tours of duty on various ships after that?

Admiral Bieri: My first assignment to duty after I left the Naval Academy was to the USS Delaware.[†] She was one of the newer dreadnoughts--first of the dreadnoughts, as a matter of fact.[‡] I went to the Delaware as a passed midshipman. In those days you graduated as passed midshipmen. The following spring, in March, we were promoted by act of congress to ensign. I remained on the Delaware until October 1912.

Q: What kind of duty did you have on her?

Admiral Bieri: I had a very good experience on the Delaware. We had a very excellent captain, and we had a good bunch of senior officers, quite a number of whom later attained top commands in the Navy: Rear Admiral J. Hood, Admiral Claude Bloch, Admiral J. O.

---

[*] The two were killed by gunfire on the night of 12-13 November 1942 during the Naval Battle of Guadalcanal.
[†] The USS Delaware (BB-28) was commissioned 4 April 1910. She had a standard displacement of 20,380 tons, was 519 feet long, and 85 feet in the beam. Her top speed was 21 knots. Her main battery comprised ten 12-inch guns. She was decommissioned in 1923 and scrapped in 1924 to comply with the Washington disarmament treaty.
[‡] The USS Michigan (BB-27), commissioned in January 1910, was actually the first U.S. dreadnought-type battleship.

Richardson, Admiral Fitch, Admiral A. C. Read, Rear Admiral Braisted.* One of our officers was Lieutenant Gillmor, who had become an electrical officer and was installing the gyrocompass on board for Sperry Company.† He had a first class, E. M. Morgan, as assistant. Both left the service shortly. Gillmor became president of the Sperry Company, and Morgan the president of the board of directors.

In those days they varied the duties of a young officer. I started out as a junior turret officer. I was also, for a period, junior torpedo officer. I was also given a tour of duty as junior engineer. In addition to that, I was "makee-learn" spotter for the main battery.

Q: Tell me a little about that.

Admiral Bieri: I was a junior watch officer, stood watches on deck and in the engine room. All in all, it was a very good experience.

We had a captain who always had considerable influence on our life. His name was Captain John Hood. He was a fine gentleman from down south and a very able seaman. At that time he had already commanded one battleship; this was his second. I subsequently served under him when he commanded his third. He was a strict disciplinarian. And the executive officer was a strict disciplinarian. They believed in working their officers and crew, and we had a very good ship.

You asked about the "makee-learn" spotter. The Delaware was one of the first class of ships that carried out what they called long-range firing. We'd fire up to about 23,000 yards. The spotting control for this battery was done from the tops of the cage masts, which we had in our day. One of my stations in the firing was as an assistant to the senior

---

* Captain John Hood, USN, commanded the USS Delaware (BB-28) from 20 November 1911 to 24 October 1912. In 1912 the ranks of the future flag officers were as follows: Lieutenant Commander Claude C. Bloch, USN; Lieutenant James O. Richardson, USN; Lieutenant (j.g.) Aubrey W. Fitch, USN; Lieutenant (j.g.) Albert C. Read, USN; Ensign Frank A. Braisted, USN.
† One of the Delaware's officers in 1911 was Ensign Reginald E. Gillmor, USN. He resigned from the Navy 7 October 1912 as a lieutenant (junior grade).

officer who spotted the battery. Of course, we had different kinds of gadgets and machines and things to train on. Subsequently, when I went to my next ship, I became the main battery spotter on that ship.

The <u>Delaware</u> cruise was, as in those days, along the Atlantic sea shores. We spent our time on the East Coast and at Guantanamo Bay. Every January the ships went to Guantanamo Bay for three months. They carried out long-range firing exercises and high-speed engineering runs and drilled the landing forces on the shore. It was a place where the whole fleet assembled. They had most of their athletic competition down there in the wintertime. There were quite a lot of facilities for athletics and recreation, such as swimming, tennis, baseball, and hiking.

We had very little so-called shore liberty, because about the only exit was to Santiago, where they ran a tug about once a week for the few people that could go. In fact, there was no liberty outside the station for the enlisted men or most of the officers. Of course, we had a great deal of self-made entertainment: smokers, shows, and happy hours which the ships put on themselves for the neighboring ships. Time went quite well. People came out of the Guantanamo cruise usually in very good shape.

Then the ships would go north. After a small amount of leave in various ports along the East Coast, sometimes in our home ports, we would have some target practices on the southern drill grounds off the Virginia Capes. Then we'd cruise up around the New England coast the rest of the summer, usually by divisions. I got to know most of the New England ports very well.

In the fall and winter we'd go back to the Navy yard, usually for about a month. During the month of December everybody would get a couple of weeks' leave. Then we'd start over in Guantanamo.

Q: Those were relatively quiet days for the U.S. Navy, weren't they?

Admiral Bieri: Those were rather quiet days. The officers and men worked hard. It wasn't too easy a life at that time for the families, because in those days we didn't have what you'd really call a home port. We were assigned to a Navy yard as a home yard for repairs. Ours happened to be New York. Presumably each ship of the division of five or four would have three months' overhaul in the Navy yard some time during the year. That was about the only time that you could have your family with you and spend any amount of time together. The rest of the time, cruising around, they had to follow you around on the train and catch you whenever they could.

Q: That was rather difficult for the families, wasn't it?

Admiral Bieri: Yes, it was. Of course, we didn't have a family at the time I was on the Delaware. As a matter of fact, I wasn't married. Later on, when we did have a family--even with one or two children--it was quite a trick to move around from place to place by train and steamer.

In those days we were allowed no family allowances. Only on shore did you get compensation for quarters, light, and those sort of things--which wasn't very much. When we got an official change of orders or station, we'd get eight cents a mile for traveling expenses to pay our own railroad fare. There was no such thing as having your household effects moved by the government. If you had any, you had to move them yourself. All those things came after the First World War.

Life in the fleet at that time was very pleasant from several points of view. One thing was that after a few years in the Atlantic Fleet you got to know practically everybody in the Navy: every officer and a great many of the senior enlisted men and, of course, your own enlisted men. It was more of a family affair in those days than it is now.

One of the duties that a junior officer was always given in those days in the big ships was that of being what they called a "boat officer." Every time that a boat of any size left the ship with any number of men or officers aboard, it had to have an ensign on board as a boat officer. Duty standing in port was quite strenuous for the junior officers, who, in addition to standing their watches on deck, had to stand by to be boat officers.

Q: That was like a double taxation, wasn't it?

Admiral Bieri: Yes. Once a year the fleet would assemble in the North River for the so-called fleet reviews.* This was usually in October. They would anchor out the ships in two long lines in the North River, extending from up around 125th Street down to the Battery. We'd be there about a week. We'd have a parade on shore. The Secretary of the Navy or the President would come and ride up and down the line of ships to receive the review. The city officials and the people in the city were quite good in taking steps to entertain the officers and the men ashore.

At the time of the review in September 1912 I got orders, along with two other classmates, to be detached and go to the USS Nashville.†

Q: Was she a cruiser?

Admiral Bieri: She was a pre-Spanish-American War gunboat, 1,300 tons--a pretty small ship after being on a 20,000-ton dreadnought.

All of us were at that age when we were interested in young ladies, so we thought here was our chance to get a few days' leave between duties. When we approached the executive officer on this proposition, he said, "No, we can't spare you. We need you right up to the last day as boat officers." So we were never able to get out of New York. I was very anxious to get down to Philadelphia to see my present wife.

The last day of the review they put the three of us in a motor launch. They put our baggage in there with us. We went down from 98th Street to the Battery and transferred to this new ship of ours, the Nashville. As we came on board, the executive officer, a rather comical guy, said, "Who's the senior man?" Well, it so developed that I was the senior man. He handed me the officer of the deck's telescope and said, "You're it. I'll relieve you tonight about 7:00 o'clock so you can get dressed and go ashore with the captain to the official

---

* North River is the name for the lower end of the Hudson River, on the west side of New York City.
† The USS Nashville (PG-7) was commissioned 19 August 1897. She displaced 1,371 tons, was 234 feet long, and 38 feet in the beam. She was armed with eight 4-inch guns and several smaller guns.

dinner. The other two ensigns will also go." That night we went with the captain to the official dinner.

Q: This was for the Secretary or the President, was it?

Admiral Bieri: Yes. We got home about midnight or so. The next morning at daybreak we got under way and went to sea. This cruise on the Nashville was not very long. They were using those old ships at that time for gunboat patrol duty down in the Caribbean.

Q: Curb budding revolutionaries or something?

Admiral Bieri: Yes, looking out for American interests.

We first went to Norfolk, where we picked up a new captain and a new executive officer. Neither of them were in my book as very good officers. Then we went up to Yorktown and participated in the dedication of the Yorktown monument.[*]

We then sailed for the West Indies. We stayed down in the West Indies until the following June. We spent most of our time going into the small ports. We went into Puerto Barrios and Puerto Cortes.[†] We spent most of the rest of the time around Santo Domingo and Haiti. There was a three-sided revolution going on in Santo Domingo at that time. The usual number of revolutions or coups in Haiti--one every month or so.

In addition, the United States at that time was collecting the revenue duties for both countries in order to see that the debts to the European countries were discharged. The European countries had threatened to go in and collect them themselves. But in order to maintain our prestige and the Monroe Doctrine, we sent down there a group of officers in small ships to guard against smuggling, collect the revenues, and pay it off to the European countries.

---

[*] On 19 October 1781 Lord Cornwallis surrendered the British Army to George Washington after the colonists' siege against Yorktown, Virginia, effectively ending the Revolutionary War.
[†] These two ports are on the Gulf of Honduras.

Bernhard H. Bieri #1 - 17

Q: We, in effect, were the tax collectors.

Admiral Bieri: That's correct, yes. There was a gentleman named Mr. Edwards who was head of it for the State Department.

They had a bunch of small costa gardas, which were something like a patrol boat. They were manned by civilian crews, and they did anti-smuggling work and that sort of thing. Most of them were commanded by little tough Irishmen from up around Boston. You had to sort of keep an eye on those fellows.

We used to moor in the Ozama River; that's off Trujillo, which then was Santo Domingo City. We would tie up parallel to the river bank with lines out to the banana trees and bow and stern anchors in the stream on the other side. We'd stay there for a month or so and then cruise around the island.

At one time we were sent around the island to gather up the different revolutionary leaders to bring them to Santo Domingo for a conference to see if they could come to terms. There was a priest, Father Noble, at Santo Domingo City who was the head of the revolutionaries there and claimed to be the head of the federal government. There was a Spanish gentleman named Madero up at Samana Bay, a very fine old man. He had staked out his claim up there. At Puerto Plata, there was a great big Carib Indian named Bordas, and he had a force.[*] Over on the northwest corner there was a fellow named Desiderio Arias, who was at one time a garbage collector in Jamaica. He was an English colored man, and he had a force. These four were fighting this revolution.

We went around to pick them up to bring them down to this conference, but the colored man refused to come. We did pick up Bordas and Madero and took them back. But nothing ever came of the conference, and their efforts to stop the revolution availed nothing until we sent the Marines in there. The Marines finally went in there and stopped it. And they stayed there for quite a number of years.[†]

---

[*] Jose Bordas Valdes was elected provisional president on 14 April 1913.
[†] U.S. Marines sent in troops to Haiti in 1915 and the Dominican Republic in 1916. The last Marine units withdrew from the Dominican Republic in 1924 and Haiti in 1934.

These fellows were very interesting, the ones I came in contact with. This fellow Bordas was an Indian of very limited education; a fine physical specimen. He could speak a few words of English because he'd been a deckhand on a merchant ship that used to go into New York. The outstanding experience in his life was his visit to Coney Island.[*] He came aboard, and he had one aide. They were both heavily armed with sidearms and pistols, which they very willingly took off for safekeeping when they came aboard.

Then we went around to Samana Bay to pick up Mr. Madero. I was sent ashore in the little steam launch to pick him up and bring him back. We got in there shortly after noon. The port was about 45 miles up inside this beautiful big bay. The captain was a very uneasy person at sea; he was not a sailor or a ship handler. He was very anxious to get out of that bay and in the open sea before dark. I don't know what he was worried about. The bay was about 20 miles across at the entrance, and all the water was navigable as far as our ship was concerned.

The instructions for me were to go ashore and pick up Senor Madero and get him back to the ship as quickly as I could. I went over there and found that Mr. Madero was living in a big house up in the middle of the city, and he was having a staff meeting. He had a whole bunch of cohorts there discussing affairs. In my rather poor Spanish I made known my mission. He said, yes, he was ready to go, but he first had to do his business with his cabinet. Finally, along about 5:00 o'clock in the afternoon, he got his business finished, and we started off for the dock.

It was my understanding that they had all been instructed to bring only one aide with them. When we got ready to leave the house, they all came down to the dock. I thought, "That's all right. They're just coming down to see the old gentleman off." We walked down to the dock, about a half a mile, and got the old gentleman in the boat. About five or six others piled in. I expostulated about this, but it didn't have any effect. He said he had to take these people along, so we went out.

In the meantime, the captain was about ready to have a fit because he was held up so long. When he saw this army that I had brought out with me on the boat, he was just

---

[*] Coney Island is a beach and amusement park in Brooklyn.

about ready to be tied. I think he had every intention of relieving me from duty. Fortunately for me, during my absence he had found displeasure with the way one of my other classmates was performing his duty, so he'd put him "under the hatches." He couldn't very well put me there, too, as that would have left him only one watch officer, so I escaped.

We made a couple of nice trips on the Nashville to the New Orleans Mardi Gras and to Galveston. Then we came back to Portsmouth Navy Yard, where I was detached. I was ordered to temporary duty on the Montana, one of the armored cruisers which was about to leave and be put in reserve in Philadelphia. I had a couple of months at Portsmouth. It was during that time that I was able to get some leave and get married.

Q: This had been in the offing?

Admiral Bieri: It had been in the offing for a little over a year. I could never seem to be able to get quite enough leave to bring it off.

Q: Mrs. Bieri is a Philadelphia girl?

Admiral Bieri: Camden, New Jersey.

After the few months on the Montana, I was ordered to the battleship Virginia.* This cruise lasted from September 1913 through April 1916. The Virginia was part of the old Third Division of battleships. It was one of the class of battleships where they had two calibers of guns: two 12-inch turrets surrounded by an 8-inch turret on the centerline and an 8-inch turret on each corner. She was a well-built ship. We had a fine old captain

---

* USS Virginia (BB-13) was commissioned 7 May 1906. She had a standard displacement of 14,980 tons, was 441 feet long, and 76 feet in the beam. Her top speed was 19 knots. Her main battery comprised four 12-inch guns, and she also had eight 8-inch guns and 12 6-inch. She was decommissioned in 1920 and sunk in aerial bombing tests in 1923.

aboard, John McDonald, a bachelor who later became the admiral who commanded the Atlantic Fleet.[*] He was a very able seaman and a hard taskmaster, but a very fair man.

On that ship, my first duty was watch officer with command of the forward combination of turrets. Each of the centerline 12-inch turrets had an 8-inch turret as an integral part of it on top.

Q: Quite a battery, wasn't it?

Admiral Bieri: Yes, quite a battery. In addition to commanding the turret, I was made the chief range finder officer and the main battery spotter. So during a firing, my turret was handled by two junior officers, and I proceeded to the foretop and did the spotting for the battery. As range finder officer, it was my job to train the junior officers who manned the range finders. John McDonald decided that I was the only one who could take ranges for him when he was coming in and out of port, so that was another small assignment.

Q: And just as exacting too.

Admiral Bieri: He apparently had a great deal of confidence in my ability to get him ranges when he wanted them. So I had that job as long as he was on there. He stayed there several months. He was a very good officer and a very good captain.

Then we had a series of captains--very fine men. One of them was Volney O. Chase, who became ill and had to be detached. He was a splendid scholarly type and made a fine naval officer.

Then we got one of the poorest captains I ever sailed with, Captain John C. Leonard. He was an ex-engineer officer. He was one of those officers, who when he left the Naval Academy, went into the Engineering Corps. He never had any line duty until he

---

[*] Captain John D. McDonald, USN, commanded the Virginia from December 1911 to October 1913. He was first commanding officer of the battleship Arizona (BB-39) when she went into commission in 1916. As a rear admiral, he commanded the Scouting Fleet in the Atlantic in 1922-23.

got to be captain. Then they amalgamated the Engineering Corps and the line. They put all these old engineer captains in the line. They were at quite a disadvantage, never having handled ships and that sort of thing. And this chap was not a good captain. He was afraid to handle the ship, he was very nervous, and never seemed to have a grasp of the situation. Fortunately for us, he was up for selection which existed at that time; which was selection out and not up.

Q: Selection out?

Admiral Bieri: Yes, they selected out a number of captains each year. He was one of those selected out.

Whereupon, we got one of the finest captains I ever served with, Captain R. H. Jackson, who is now the oldest graduate of the Naval Academy. He was a splendid captain: a strict taskmaster, a most able ship handler, and had unlimited nerve. He always gave everybody their due. He had a very good ship. He's been a friend of mine ever since. I saw him about two years ago, when he was 101.*

Of course, at that age, and mine, too, you remember things that happened long ago much better than you do things that happened last week. We had a very pleasant visit of about an hour or so, about our old ship and shipmates, of which there are not too many now left. It was a very pleasant experience.

When I joined the Virginia, that was September 1913. The Presidential election was on, and the affairs in Mexico were in quite a turmoil. They sent our division down to the Mexican coast.

Q: In the Gulf?

---

* Richard H. Jackson graduated from the Naval Academy in 1887 and served until his retirement in 1930. He was advanced to the rank of four-star admiral on the retired list in 1942. He died in 1971 at the age of 105.

Admiral Bieri: In the Gulf. Two of us used to anchor off of Vera Cruz, and two of us would anchor off Tampico. We remained there from September 1913 until late March 1914. The ships would alternate between Vera Cruz and Tampico anchorages. We had the admiral aboard, Admiral Coffman.[*] We carried out some ship and division exercises off the port, but we were generally anchored in port. Supposedly keeping an eye on the situation ashore, which was going from bad to worse.

In February 1913, Huerta had Madero and Suarez shot and assumed the presidency.[†] That was still in the Taft administration. Henry Lane Wilson was still the ambassador, and he was backing Huerta. But when Wilson came in, in March, he refused to recognize Huerta.[‡] Things began to get a little tense. Carranza and the other revolutionaries had launched their Guadalupe plan, disavowing Huerta.[§] Wilson replaced Henry Lane Wilson, who was the ambassador down there, with a series of misfits, the former Governor of Minnesota, John Lind, being one.

We stayed there from September 1913 until early April 1914. The only thing that we did out of the ordinary was that on one or two occasions we acted as hotels for the American evacuees from Mexico. Refugees who were getting away from the revolution, until some other ship came along and took them up to the United States.

Q: Did you get ashore at Vera Cruz?

Admiral Bieri: At that time, no, we didn't go ashore to Vera Cruz. There were a couple of outlying islands in the reefs. One of them was Sacrificio, which lent itself to shore parties.

---

[*] Rear Admiral DeWitt Coffman, USN, Commander Third Division, Atlantic Fleet, December 1914 to May 1916.
[†] General Victoriana Huerta seized power in Mexico and had President Francisco Madero and Vice President Jose Pino Suarez arrested by his forces. On 23 February they were reportedly "shot while attempting to escape." Huerta became the new President.
[‡] On 4 March 1913, Woodrow Wilson was inaugurated as U.S. President, replacing William Howard Taft.
[§] Don Venustiano Carranza, governor of the state of Coahuila, became commander in chief of the Constitutionalist armies.

They would send parties of officers and enlisted men over there to run on the beach and have beer parties and that sort of thing. This was before the days of Prohibition.*

Q: Before Josephus Daniels's famous order.†

Admiral Bieri: That was about the time it was put in.

Also, at that time, one of the things that we undertook in the fleet was to educate the enlisted men. Most of the enlisted men weren't about to be educated. They came in the Navy to get away from book education. So the plan never worked out very well, in spite of everybody's effort to make it go. That finally fell through.

In the later part of March 1914, our division was finally relieved and sent north. My ship went to Boston Navy Yard; this was our home port. We got up there about the fifth of April. I hadn't seen my family, and the other people hadn't seen their families since October previously. There was a move afoot to give us all leave, and fortunately I drew the first leave party.

I went down to Camden, where my wife lived. We decided to go down to South Jersey and get away from civilization for a few days. I no more than landed down there, than I got recalled to the ship. The American Fleet had landed in Vera Cruz, and we were to proceed immediately to reinforce it.‡ So I went back on the Virginia, and back to Vera Cruz. We stayed there all during the occupation. The occupation was ended in November 1914. We stayed there until then.

Q: Did you get involved in any of the street fighting?

---

* The 18th Amendment to the Constitution was ratified in 1919 and went into effect in 1920, prohibiting the consumption of alcoholic beverages in the United States. The Volstead Act, enacted by Congress in 1919, spelled out the penalties for violations. In December 1933 the ratification of the 21st Amendment to the Constitution repealed the 18th Amendment and thus ended national prohibition.
† Josephus Daniels was Secretary of the Navy under Wilson from 1913 to 1921. On 1 July 1914 Daniels abolished the traditional officers' wine messes on board Navy ships.
‡ The landing occurred on 21 April 1914. For details see Jack Sweetman, The Landing at Veracruz: 1914 (Annapolis: U.S. Naval Institute, 1968).

Admiral Bieri: No, we didn't. We were away at that time. We were not there at the time of the Mayo boat incident.* We were en route to Boston when all this happened.

Q: That's where Paul Foster got involved.†

Admiral Bieri: Yes, Paul Foster. That was where they had the big hand-out of Medals of Honor.‡

As I said, we barely got into the Boston Navy Yard when they recalled us. Why I don't know, but they recalled us. We went tearing back down there, and we stayed again from April until November. Then we came back to the Navy yard, and had a little leave, and a month's overhaul by the yard. Then we left for Guantanamo in the early part of 1915. We had a full year of operations then with the fleet, the same routine we had before up and down the coast from Guantanamo. On the second trip to Guantanamo in 1916, we broke an engine shaft, and had to return to Boston in February or March in the middle of winter. They decided then to put the Virginia out of commission.§ All the officers and men were detached.

I was ordered to the Texas, which I joined in April 1916, at the New York Navy Yard.** I served in the Texas from that date until June 1919.

---

* Rear Admiral Henry T. Mayo, USN, commanded the Fourth Division of the Atlantic Fleet. He demanded an apology from the Mexican government on 9 April when a U.S. Navy boat party was seized and detained for half an hour when it inadvertently strayed into a Mexican military area.

† Ensign Paul F. Foster, USN.

‡ All told, 55 men received Medals of Honor for Veracruz, the most ever granted for a single engagement.

§ On 20 March 1916 the Virginia was placed in reserve but not out of commission. She was reactivated for World War I and eventually decommissioned 13 August 1920.

** USS Texas (BB-35) was commissioned 12 March 1914. She had a standard displacement of 27,000 tons, was 573 feet long, and 95 feet in the beam. Her top speed was 21 knots. Her main battery comprised ten 14-inch guns, and her secondary battery included 21 5-inch guns. She served in both World Wars and was eventually decommissioned in 1948.

Q: During the war period.

Admiral Bieri: During the First World War. The Texas was a brand-new ship, just having gone in commission, and had an excellent bunch of officers on board. I was very happy to again have John Hood as my captain.* I was given command of the number-one turret. That fall at the short-range firing, my turret made a perfect score in shooting. It was the highest score that had been made by a 14-inch gun up to that time.

We were at that time, I think, manning guns on merchant ships--or very shortly after that.† One of the jobs of these ships in the fleet was to train crews for these merchant ships. I was given the job on the Texas of supervising the training of the enlisted men who were going on as these crews, particularly in training them how to spot their gunfire.

Subsequently, I continued as a deck officer. That was in 1916, and that fall we went to Guantanamo with the fleet, but we didn't stay long. We came back up and went into York River.‡ They took the whole fleet into the York River, behind the submarine nets, in early 1917.

We spent the winter of 1917 in the York River and the Chesapeake Bay. I'm not sure whether we went to Guantanamo that fall or not. I'm inclined to think that we went directly to the Chesapeake Bay.

Q: Were the German submarines prowling in the Caribbean at that time, along the coast?

Admiral Bieri: Nobody knew. They were prowling in the Atlantic and sinking ships all over the Atlantic. So we had nets up, and they put us back of these barriers in the Chesapeake Bay, where we carried out our target practices. We spent the winter in the York River. The York River and the bay froze up very hard. We had some of the old battleships that were used as icebreakers; they broke up ice in the channels.

---

* Captain John Hood, USN, commanded the Texas from 10 June 1915 to 14 August 1916.
† Generally these were 5-inch guns mounted on the decks of merchant ships as protection against German submarines.
‡ Yorktown, Virginia, is at the mouth of the York River, which feeds into the Chesapeake Bay.

We stayed there all the next summer carrying out target practices, training men. It was in April 1917 that we declared war on Germany. There was no call for the battleships at that time. Our destroyers started to go to Europe. The fleet, towards the end of the summer, rendezvoused at Port Washington in Long Island Sound on the north shore of Long Island. Long Island Sound got closed off with mines and some nets around the harbor.

The Texas went to the New York Navy Yard for overhaul. We were in the New York Navy Yard in the fall, when it was decided to send a division of coal-burning battleships to Europe under Rear Admiral Hugh Rodman.* This was the New York, Texas, Arkansas, Wyoming, and Florida--five ships. They were coal burners, because there weren't sufficient oil supplies in Britain.†

We were at the New York Navy Yard, and we were to go around and join the other ships at Port Washington, and sail from there to Europe. We completed our overhaul, and we got a new captain, Captain Victor Blue.‡ We also got a new navigator, Commander Frank Martin.§ These two gentlemen had spent a long time on shore, and were not too confident of themselves. They didn't have too much trust in each other, apparently.

Q: That was a bad combination, wasn't it?

Admiral Bieri: We left the New York Navy Yard one day and started for Port Washington. I had the officer of the deck watch, beginning at 2000, at which time we were down about west of Fire Island. The ships were running darkened, of course. In those days, we didn't have any radar. We met a great big merchant ship, enormous fellow. I think when we

---

* Rear Admiral Hugh Rodman, USN, commanded Battleship Division Nine of the Atlantic Fleet, November 1917 to February 1919. As part of the British Grand Fleet, the five U.S. battleships were designated the Sixth Battle Squadron.
† Some of the newer American battleships, which burned oil, remained behind in the Chesapeake to train gun crews.
‡ Captain Victor Blue, USN, commanded the Texas from 14 August 1916 to 31 December 1918.
§ Lieutenant Commander Frank C. Martin, USN.

passed each other, we could have reached out and shaken hands with each other. I was very grateful we didn't have a collision.

At midnight, I was relieved by Lieutenant Fitzhugh Green.[*] He was quite a fellow. He was a Naval Academy man. He'd been up there on two trips to the Arctic. Fitzhugh Green relieved me, and some hours later--when the ship started around Block Island to make the turn into Long Island Sound--the captain and the navigator got confused about the lights on the beach. The captain was very much concerned about the mine field. He didn't want to run into the mine field. They made the turn at the wrong time, and instead of heading into the opening in the mine field, they ran nose on onto Block Island.

I was in my bunk at that time, which was right up in the forward part of the ship, next to the hawsepipe. The officers' quarters were forward. I heard this terrible grinding noise, and the first thing that occurred to me was that we had hit a ship.

Q: Having come so near earlier.

Admiral Bieri: Yes. I grabbed my bathrobe and slippers and jumped up on the deck. Here was Block Island, a great big yellow cliff, right up ahead of us. You could almost reach out and touch it. We had run aground with a full load of ammunition, a full load of coal, a full load of stores, and our spares--completely loaded. We went aground from the bow all the way aft beyond the cranes, which was well beyond midships.[†]

Q: Really did a good job of it.

Admiral Bieri: Fortunately, it was a calm period, and we turned to. We had to take out all the ammunition, all the coal, and all the stores. We laid out a couple of enormous kedge anchors from the stern to hold her in position and from going up on the beach.

The naval constructors came up from the New York Navy Yard and installed air compressors to blow the water out of the wing tanks, which had taken water from the

---

[*] Lieutenant (junior grade) Fitzhugh Green, USN.
[†] This grounding occurred on 27 September 1917.

double bottoms. Fortunately, the inner skin of the ship was not pierced any place. They rigged these air compressors, and eventually they blew the water out. By draining the water, and the hauling on the huge cables which we had astern, the ship slid off after about a week of hard work unloading night and day.*

We were taken back to the New York Navy Yard, while our friends in the rest of the division proceeded to Europe. We went back to the Navy yard to have the damage repaired.

Q: What happened to Captain Blue?

Admiral Bieri: He remained. Captain Blue was a protege of Josephus Daniels. I don't think he was ever court-martialed; in fact, I know he wasn't. They had a court of inquiry. They court-martialed Martin, the navigator, and he was detached, but Blue remained. The ship was finally repaired about the end of January 1918, and then we proceeded on our own to join the Grand Fleet in Europe.

Q: I think that the crew under those circumstances wouldn't have had great confidence in their captain any longer.

Admiral Bieri: There was some question there. I think it was a very poor move myself. As I say, he was a protege of Josephus Daniels, and eventually he was made a rear admiral.

Q: So you can run aground and get promoted to flag rank.

Admiral Bieri: I think after he left the Texas, he went back to the Navy Department. Daniels made him Chief of the Bureau of Navigation. That carried with it an automatic promotion.†

---

* The ship was refloated on 30 September.
† Blue had previously been Chief of the Bureau of Navigation from 1913 to 1916 and returned for another stint, 1918-19. He retired from active duty in July 1919.

My cruise on the <u>Texas</u> was a very satisfactory cruise, as far as I was concerned.

Q: Once you got out of the Brooklyn Navy Yard.

Admiral Bieri: I had a great deal of separation from my family. I always had responsible duties on board. I had the number-one turret and trained the crews for the merchant ships. I became the fire control officer of the ship. The next time I was on there, I was in charge of main battery fire control. I was also number-one main battery spotter.

The ship was a good ship. We won, not only the gunnery trophy; but we won the engineering trophy under Captain John Hood. We had a fine ship's company, very experienced.

We went to Europe in February of '18. We had a rather rough passage up in the rolling 40s. We had one escort out at that point--a destroyer; she was a converted yacht. She was going to France to join the destroyer force. Then we went on our own. We got in this storm, pretty heavy weather, and we had to slow down. We were still making too much speed for the weather, I think.

Q: How many knots was she capable of?

Admiral Bieri: She was capable of making 21 knots. We were steaming about 15 at that time. Harry Hill had joined the ship during the year.* I was relieving him as officer of the deck on this morning, at 4:00 o'clock. He had had the midwatch. I came up on the bridge, and Harry was very happy to see me. He said, "We've lost the two top masts. The boats on the port side are all stove in. We've lost one of the life boats. The gasoline cargo which we had on deck, lashed to the barbettes of the turrets, is adrift. The drums are rolling all around the deck, and the ship is full of gasoline fumes. The smoking lamp is out. The deck is yours."

---

* Lieutenant Harry W. Hill, USN, was a Naval Academy classmate of Bieri. Hill's oral history is in the Columbia University collection.

We finally got rid of the gasoline on the topside, got squared away, and ran out of the storm. We arrived off the northwest coast of Scotland, where we were picked up by some British destroyers as escorts into Scapa Flow.* We spent from February 1918 until early December 1918 as part of the Grand Fleet, in Admiral Rodman's division.

Q: What did that entail?

Admiral Bieri: We were part of the fleet. Whenever the fleet went to sea as a unit, we went as one of the battleship divisions. We were usually stationed next astern of the battle cruisers and British fast battleship division. The other British battleships were astern of us.

It entailed also, considerable convoy duty in the North Sea.

Q: Convoy duty with battleships?

Admiral Bieri: Yes. At that time, the U.S. Navy was laying a mine barrage across the North Sea from Scotland to Denmark. We had these minelayers out there, which were convoyed or protected against submarines by British destroyers that went with them; we didn't have any destroyers there. They were supported against attack by surface ships by the battleships. So that took up some of our time.

In addition to that, the British ran regular convoys from Aberdeen, Scotland, to Bergen, Norway. These convoys were merchant ships which brought back from Bergen, Norway, dairy products and food. I think we took coal over there, because the British didn't have anything else to export.

A little side issue, I think, was an attempt to get some of the German fleet to bite on the bait and come out and try to get the convoy.

Q: You were trying to draw out the German fleet for a battle, weren't you?

---

* Scapa Flow was a Royal Navy anchorage in the Orkney Islands, north of Scotland.

Admiral Bieri: Yes. For that reason, they always convoyed or escorted these ships very heavily. They would have a squadron of destroyers, a division of cruisers, and a division of battleships. The battleships usually stayed in the offing, well clear of the convoy.

Q: That was pretty obvious bait, wasn't it?

Admiral Bieri: I think it must have been eventually. There wasn't any occasion that the Germans did come out, that I remember. Or even started out.

Whenever these convoys went out, the whole Grand Fleet would be at the ready, ready to go to sea. The apparent hope was that the Germans would come out where they could get rid of them, but they never got them out.

On one occasion, there was intelligence information that some of the Germans' battle cruisers, or heavy cruisers were about to break out into the Atlantic to attack shipping again. We spent one week up there guarding one of the passages through the Shetland Islands, up around the Faeroes. Nothing came of that.

The rest of the time we spent mostly, the first winter, in Scapa Flow, where the British had this immense anchorage. We carried out our target practices with the British ships inside the Scapa Flow. Of course, we engaged in all the intership social activities they had around there. It made life more or less bearable and interesting.

In the spring of 1918, the British moved the fleet down to the Firth of Forth. The rest of our time over there was spent using the Firth of Forth as an anchorage. We would come out and proceed to Scapa Flow for our target practices, usually by divisions. We made several sorties with the British fleet from Scapa Flow, on I suppose intelligence which the British had. We never encountered the Germans.

Q: I guess their fleet was of more value to them as a constant threat, than anything else, wasn't it?

Admiral Bieri: Yes. We were in the Firth of Forth when we got word that the armistice was signed.* We stayed and participated in the surrender of the German fleet, which was quite a sight. The Grand Fleet and cruiser forces went out and escorted the German High Seas Fleet in and took the surrender. They escorted them into Scapa Flow. The destroyers took the German destroyers, I think, into Harwich. The submarines were turned over on one of the east coast ports of England also.

When the German battleships had been anchored in Scapa Flow, the cruisers reduced to ship-keeping status; the British kept just a small force of ships up there. I don't recall the size of it, but I imagine it might have been a battleship or two, some cruisers, and a destroyer; just watching.

The rest of us came back to Firth of Forth. By Thanksgiving Day life had changed for everybody in the fleet. British sailors were getting ashore, officers were getting ashore, and some of the ships were being sent here and sent there.

We had orders to return to the United States, but to go to Plymouth and escort the George Washington that was bringing President Woodrow Wilson to Europe, into Brest.

We were still at the Firth of Forth on Thanksgiving Day. The British decided that every ship in the British fleet was going to celebrate Thanksgiving with us. So they had Thanksgiving parties on all the British ships. The officers and men of the American ships, except those needed to stand watch, were divided up into parties amongst all these different ships: battleships, cruisers, destroyers, and so forth. We all went over for Thanksgiving dinner, and it was quite a party.

Q: Day of feasting. What did they do? Did they provide entertainment as well as food?

Admiral Bieri: We had some entertainment, not much, but a little. A lot of food and drinks and chitchat and singing afterwards. I remember the ship I was on. We were due to sail, I think, the next day. They were to have boats over there for us at midnight. We were having a good time, and the British were having a good time; but we were very cognizant of

---

* The armistice ending the fighting in World War I took effect on 11 November 1918.

the fact that we should be getting in our boats. Every time we made a move to get into our boats, the British insisted that they were broken down. They were trying to get them to run, but they couldn't. Eventually, about 2:00 o'clock in the morning, they got them running and we went home.

Q: Had they provided you with turkey and that kind of thing?

Admiral Bieri: Oh, yes, I think they had everything. As I remember, mostly beef, but we had fowl of various sorts--a very good meal. A lot of speeches by different officers during the dinner. The captain of each ship would come down to the wardroom and join the party. The British are quite good at giving those sort of ship parties, with the singing of naval songs and individual instrumental talent.

Then we sailed for Plymouth.

Q: In very good shape the next day?

Admiral Bieri: Yes, we were in good enough shape, quite able to do it. We went out to escort the George Washington in and took her to Brest.[*] We left her, she went into port, and we came back and joined up with some other ships and started for New York.

We were due to be in New York well before Christmas. Everybody was looking forward to spending Christmas with their families, or visiting the United States. When we got about halfway across, we were informed that the U.S. Fleet would pass in review for the Secretary of the Navy sometime between Christmas and New Year and that we would parade in New York City.

---

[*] President Wilson went to France to take part in the negotiations leading to the Treaty of Versailles.

In order to kill the time, we eventually anchored off Ambrose Channel light ship to wait for the propitious moment to go in.* As I remember it, they didn't even send our mail out to us. They were a pretty mad bunch of people by that time, but they paraded and did their stuff. Then we went about our business. We went back to New York Navy Yard and finally met up again with our families.

After the war, we weren't in the yard very long. We almost immediately started the Guantanamo routine again. I was then made first lieutenant of the ship.

Q: At that point, things were complicated, weren't they, by all these people leaving the service?

Admiral Bieri: Oh, yes. We were in New York, and we paid off a great many people. The recruiting service was apparently unable to furnish men, so they authorized the ships to recruit locally themselves. We recruited some awful people, as you can imagine.

Q: Did you go down in the Bowery, or where?

Admiral Bieri: They got them off the street, and every place. I know we had a lot of misfits, people that an experienced recruiter would never have taken. But these recruiting parties that were sent ashore, impressment gangs, came off with these people.

Q: They were just looking for bodies.

Admiral Bieri: We were at sea with them, and it wasn't many months before we had to get rid of most of them.

I was made first lieutenant about that time. This was 1919. We made the Guantanamo cruise and did some target practice work off the Virginia Capes. Then we came back into Norfolk, and I was detached in June 1919 for my first shore duty.

---

* The ships arrived off Ambrose Light on Christmas day and entered New York on the 26th.

I went ashore at the Fifth Naval District, naval operating base at Norfolk as personal aide to Admiral Fechteler.*

Q: Is that the father of Admiral Bill Fechteler?†

Admiral Bieri: The father of Admiral Bill Fechteler.

Q: That was actually your first shore duty.

Admiral Bieri: That was my first shore duty, eight years after I left the Naval Academy. My wife and son, that we had then, joined me at the base, and we were assigned nice little government quarters. We stayed there until fall of 1920, I think. I went to the West Coast in '21.

Q: In July '21, you were assigned as personal aide to the commandant while he was a member of the official U.S. Commission to visit South America.

Admiral Bieri: Oh, yes, that's right. It was longer than that. I was aide to Admiral Fechteler, a very pleasant duty, I must say.

Q: What was he like as a person?

Admiral Bieri: He was a fine gentleman. He was born in Germany, and that's one of the reasons he didn't get a job during the war.‡ He was a grand gentleman, a fine seaman, a fine naval officer, but he was, at that time, approaching retirement age. He was quite active, and I used to walk with him quite a bit. Then he wanted to play tennis. I tried to dissuade him

---

* Rear Admiral Augustus F. Fechteler, USN, Commandant Norfolk Navy Yard and Commandant Fifth Naval District, 1918-1921.
† Admiral William M. Fechteler, USN, was Chief of Naval Operations from 1951 to 1953.
‡ During World War I Fechteler was Commander of the Sixth Division, Battleship Force, Atlantic Fleet, on the East Coast of the United States.

from playing tennis. I wasn't much of a tennis player, but I was still young. I tried to get the doctor to persuade him not to play tennis, but to play golf. No, he didn't want to play golf. So we used to go out every afternoon and bat the ball around the tennis court. It was pretty hot down there in Norfolk in the summertime. Following one of these exercise periods, in late summer, he had a stroke. He lasted for several months and then passed away.[*]

Admiral Hugh Rodman came as commandant.[†] They were two people who were as different as night and day. Fechteler was a very courtly, gentlemanly man. Uncle Hughie was a blustering, rough and ready seaman. I'd never served with him before. I'd served under him, of course, when he had command of the ships in the North Sea. He just came and joined me; he didn't bring an aide with him. So I was there, and he took me on as an aide.

I was talking to him one day, and he said, "When I came here, I wanted this fellow Jonas Ingram to be my aide." Of course, Jonas by that time was full commander.[‡] They told him he couldn't have Jonas Ingram. He said, "I don't care who you send me. Give me anybody you've got. So when I came here and found you, I just took you. You're all right."

Q: A great accolade, wasn't it?

Admiral Bieri: We got on fine with Admiral Rodman. In July of 1921, we went down to the Centennial of Independence at Peru.

President Harding sent down this mission.[§] It was composed of an ex-representative from Ohio named Douglas and an industrialist from New York. I've forgotten his name; he was treasurer of the Republican Party for a number of years. We had Admiral Rodman as

---

[*] Fechteler died 26 May 1921.
[†] Rear Admiral Rodman served as Commandant of the Fifth Naval District, June 1921 to January 1923.
[‡] Actually, at the time Jonas H. Ingram was a lieutenant commander. He later became a four-star admiral and served as Commander in Chief Atlantic Fleet in World War II.
[§] Warren G. Harding was President of the United States from 1921 to 1923.

naval representative, and Lieutenant General Hunter Liggett, USA, a very fine-looking Army officer, and his aide. We had the ex-ambassador to Mexico. And a Dr. Feraby, curator of the museum art the University of Pennsylvania, who was an authority on Inca civilization and archaeology. Most of the members of the mission had their wives with them, except Rodman didn't take his wife. And Feraby didn't have his wife with him.

I had some very interesting experiences with Dr. Feraby, who took me around to various private archaeological collections, and that sort of thing while we were there. We were in the city for about a week, I believe.

Q: Did you get up to Cuzco?

Admiral Bieri: No, I never got outside of the city. In connection with the centennial, there were official visits for the officials to make. And there were entertainments every day, beginning in the morning and usually lasting into the evening. Several evenings of the week they had opera. There were dinners, horse races, and all that sort of thing, to which I had to accompany the admiral. Still, there was some time left over. Dr. Feraby and I used to go around and see some of the interesting things.

Q: Private collections?

Admiral Bieri: Yes, private collections.

Q: And there were some excavations right outside Lima, somewhere, weren't there?

Admiral Bieri: We never went there; we never got that far out.

The missions were quartered in a suburb of Lima called La Flora. They were just paving the roads between this suburb and the city. At the time of our arrival, they had just changed their driving rules--from driving on the left side of the street to driving on the right side of the street. And there was a great deal of confusion in the automobile traffic, foot traffic, burro traffic, and whatnot in the city.

Q: It still is.

Admiral Bieri: I don't know whether they ever changed back or not.

We were assigned a car and a driver. This driver was a civilian Peruvian, and he had what probably was an old taxicab, a pretty good-sized one. But he never used his horn. He always used the cutout on the muffler.

Of course, the President had a big dinner. Do you remember the name of the President? President Leguia--a very famous Peruvian President, dictator there for many years.* His son was a young officer in the Peruvian Naval Aviation. He was about 25 years old, and he was the head of the aviation. He was detailed as aide-de-camp to Admiral Rodman. He drove a big Mercedes-Benz. He took care of the admiral and myself for official functions.

Q: You really got around in style.

Admiral Bieri: We really got around in style, and we really met all the people. The mission lived out in this suburb. They had several houses. They all messed together in one of these larger houses. Usually the only meal we had together was breakfast, and occasionally lunch.

My memory runs in spurts and bounds, as you notice.

Q: It seems very good to me. In those days, the Peruvians thought well of the United States.

Admiral Bieri: Yes, we had a naval mission down there. We also set up their Naval Academy. The superintendent of their Naval Academy was a man named Davy of the class

---

* President Augusto B. Leguia.

of 1907, Naval Academy.* He was no longer in the service, but he had been appointed by the Peruvians as superintendent of their Naval Academy.

We had a naval mission down there, which supposedly supervised and looked out for the training of the Peruvian Navy. At this time, this mission was headed by Commander Dean Causey.† He was from the class of 1906 at the Naval Academy. He had several other officers with him.

I've been doing a little writing, off and on, for my grandchildren.

A very interesting thing about our stay in Vera Cruz --I've gotten beyond that subject.

Q: Just revert back to it.

Admiral Bieri: During the months before the occupation, when we were down there, a large number of foreign ships had gathered there. There were British, French, two Germans, Spanish, and I think a Swedish ship. All were presumably there to look out for the interests of their nationals. There was a considerable amount of visiting back and forth among the ships and nationalities, especially officers.

There were two British ships there as I remember it, commanded by a flag officer, Admiral Sir Christopher Craddock. All these ships were there in '14, before war was declared in Europe. Things were getting very tense. Everybody was reading the radio news with much interest.

All of a sudden one night, the two German ships disappeared. They had been playing around the outskirts of the harbor, exercising or something during the day. And that night, they disappeared. The next day, war was declared.‡ One of them was the Dresden, and the other was the Karlsruhe. We never saw them again. The Dresden was

---

* Charles G. Davy had resigned from the U.S. Navy as a commander in December 1919.
† Commander Lewis D. Causey, USN.
‡ Germany declared war on Russia on 1 August and on France on 3 August 1914. Britain declared war on Germany 4 August.

sunk by the British in the Falkland Island battle. The Karlsruhe was lost; just what the circumstances were I don't know. I think the British got her down around the West Indies.

After the Germans left, this gathering of ships broke up. Sir Christopher Cradock was the next man to leave. He was a fine old gentleman, very much liked by the Americans there. He left the harbor with all his flags flying, with cheers and salutes from the other ships. We never saw him again. He went down in the Battle of Coronel off the west coast of South America.[*]

To revert to my shore duty, I stayed at Hampton Roads until December of 1921. I had orders then to go to sea and report to Commander Destroyers Pacific for duty.

We were ordered to take passage on the Navy transport Chaumont from the East Coast to the West Coast through the canal.

Q: You were taking your family out there too?

Admiral Bieri: This was in line with saving money on transportation. We had a few days' leave before we left, and we went up to see my wife's family in New Jersey. Then we got on the ship at Philadelphia and stopped at Norfolk.

This ship was lousy. She had been used just previous to this for a junket trip by a bunch of congressmen to go down to the Virgin Islands.

Q: They were on junkets in those days?

Admiral Bieri: Oh, yes. This was just before Christmas. I presume the idea of the junket was not only to get warmed up, but to get some other things that they could get down there.[†]

---

[*] In a battle in November 1914 off the coast of Chile, near Coronel, a force of three British cruisers and a troopship under Rear Admiral Sir Christopher Cradock, RN, was soundly defeated by five cruisers of the German Far East Squadron.
[†] Probibition against alcoholic beverages was then the law in the United States.

She came back just about Christmastime. Of course, they let the officers and men have their Christmas leave. She hadn't been cleaned up when we got to her. She was in terrible shape, dirty.

We were given one little stateroom for my wife, myself, and two boys; they were seven and two. It had one bunk up over the other and a little transom. It was terrific. They had a load of officers and families aboard, many of them with small children like mine. They hadn't even rigged the ship with safety lifelines.

We went down to Norfolk; we were going to be in there several days. Admiral and Mrs. Rodman came down and rescued us from the ship, and took us up to their quarters for our stay there. The admiral was a great stickler for cleanliness, especially aboard ship. He took one look at the ship, and he said to me, "What's the condition of that ship?"

I said, "She's lousy, admiral. She's the filthiest thing I've been on in years."

He said, "You won't go out on her filthy. I'll get her cleaned up before you go back on." And he did.

He exercised whatever authority his rank gave him where he didn't have any command of the ship. He got her cleaned up, and he got lifelines rigged on her. We left port in pretty good shape.

In addition to taking passage on this ship, all those officers who were qualified to stand watch were detailed as officer of the deck. The watch standing was not very strenuous, because there were about 24 of us on the watch list. So we got a watch every six days. There were several of us who had more or less service and experience.

Q: Oh, my, you didn't escape that then either?

Admiral Bieri: A lot of these officers that were officers of the deck were young and inexperienced. Some of them had come in from the reserve. They had an exec on there who was notorious in the Navy as being no good. Of course, as soon as we left port, the old ship began to slide down again. The exec never had a field day from the time we left Norfolk until these senior officers on the watch list decided they'd have field days. So every time one of us came on watch, we'd order a field day. We'd get the old ship cleaned up, and then we'd turn her over again. We finally made the West Coast.

Q: Part vacation and part work.

Admiral Bieri: Part vacation and part work.
    That was about it up until the time I joined the destroyers.

Q: That's probably a good breaking-off place.

Interview Number 2 with Vice Admiral Bernhard H. Bieri, U.S. Navy (Retired)

Place: Bethesda, Maryland

Date: Friday, 25 July 1969

Interviewer: John T. Mason, Jr.

Q: Admiral, it's good to be with you again this morning and to have the second chapter of your very interesting account.

Admiral Bieri: We'll start this morning with my detachment from the Fifth Naval District in January 1922.

On the fifth of January, 1922, I took passage from Norfolk, Virginia, to the West Coast with my family on the USS Chaumont. I was attached to that ship for duty during passage and then to report to Commander Destroyer Squadrons Pacific on arrival in San Diego.

Q: You say "duty during passage."

Admiral Bieri: I was attached to the Chaumont myself.

Q: It was a military transport, was it?

Admiral Bieri: Yes, the USS Chaumont. On arrival at San Diego on the 28th of January, 1922, I assumed command of Destroyer Division 29 and the USS Bailey for the purpose of decommissioning these vessels. These First World War destroyers had been operating in the Atlantic and Pacific with inexperienced and small crews. They were in rather poor condition. But at that time it was finally decided to place them all out of commission in San Diego.

Bernhard H. Bieri #2 - 44

Q: Put them in mothballs, so to speak.

Admiral Bieri: No, at that time the Navy had not yet developed their mothball system. This was a question of removing the stores, accounting for the stores, removing the ammunition, and getting the ships in supposedly good material condition by removing the rust and that sort of thing. Labeling all the spare parts and putting them in good condition. Eventually, greasing them up so they wouldn't rust and hauling them down and putting them down in the back channel in San Diego.

Q: How many destroyers were involved in this operation?

Admiral Bieri: I had a division of six destroyers, and we eventually got the seventh. The whole operation probably had about two squadrons, 30-odd ships.

Q: Admiral, were they ever used again, to your knowledge?

Admiral Bieri: Yes, some of them were used again. Some of them were later on traded to the British in their base deal.

Q: Part of that 50-destroyer deal?*

Admiral Bieri: Yes, whether these particular ones were or not, I don't know; but they did the same thing on the East Coast and had them laid up at Charleston.

The destroyers that I got, and particularly the <u>Bailey</u>, were in extremely poor condition. The <u>Bailey</u>, somewhere on her last trip at sea, had somehow or other filled up the reduction gears with salt water. They had not drained it off or properly cleaned it out.

---

* In September 1940 President Franklin D. Roosevelt concluded a deal with Prime Minister Winston Churchill of Great Britain whereby the United States transferred 50 destroyers to the Royal Navy for use against German submarines. In return the United States received 99-year leases to British bases in the West Indies, Bermuda, and Newfoundland.

These were just frozen together in one solid mass. We worked for weeks and weeks, attempting to get these gears so they would operate again. I don't think that they ever used the Bailey again.*

Q: I would think under those circumstances, scrapping would have been the solution.

Admiral Bieri: Yes, but they weren't scrapping them at that time.

The destroyers were then taken down and tied up at the base. I finished that job at the end of five months.

Then I received orders to command the USS Corry.† That was in June 1922. I remained in the Corry until March 20, 1925. This was a very interesting cruise. The Corry was a new destroyer, had not seen any war service, and was in excellent material condition. She had only been in commission a few months under command of Captain Foote, who later became Commodore Foote.‡ They hadn't done any operating to amount to anything.

The Navy was going through a very strenuous economy program at the time, even to the point of not using any lights aboard ship, and certainly not carrying out any military training or cruises of that sort. The young officers on the ship told me that the only trip that they had made in the previous six months was one trip from San Diego to Long Beach. It was an overnight run, although it was only 90 miles or so, and that the whole complement of ship's officers stayed up all night to experience this operation.

Very shortly after I joined the Corry . . .

Q: Was she of the new design?

---

* USS Bailey (DD-269) was transferred to the Royal Navy on 26 November 1940. She became HMS Reading.
† USS Corry (DD-334), a Clemson-class destroyer, was commissioned 25 May 1921. Standard displacement was 1,190 tons, length 314 feet, and beam of 32 feet. Top speed was 35 knots. She was armed with four 4-inch guns, one 3-inch gun, and 12 21-inch torpedo tubes.
‡ The first commanding officer was Lieutenant Commander K. E. Hintze, USN. Bieri's predecessor as CO was Commander Percy W. Foote, Jr., USN, who served as Commander Destroyer Division 36 at the same time he commanded the Corry.

Admiral Bieri: Not particularly, no. She was a little more modern, a few improvements, but not much different than the old four-stackers.

We went to the Mare Island Navy Yard for some post-commissioning repairs.* It was during that summer that they installed on the Corry the first so-called sonic range finder. These were installed on the Corry and the Hull, the sister ship.

It was a depth recorder or finding machine. Instead of being recorded electrically as they are now, the operator had to operate it and yet do it orally. In other words, he sent out an impulse from the machine, and when it bounced off the bottom and came back, he heard the echo. He superimposed the echo on the outgoing sound. When he had that, he could look on the scale and see how deep the water was.

Q: Is this comparable to what the British call the echo-sounding gear?

Admiral Bieri: Yes, that was the beginning of it, part of it. It was probably more nearly comparable to the fathometer, which we had later.

We were the first ships that were supplied with this thing. It was interesting, too, to note that at this time the destroyers in the fleet were still equipped with magnetic compasses. None of them had gyrocompasses.

In late 1922, or maybe in the new year, the fleet made one of its first fleet trips in several years. The entire fleet sailed from the West Coast to Panama, held some maneuvers en route and on the way back, and spent several days in Panama.

Q: Were these maneuvers in connection with the defense of the canal, that kind of thing?

Admiral Bieri: It was more in connection with training the fleet, ordinary steaming and that sort of thing. We had no gunnery during this cruise, but we did a lot of various tactical problems and development formations.

---

* Mare Island Navy Yard, Vallejo, California.

On the way down we stopped at Magdalena Bay on the west coast of Mexico. I think this was the last time that the Pacific Fleet was able to use this bay, on account of the Mexicans desiring us not to use it.

We did some sonic work on this trip. Every time somebody reported a shoal someplace which didn't show on the chart, they would send either the Hull or the Corry out there to look for it. That was a little additional for us. On return from the south in 1923, the Hull and the Corry were directed to make a sonic survey of the West Coast from San Francisco to the southern border of the U.S., from the shore out to the 2,000-fathom curve.

Q: That was quite an operation, wasn't it?

Admiral Bieri: Yes. We spent several months on that job, night and day practically. We did stop occasionally. We had to stop and get oil and spend a weekend in one of the ports along the coast some place. The results of this survey were very good.

Q: And the equipment worked well?

Admiral Bieri: The equipment worked well. The Carnegie Institute was very much interested in this thing. When it was finished, the Navy Hydrographic Office took the soundings and made what was the first bathymetric chart that the Navy ever had. I think that the bathymetric chart is still being issued.

Q: It's still being issued?

Admiral Bieri: I think so.

Q: So accurate it was.

Admiral Bieri: Yes.

Q: Did you have BuOrd men on board?*

Admiral Bieri: No, this work was all done by ship's officers and ship's men. We trained our own men to use this gear. Occasionally we would take with us a man from the Mare Island Navy Yard who would supervise the installation of this material and was interested in it. He just came on to see how it was working. A man named Mr. Bruck.

On the completion of this survey, both Commander Schuyler Heim, captain of the Hull, and I received letters of commendation from Carnegie Institute and the Hydrographic Office for the excellent work the ships had done.†

Q: Tell me about the interest of the Carnegie people in this.

Admiral Bieri: They were interested in it, I suppose, from the scientific point of knowing what the variations of the bottom of the ocean floor were and trying to figure out the effects of that on the coastal currents, the aquatic life, and that sort of thing. Of course, the Navy's interest was primarily in navigation.

Q: Was the Carnegie Institute interested in other parts of the world also, in this kind of thing?

Admiral Bieri: If they were, nobody was doing any work on it. We were the only Navy apparently that was doing any of that sort of thing at that time. This survey was completed in April of '23.

The early summer of that year, the Hull and Corry were detailed to make a trip to Alaska with a convoy carrying President Harding.‡ President Harding, some of his Cabinet,

---

* BuOrd--Bureau of Ordnance.
† Lieutenant Commander Schuyler F. Heim, USN.
‡ Warren G. Harding was President of the United States from March 1921 until his death on 2 August 1923.

and their families had taken passage on the USS Henderson transport. The two destroyers that were equipped with the sonic range finders were detailed to convoy them to Alaska.

Q: Was this a protective measure? Or was it also scientific?

Admiral Bieri: In a way, a protective measure, but it was just to have someone with them as escort. We had this sonic range finder so that we could be of use to them if they got into navigational difficulties.

We left Seattle and went up through the inside passage to Alaska. We stopped at all the ports in Alaska: Ketchikan, Juneau, or up and across to Seward. Then we came back through Cordova and stopped at Sitka. Then we turned down the coast again through the inside passage. The President made a visit to Vancouver.

The President's schedule was such that we arrived at all these ports in the early forenoon, as a rule. He would spend a day, and maybe two days in some of them. Then we would proceed again at night to run to the next port. So it got to be rather strenuous cruising for the officers and men on the destroyer.

Q: Were you invited on board the Henderson at all?

Admiral Bieri: No, I never went on the Henderson. But on our return trip--when we stopped at Sitka on a weekend--President Harding and Mrs. Harding and one or two other couples that were with them came on board the Corry. They inspected the ship, and we had tea for them in the wardroom. The President appeared a little grumpy, but I had previously met the President when I was aide to the commandant at Norfolk and knew his peculiarities to a certain degree.

Q: Was this a natural state with him, being grumpy?

Admiral Bieri: No, not as a rule. Mrs. Harding was most genial and very nice. I think he probably didn't want to visit any ship and was more interested in getting some sleep or something like that, maybe a game of cards.

We then came on back and stopped at Vancouver. There the Canadian citizens had a parade and a lunch for the President at the principal hotel in town. To this all the officers were invited. The rest of his stay in Vancouver used up the day until about sundown, when we left for Seattle.

Very shortly after we got out of Vancouver and headed south through the sound, we ran into a very, very heavy fog. The captain of the Henderson, Captain Buchanan, ordered the Corry and the Hull to drop astern and to take station one on each quarter.* He was going to proceed at 15 knots, regardless of the fog. In the interval sometime before that, the naval people had ordered out a squadron of destroyers from Seattle to meet the Henderson down at Juan de Fuca Straits and escort her into Seattle for the purpose of making a big show.

The fog continued. We had a Finn on board who was a pilot, and he was supposed to be acquainted with the Alaskan waters and was. We didn't have too much use for him, but we had him along. He came down about 4:00 o'clock in the morning and he heard a fog whistle, almost up ahead. The old pilot said to me, "That sounds like a 10,000-ton ore ship."

I thought to myself, "If that's a 10,000-ton ore ship and the captain of the Henderson doesn't slow down, we're liable to get in trouble with him. And I'm not going to get caught in too much of a mess."

So I took my station at the engineering telegraphs and followed along astern of the Henderson. This whistle continued without change of bearing. All of a sudden, there was a crash. The Henderson had hit one of these destroyers that had come up from Seattle.

The Hull was apparently also standing by, and we swung onto our engine room telegraphs for full speed astern. We cleared the melee and back in a couple of minutes we were lost in the fog. We didn't know where they were; the general direction was ahead.

---

* Captain Allen Buchanan, USN.

Then we received a signal from the Henderson that the Corry was to stand by the destroyer. And that the Hull would continue with the Henderson to Seattle.

Q: Then neither one was badly damaged?

Admiral Bieri: The Henderson was not particularly badly damaged. She hit her bow line, so she just had a dent in her bow more or less.

The destroyer had been hit in the starboard fireroom tanks. She had taken considerable water aboard, she had a hole in her, and she assumed a bad list. By the time we found this destroyer in the fog, she had been abandoned.

Q: Been abandoned by her crew?

Admiral Bieri: Been abandoned by all the officers and crew. The fog cleared somewhat at that time, but we had no idea what became of the officers and the crew. I had a discussion with my chief engineer. He said, "I think I can go over there with about four or five men. She isn't listing anymore, and she isn't going to sink. I think I can get the steam up on her, and we can steam her in."

I sent this officer over there with four or five men, and he got up steam. We were just about ready to take him in tow as well. The fog cleared off momentarily, and we saw this crew all around the place there in lifeboats and rafts, and so forth. Of course, when they saw us, and saw their ship making some smoke, they all came back on board.

Q: Had they acted in accordance with Navy regulations in abandoning their ship?

Admiral Bieri: Hardly the best practice. They came back on board. About that time, a second destroyer of that squadron showed up and said he would take the destroyer in tow and take her down to the Navy yard. In the process of doing this, they got their towlines fouled in the destroyer's propeller. It was quite some time before the mess was finally straightened out, and we were able to proceed on our way. The other destroyer took the crippled destroyer in tow and took her to the Navy yard.

Q: Pre-radar days were strenuous, weren't they?

Admiral Bieri: We went on down to Seattle and joined the part of the fleet that was there.

The President had arrived approximately on time in the early forenoon at Seattle, and they had a big parade for him. Immediately after the parade, he left by train for San Francisco. It was there that he died a day or so later.[*]

Q: I believe your colleague, now Admiral Joel T. Boone, was his physician at that point.[†]

Admiral Bieri: Yes, I think so.

The Henderson was given orders to proceed to San Francisco from Seattle as soon as the President left. She was to stand by at San Francisco for whatever use the President wanted to make of her. On the way out through Juan de Fuca Straits, she had another collision--with a windjammer that had just arrived in the straits from Australia. Fortunately, all she did was carry away a bunch of the lower yardarms of the ship, and she was able to proceed on the way.

Q: Captain Buchanan sounds like a rather belligerent man.

Admiral Bieri: The captain had a little hard luck on that cruise. He was a very dashing sort of a fellow. His son is Admiral Buchanan.

We joined the fleet. That summer the fleet remained up around Puget Sound for summer operations, but my ship was detached and sent down to San Francisco to do some sound work with submarines.

---

[*] Harding died 2 August 1923.
[†] Lieutenant Commander Joel T. Boone, MC, USN.

At that time, we were also equipped with the old listening gear. We worked out some problems with these submarines. In the course of one of the problems, one of the submarines we were working with unfortunately ran up on the Farallons.* Luckily she got off with no help and not much injury. That resulted in a court-martial for the captain of the submarine, to which I was called as a witness later on in the year.

The fleet then came down to San Francisco on its way south. In the meantime, we had completed our work with the submarines. I was told by the squadron commander to moor at a certain berth at San Francisco and await the arrival of the squadron. While moored at the dock, where other destroyers were coming in, one of them had a little difficulty coming alongside and she punched a hole in my port quarter. That resulted in another trip of mine to the Navy yard for two or three weeks to get that fixed up. Then I rejoined the fleet in San Diego.

Q: For an accident of that sort was a board of inquiry held?

Admiral Bieri: I forget just what it was, but I don't think there was. He was handling the destroyer in a very heavy current and tide, and so the tide was apparently running in. When one made a dash in to the dock, you had to come in at right fast speed to do it; he hadn't allowed himself enough room. The current inside the dock line stopped, and the current outside carried the stern around a little. They usually just take administrative action in those cases. Of course, it never does the officer's record any good to have it happen to his ship.

We did several jobs around. I was repaired and back in the fleet in time to go south.

They had a report from one of the battleships, that she on occasion had picked up a five-fathom spot off Point Sur where there should be several hundred fathoms of water. The commander in chief directed the squadron commander to send the <u>Corry</u> down there to look for this thing. I left before the fleet left San Francisco and searched the area quite thoroughly and found nothing. And I don't think anything has ever been found since. So I

---

* The Farallon Islands are about 30 miles west of San Francisco's Golden Gate.

imagine the battleship got into some shallow water or got a faulty sounding of some sort. I think it was 15 fathoms and not five.

The fleet left San Francisco, and I was then told to proceed on my own to San Diego, which I did. I rounded Point Arguello in the fog, steamed down the channel, and made San Diego the night that all the destroyers ran aground on Point Arguello.[*]

Q: The Honda thing?

Admiral Bieri: The Honda affair. My first knowledge of it, of course, was when I awoke at home the next morning and read about it in the newspaper. We had just made the same trip the day before.

Q: But not subject to the same temptation?

Admiral Bieri: Not subject to the same error.

We made another trip that winter to Panama, which was an extensive trip. We went all the way over to Puerto Rico, to Roosevelt Roads.

While we were at Colon, Panama, we got word that one of our cruisers had grounded on a reef at Vera Cruz.[†] She was attempting to enter the port during the night, was caught there by a "northern," and was being badly beaten up. So they sent our division, including the Hull and the Corry, under Captain Church to see what we could do for them.[‡] The flagship of the destroyers, with Admiral Kittelle, also led the way for us.[§] We arrived in Vera Cruz after a very stormy passage.

---

[*] On 8 September 1923 seven ships of Destroyer Squadron 11 ran aground in heavy fog at Point Arguello, also known as Point Honda, off Santa Barbara, California. Twenty-two men were killed, and all seven ships were wrecked.
[†] The cruiser Tacoma (CL-20) grounded on Blanquilla Reef, off Vera Cruz, Mexico, on 16 January 1924 with four lives lost.
[‡] Captain John G. Church, USN, Commander Destroyer Division 36.
[§] Rear Admiral Sumner E. W. Kittelle, USN, Commander Destroyers Battle Fleet. His flagship was the light cruiser Omaha (CL-4).

The cruiser flagship was able to handle the seas much better than we were. So when we came out of Colon making 20 knots, he was able to keep right on going, but the destroyers had to slow down. We followed him on up, arriving a day or so after he did. By the time we arrived, the old cruiser on the rocks was a complete wreck and was abandoned by the officers and crew who had been taken ashore.

We left the destroyer division there for a few days, and then we proceeded over to Puerto Rico to join the fleet. We had some maneuvers over there. In March, we got a signal from the commander in chief that the Navy Department wanted the <u>Hull</u> and the <u>Corry</u> to make a survey for a new Alaskan cable which the Army was laying between Seattle and Seward. We were to depart immediately.

Q: You certainly were much in demand for these jobs. Had they not outfitted other destroyers by this time with sounding gear?

Admiral Bieri: No, they never did, until they got the electrical equipment.

So we had a very active cruise, did a lot of cruising. In the meantime, I continued in command of the <u>Corry</u>. My friend Schuyler Heim had been detached. Another officer, Lieutenant Commander Raguet, had her for about a year.[*] On this particular occasion he was detached at Panama, and the third officer, Commander John Hilliard, came.[†]

On our way across the Caribbean, which was pretty rough at that season of the year, we got a message from the commandant at Panama that he had a very sick man down at Port Obaldia on the Colombian border. We had a radio station there. The commandant wanted one of the destroyers to go down and pick him up and bring him to Panama.

About a year before that, the <u>Hull</u> and the <u>Corry</u> were down in the same area in Colon trying to find a shoal spot which one of the transports had reported on the track approaching the canal. We spent a week or so out there covering an area of about 50 miles square, thoroughly combing the area for this shoal spot, which we never found.

---

[*] Lieutenant Commander Edward C. Raguet, USN.
[†] Lieutenant Commander John C. Hilliard, USN.

We had a rough week, and the Hull got in from that particular trip several hours ahead of me. I came in later on in the evening. I had just allowed my officers and chief petty officers to go ashore when I got a message from Captain Heim that he'd like to see me on board. I went over there, and he handed me a message which said, "Commandant wants a destroyer to go down to Port Obaldia to pick up a man who has a bad case of appendicitis."

Being the junior one, I was detailed to go down and get him. We rounded up our few officers and all the chiefs that had gone ashore. We left about 4:00 o'clock in the morning. In the meantime, we took out a young doctor from the shore station there. We proceeded down to Obaldia; this was a very rough passage. We went down at about 25 knots, and that didn't add to the comfort.

We arrived down at Port Obaldia, and sent a boat ashore. There was no harbor there, but the boat got the man aboard and brought him out to the ship. The young doctor, in the meantime, had gotten very seasick, so he wasn't any use to us. The corpsman took care of this young fellow when he came aboard. The doctor was able to give instructions what to do, and we did them. After the radioman was aboard for several hours on the way back, we were still making 25 knots with this heavy sea we were in, he got very seasick. By the time we got to Colon, he was quite well again.

Instead of having appendicitis, he had a case of lead poisoning from painting in a closed compartment. The seasickness rid him of both.

Q: Quite an antidote.

Admiral Bieri: The doctor was able to walk off the ship. He wasn't too impressed with duty on the destroyers.

That was the year previous to our going to Alaska for making the survey for the new Alaskan cable in March 1924. We left Seattle with a full load of oil, with instructions from the Navy Department to steam at economical speeds and not burn up an excess oil or take any in Alaska. It cost something like $7.00 or $8.00 dollars a barrel in Alaska. They weren't about to spend that much money, I guess.

We started this sounding. We steamed several miles apart, I think maybe about five miles apart. We took soundings at intervals and eventually made a very good chart for them. At the same time that we were doing this, four Army aviators left Seattle and were going to fly around the world by way of Seward, Alaska, and then on over to Japan. We figured that we might get mixed up with these fellows, because it had been our experience every time we were at sea when there were any aviators around, we were picked to get them up out of the water.

Q: Who was leading this flight?

Admiral Bieri: A major named Martin, there were three other young lieutenants.[*] I think most of them were lieutenants. They flew on wheels to a place up in Canada. Then they put on some floats and flew from there to Seward, Alaska. They left Seward before we got there. In fact, we were approaching Seward with the intention of turning around and running the other line of soundings back to Seattle. We got word that Martin in his plane had broken a piston rod and had to make a forced landing out on the Alaskan Peninsula, somewhere near Wide Bay.

Q: The Alaskan Peninsula, is that the Aleutian Islands?

Admiral Bieri: Yes. This was in the evening about 8:00 or 9:00 o'clock, still daylight up there. The Hull and the Corry made a full-speed run down there. While the Hull went in and searched one of the bays, I went down and searched Wide Bay, which was quite an enormous place. It was unsurveyed at that time, so we didn't feel like entering the bay. We sent in a boat. She was soon out of sight, and we lost contact with it. Then we got a message from the Hull that he'd found this aviator and was taking him up to a Coast Guard vessel which had appeared on the scene nearby.

---

[*] Major Frederick L. Martin, USA.

I had to round up my boat, which took considerable doing. We blew the whistle, and we blew the siren, and hoisted the flags, but apparently he couldn't see us. Eventually, the executive officer suggested that we fire a star shell over in that direction; maybe that would bring him back. So we fired a star shell. Unfortunately, the star shell fell on a little island and set it on fire. But that brought them back. The two boat parties had to first go ashore and put the fire out. So we were somewhat delayed in getting back.

All the time that this thing was going on, the sea was as smooth as a billiard ball. It was very mild, the climate was mild. We went back up, and when we approached the place where they had found the aviator, I got a message from Hilliard in the <u>Hull</u>. It said that he would complete the survey to Seattle, and that I was to take my ship and go to Seward, Alaska, to get an engine which these fellows had cached there for possible use.

I ran across the Gulf of Alaska, and the weather kept getting worse and worse as we went over in that direction. We got to Seward in the late afternoon to find out that the people in Seward had put this engine on a merchant ship and sent it back to Seattle the afternoon before. The merchant ship was to stop in various ports in Alaska on the way down. I figured out that I could intercept her in Juneau by going south up into Frederick Sound, around Cape Ommaney, and pick up the engine the next morning and come back.

We left Seattle at 25 knots, and the seas were running very high on the quarter. We did some terrific rolling and pitching. Finally we rounded up around midnight into Frederick Sound, where the water was nice and smooth. My navigator, Lieutenant Von Heimburg, set the course for the night, and we turned the deck over to the officer of the deck.* The navigator and I had hardly gotten into our bunks when the officer of the deck called up and said, "This course is taking me right to the beach." So we had him head off. We went up there and found out that this heavy rolling that we did, especially this terrific roll that we took just as we rounded into Frederick Sound, had thrown open the doors on the magnet holders of the magnetic compasses. The magnets had slipped out.

Q: A timely discovery, wasn't it?

---

* Lieutenant Ernest H. Von Heimburg, USN.

Admiral Bieri: Fortunately, our records were complete. We were able to slip the magnets back in again. Just as we finished doing that, the fog set in, and we had no way of checking them to see if they were all right.

So we spent the night steaming up Frederick Sound at slow speed. We were sounding our whistle to get the echo off the cliffs, to make sure that we were not going in on the shore. The next morning it cleared off, and by observing the stars and so forth we were able to check our compass enough to get to Juneau.

Q: Admiral, why wouldn't you, instead of steaming, drop anchor?

Admiral Bieri: It was a large, deep sound, very wide. There's plenty of room there. As long as we could get an echo from the beach, from the cliffs, we were safe enough.

The next morning, when everything cleared off, we got in to Juneau. We found the engine, and about noon we headed back again across the Gulf of Alaska. By that time, the storm had really piled up. We had a very rough passage across the Gulf of Alaska. Naturally, we used up a lot of oil, because we had been doing all this high-speed running. So we did have to stop in Seward and buy a carload of $7.00-a-barrel of oil, which we had to explain to the Navy Department for several months thereafter.

We got almost into Seward, and we ran into a terrific snowstorm which blacked out everything. Snowflakes bigger around than a dollar would hit you in the eye. The old destroyers had practically no protection on the bridge. It would blind a person for a minute or so while he was trying to get his eyes cleared out.

We made a couple of passes at the entrance to Resurrection Bay. They had no lights there at that time. Neither my executive officer, Von Heimburg, nor I recognized any of the landmarks. We'd been in there before, when we were up there with the President. So we stood back out to sea, and just before nightfall we decided to try it once more.

So we stood in, and fortunately this time we picked up one of the big rocks at the entrance with which we were familiar, and we got into the bay. It was still snowing very heavily, and we steamed slowly up the bay during the night, toward the oil dock, which we almost overran, but discovered our mistake in plenty of time. It took us all day to take a load of oil, because they had no way of heating the oil tanks at that place.

Q: It was sluggish.

Admiral Bieri: The oil was very thick. We finally got a load of oil and started off down Resurrection Bay. We thought we would have a good trip, but unfortunately as soon as we got our nose out into Kodiak Sound, we ran into the tail end of this storm. It turned very cold. We took the seas over green, and they froze as they came over. We ran all night in this condition. We finally got down to where the Coast Guard ship had this Army plane, and we gave them the engine. We took their mail and asked if there was anything else we could do for them. They said, "No." So we took off for Seattle, around the southern end of Kodiak Island.

We'd been out about two days when we got word that Martin had taken off and managed to hit a mountain. So we were sure there was nothing we could do for him up on top of the mountain, and we kept on going to Seattle. Very rough trip, but we finally made it.

Q: Was the party killed? Were they killed?

Admiral Bieri: No, they slid upon the snow on top of this mountain. Of course, they crashed the plane, and that was the end of his flight. They walked down to an Indian village nearby, and the Indians took them back down to the coast, to the Coast Guard ship. They got back all right. The other three continued on, and eventually made it back across the Atlantic. I think two of the three made it to New York.

There was a sequel to this story. Quite a number of years later, about 1939 or '40, I was out in Hawaii. I was invited to a party one night given by an Army officer. I met this fellow, Major Martin, who was then a colonel. I said, "You may not know it, but I'm the fellow that brought you that engine from Seward, Alaska, over to Wide Bay when your plane was down on your flight around the world."

He looked at me, and he said, "I never knew how that engine got over there."*

Following our return to Seattle, we rejoined the fleet. We had another year in which we did a lot of these side trips, in addition to doing all the work the other destroyers did, target practices and so forth. It was a very active cruise. Unfortunately, we missed an awful lot of time in port that these other ships had. Our crew were quite attached to the ship, and we didn't have too much trouble getting them to ship over.

Q: They probably got a kick out of some of these special duties.

Admiral Bieri: A great many of them had families, and they were getting kind of sick of being away from their families while everybody else was in port. But they were loyal, and they stuck by her. In 1923, we won the trophy for excellence in engineering, which showed that the ship had good spirit. We went through another year of training with the fleet in squadrons.

On the 20th of March, 1925, I was detached from the Corry and ordered to duty as communications officer in the Navy Department. I stayed in that assignment from May 1925 until the end of December 1927.

Q: So you were able to have your family in Washington.

Admiral Bieri: Yes, we moved to Washington. That was when we first came to Washington. Our two youngest sons were born here in Washington during that period. The fifth one had been born in San Diego during my destroyer experiences out there; he was the middle one.

During the two years at the Navy Department I had quite interesting duty. It was a rather odd duty to assign me to, as I had never had any particular duty as a communication officer or a radio officer.

---

* As a major general, Martin was commanding general of the U.S. Army Air Forces in the Hawaiian Islands when the Japanese attacked in December 1941. He was relieved of his command in mid-December.

Q: How do you explain an assignment like that?

Admiral Bieri: It was largely an administrative job. I had plenty of technical assistance and that sort of thing. My job was to keep the communications going to and from the Navy Department. We had, of course, a lot of side things, like the cryptographic section working on Japanese codes. One of the interesting things we did at that time was the beginning of the use of high frequency in Navy communication.

At that time, Dr. Taylor of Bellevue was in the process of developing transmitters for the Navy's use on the different high frequencies.[*] I had very close touch with Dr. Taylor. As he would develop a transmitter, they would install it on one of our circuits as a secondary transmitter, and we would try it out for him. We had some very excellent results. For instance, this was the first time that the Navy Department was ever able to communicate directly by radio from Washington to such outlying stations as the Asiatic Commander in Chief and Admiral Bristol in Turkey, to London and Panama.[†]

As he developed these transmitters, we had to use them at the hours in which these particular transmitters would carry the high frequencies to those places. We got a great many communications through much faster than they used to get through.

By the time I left there . . .

Q: May I ask a question about that, sir? Because of this new means of communication to the fleet units in all parts of the world, was there any noticeable increase in the effectiveness of the Navy as a whole, in the unity of the Navy?

Admiral Bieri: Oh, I think so, yes. Yes, but like all these things it took away again a certain amount of requirement of the man on the spot to make his own decision.

---

[*] Dr. A. Hoyt Taylor of the Naval Research Laboratory in Anacostia, D.C. For details see L. S. Howeth, History of Communications-Electronics in the United States Navy (Washington, D.C.: Bureau of Ships and the Office of Naval History, 1963).
[†] Rear Admiral Mark L. Bristol, USN, U.S. High Commissioner to Turkey, 1919-27.

Q: Yes, it became a centralized authority, didn't it?

Admiral Bieri: Yes.

Q: Is that good or bad in terms of the Navy?

Admiral Bieri: I think as it eventually worked out, it was good. The Navy got past the point where one man with not enough information should be called on to make decisions of that sort.

Before I left there, Dr. Taylor had developed what he called a Cornet transmitter. It transmitted on about four different high frequencies simultaneously from about, as I remember, 4,000, 5,000, or 6,000 kilocycles up to 14,000. By transmitting messages on all four of these, we could almost cover the clock around to all these outlying stations. Of course, these messages that we sent out this way had to be broadcast, because the other people at that time had no transmitters to acknowledge them. They could acknowledge them by the regular low-frequency radio. We would get an acknowledgement the next day or the day after.

Q: Tell me, sir, a little about this Dr. Taylor.

Admiral Bieri: Dr. Taylor was a radio expert. He was at the University of Wisconsin at the beginning of the First World War. He was a research man. The Bureau of Engineering got ahold of him and put him in charge of radio research at Bellevue Laboratory. Dr. Taylor stayed there for many years. I think he died very shortly after he retired from the Civil Service. He was very able, a very productive man, and did an excellent job for the Navy in developing this high frequency. He worked on a great many other problems, too, like the radar and that sort of thing.

Q: That concept was already in being. The Army was doing something in the field of radar too.

Admiral Bieri: Yes, I think the Navy had a little jump on them with that. He was also involved in sonar. He was a very valuable person.

Q: One other question I'd like to ask at this point. You made some reference to the fact that your communications people were working with Japanese codes.

Admiral Bieri: Of course, that was very secret at that time, but it's all come out since then. We had no way of knowing what the Japs were doing particularly, getting information on their methods, or maneuvers, communications and whatnot. It was a very difficult job, because the Japs had a couple of different alphabets that they used. We had to train sailors and officers to copy their transmissions. Then we stationed these various men around on shore and on ships. At one time, we had great many of them riding around on merchant ships. They would copy these Japanese transmissions and send them in to Washington, to the cryptographic section, where they attempted by the old methods to reconstruct the Japanese naval code and break them down. They had very material success, despite the fact that they didn't have the computers and all that sort of thing to work with. It was all hand work and head work in those days.

Naval officers named Safford and Rochefort were the heads of that at that time.[*] They stayed there for quite a number of years and did a very remarkable job. Safford was highly commended for it later on in his career. Up to the time that the war started, that was the only method that we had of breaking down the Japanese codes. We had broken down a great many of their codes. It paid dividends in the Battle of Midway.[†]

---

[*] Lieutenant Laurance F. Safford, USN; Lieutenant (junior grade) Joseph J. Rochefort, USN. The oral history of Rochefort is in the Naval Institute collection.

[†] During this battle in June 1942, Admiral Chester W. Nimitz, USN, Commander in Chief Pacific Fleet, was able to station three U.S. aircraft carriers in an advantageous position to intercept the Japanese, based on intelligence from Rochefort.

Q: Did they have any knowledge that we were working on this?

Admiral Bieri: They must have, but there was no way for them to get around it. They undoubtedly also were working on our code. They probably had a much easier job than we did. So we had to be extremely careful in the protection of our codes.

Q: Did you know this Captain Rochefort?*

Admiral Bieri: Yes, he was one of those people?

Q: Was he involved while you were in the department?

Admiral Bieri: He was involved in the same thing, yes.

Q: One other question about that. Do you infer, then, with the advent of the computer, the problem of breaking codes is much easier accomplished?

Admiral Bieri: Oh, very much easier, yes.

Q: Codes are then very vulnerable.

Admiral Bieri: Yes, they're very vulnerable. Not only that, they had the machines to copy this code. Copies came in on receivers, and they put it right into these computers. They could go through an enormous amount of material, compared to what the old hand method used to be able to do.

    I remember during the war, I one time went out with Admiral King to the center where they were doing this work.† It was remarkable the amount of material they were

---

* Rochefort eventually retired as a captain.
† Admiral Ernest J. King, USN, served as Chief of Naval Operations from 26 March 1942 to 15 December 1945; he was promoted to the rank of fleet admiral in December 1944.

processing on these machines. Of course, we have very excellent results from the machines. If they had been used a while, you could read some of these codes just as fast as they would send them in.

Q: Another man involved in that was Redfield Mason; he's now Admiral Mason.

Admiral Bieri: He might have been, he wasn't around Washington.*

Q: He was out in the Pacific.

Admiral Bieri: As a matter of fact, I really didn't have much control or anything to do with these people, except to see that they got all the help that they needed from the Navy Department--space and so forth--and handle their communications. I came in on hearing what they were doing.

Q: And still one other question, before you continue your narrative. This is in a personal sense. The fact that you were assigned to a job like communications for which you had had no background or experience, was this indicative of the fact perhaps that you were being prepared for flag rank?

Admiral Bieri: No, I don't think so. A lot of those assignments were just happenstance. For instance, I came ashore at that time. The officer in charge of naval communications was Commander Raguet. Raguet was an old communicator. He'd been in communications for years. Captain Ridley McLean was Chief of Naval Communications out there. He also had direct control of the Washington communication office. He, undoubtedly, asked the Bureau of Navigation for an officer of experience to take this job.† My name was on the list, and they said, "Here, give it to this fellow. He'll do it." That's the way it came about.

---

* Ensign Redfield Mason, USN, was commissioned in 1925 and went initially into the fleet.
† The Bureau of Navigation made officer assignments to various duties in the years prior to World War II.

McLean was a strict taskmaster, and we got along fine. I think we did a good job of it.

Among other things that we were playing with at that time was the facsimile machine. This was for sending facsimiles to outlying stations. We had a machine, and I think the second machine was in San Francisco or one of the other stations on the continent. We worked on that. They had not made too much progress with it. The machine that they had at that time was an enormous thing, probably the height and width of the side of the room there and about four or five feet deep. Subsequently, they got these things so that you could almost carry them around by hand. The thing hadn't gotten very far then. The Bureau of Engineering was working on it, and we were trying it out for them.

We had a lot of things of that sort to do in the communication department of the Navy Department. To me, it was a very interesting experience. It was particularly interesting as it brought me in touch with a great many officers in the Navy Department that I had never met before, senior officers.

Q: This was your first assignment in the Department.

Admiral Bieri: Yes, it was my first assignment. I learned a very considerable amount about the organization of the Navy Department at that time.

On December 27, 1927 I was detached from the Navy Department and ordered to the USS Utah, as the navigation officer.* I proceeded immediately to join the Utah at the Boston Navy Yard, as she was about to go with the fleet on the annual cruise to Guantanamo.

Q: Who was her skipper?

---

* The USS Utah (BB-31) was commissioned in August 1911. She had a standard displacement of 21,825 tons, was 522 feet long, and 88 feet in the beam. Her top speed was 21 knots. Her main battery comprised ten 12-inch guns. In 1931, she was converted to a mobile target ship.

Bernhard H. Bieri #2 - 68

Admiral Bieri: The skipper was Captain W. L. Littlefield, and her executive officer was Commander Harvey Delano.* Most of my acquaintances, when they found out where I was going, and with whom I was going to serve, commiserated very generously with me.

Q: Why, the men had a reputation?

Admiral Bieri: They had a rather tough reputation, but I got along fine with both of them. Never had any trouble.

Q: Were they supposed to be martinets, or what?

Admiral Bieri: Yes. Delano was a martinet. Littlefield was one of these "picky" naval officers--always after little details and that sort of thing.

Q: Old Navy style?

Admiral Bieri: Old Navy style.

Q: Was Delano related to FDR?†

Admiral Bieri: No. Delano was a very good officer, but he had a reputation amongst all the younger officers in the Navy and Marines as rather a martinet type. Harvey Delano and I got along fine. We became very good friends, and worked together very well. After I established myself, Captain Littlefield got some confidence in me. He left me alone and didn't bother me any.

We had a very good cruise; it didn't last too long. I sometimes wondered why I got along with them so well. The only thing that I could figure out was, with the exception of

---

* Captain William L. Littlefield, USN, commanded the battleship Utah (BB-31) from 23 January 1927 to 29 August 1928. Commander Harvey Delano, USN, was the exec.
† Franklin Delano Roosevelt was President of the United States from 1933 to 1945.

one other head of department, they had a pretty poor lot of officers. The fellow that I relieved was a classmate of mine who succumbed to "John Barleycorn" so badly that he was not able to do his job.[*] That was one reason that I went there.

Q: It was hardly a happy ship then, was it?

Admiral Bieri: Not particularly, and she wasn't a very good ship. She was a good engineering ship because they had a good chief engineer, Commander La Roche.[†] I think the navigation department was all right, but the rest of it you couldn't say too much for.

Suddenly, in the early part of August 1928, when I'd only been on there about seven months or so, I was detached. I was ordered to report to the USS Texas, the fleet flagship, as the navigating officer. The Texas, at that time, was operating independently of the fleet. It carried the Commander in Chief of the U.S. Fleet, and at this particular time was in the New York Navy Yard.

It appeared that when she was in San Diego, a short time previous to that, she had the unhappy experience of running aground coming out of the harbor. The Commander in Chief was Admiral Wiley.[‡]

Q: Was he aboard?

Admiral Bieri: He was on board, with all his staff. He demanded the detachment of the captain and the navigating officer, so that was how I got into that job.[§] They detached me from the Utah and sent me to the Texas. They detached my unfortunate classmate, Jack O'Brien, from the Texas and sent him to the Utah.[**] I stayed on the fleet flagship during the tenure of three commanders in chief and two captains.

---

[*] "John Barleycorn" is a euphemism for alcoholic beverages.
[†] Lieutenant Commander Francis A. La Roche, USN.
[‡] Admiral Henry A. Wiley, USN, served as Commander in Chief U.S. Fleet, 1927-29.
[§] Captain Zeno E. Briggs, USN, commanded the USS Texas (BB-35) from 2 June 1926 to 4 January 1928.
[**] Lieutenant Commander William H. O'Brien, Jr., USN.

Q: Always serving as the navigator?

Admiral Bieri: Serving as navigator, until April 1931. During that time, I was very largely separated from my family because they had to remain in one place. The Texas was continually cruising from one coast to another, up and down the coasts, and as far out as Honolulu. I had a great deal of navigation experience as the result of that. I also had a great deal of experience in maneuvering the ship. Handling the ship in formation, and changing stations, that sort of stuff. I got excellent reports from the captains.

Q: That was a strategic spot to be in, wasn't it--under the watchful eye of the CinC.

Admiral Bieri: Yes, we had three commanders-in-chief during that period: Admiral Wiley, Admiral Jehu Chase, and Admiral William Veazie Pratt.*

We did, as I said, a great deal of cruising. We visited a great many ports up and down the coasts, from Panama to Honolulu to Seattle and back up around to Boston. We would always be with the fleet when they made their annual cruises. The fleet, of course, at that time, was based on the West Coast. We always joined them for the maneuvers of the fleet.

I was a lieutenant commander during this period, until June 4, 1931. That meant that I had been a lieutenant commander, temporary and permanent, for 12 years.

In April 1931; I was detached from the Texas, fleet flagship, and ordered to the Navy Department for duty as detail officer in the enlisted men's detail section.

It was in June of that year that I was promoted to commander.

Q: What did that assignment entail?

---

* Admiral William V. Pratt, USN, served as Commander in Chief U.S. Fleet, 1929-30. Admiral Jehu V. Chase, USN, served as Commander in Chief U.S. Fleet, 1930-31.

Admiral Bieri: That assignment entailed all special assignments for enlisted men: such as shore duty, schools, and just about anything that you could think of that had to do with enlisted personnel, except enlisting them and training them. When they came due for changes, we saw that the men were rotated in different shore billets, between the different shore billets and sea billets. We made details to billets that required special qualifications. We also handled the detail of enlisted men to the Naval Academy Preparatory School. And that was about it.

It was a pretty good-sized job.

Q: At that point, your ability to select men was greater, wasn't it? Because they were coming in then, there being a Depression.[*] Weren't there more men enlisting or wanting to enlist?

Admiral Bieri: We never had a shortage of enlisted men, at that time, for the complements we had. Because the complements we had were not too large. They were never large enough really to fill the war needs of the ships. As far as enlisted men were concerned, we never had any trouble meeting the quotas that were set by the budget and so forth.

At that time the chief of the Bureau of Navigation, which it was called in those days, was Admiral Upham.[†] The officer in charge of all enlisted affairs was Captain Claude.[‡] His first assistant was Randall Jacobs, captain at that time.[§] I worked directly under Jacobs. I'd known him for many years. He was an old friend of mine. In fact, I roomed with his brother at the Naval Academy.

---

[*] Following the crash of the New York Stock Exchange in late October 1929, the United States was plunged into the Great Depression, from which it did not recover until the nation geared up for World War II at the beginning of the 1940s. The Depression was marked by high unemployment and many business failures.

[†] Rear Admiral Frank B. Upham, USN, served as Chief of the Bureau of Navigation from 22 May 1930 to 30 June 1933.

[‡] Captain Abram Claude, USN.

[§] Captain Randall Jacobs, USN. Later, as a flag officer, Jacobs served as Chief of the Bureau of Naval Personnel from 1942 to 1945.

Bernhard H. Bieri #2 - 72

Q: Oh, really. Then you could work in tandem with him when World War II came along, because he was right there.

Admiral Bieri: Yes. This was a very interesting experience, this detail in the Navy Department. I had under me usually two other officers, several chief petty officers, and a civilian force of stenographers and clerks of about eight or ten. It was a fairly busy job.

One of our jobs was answering correspondence from Congress and the White House, and so forth. We received a large amount of correspondence from these people, interceding for the people to be assigned here or there.

Q: What was your general policy?

Admiral Bieri: The general policy was to write them a very polite letter and explain just how it was handled, where these particular people stood on the list for the assignment they wanted, and why it would be poor policy to make any special assignment. Occasionally, when there was a humanitarian need for a change or something like that, we would make a change.

Q: Were the members of Congress always willing to accept this explanation?

Admiral Bieri: Most always. We never had any difficulty that I recall. Once in a while, we'd repeat. We realized that we had to do that for political purposes. There's one thing about it--all letters to congressmen and senators and people on the Hill were always signed by the chief of the bureau. Of course, they got a lot of them in the officers' section. As far as enlisted men were concerned, my group prepared the letters. I scanned them before they went up to see that they were in the proper form. We had very few of them that were ever questioned. That wasn't to say that they didn't continue; the volume of them continued right along. There were always plenty of requests on the congressmen. We knew that they had to handle them, and they knew we had a system.

Q: You had to have a letter which they could show to the constituents from the authority in the department.

Admiral Bieri: That's right.

Q: What about the White House pressure?

Admiral Bieri: We didn't have much from the White House. When we got one from the White House, they seldom asked for anyone to be given a job anywhere, except at the White House. If they wanted a certain officer or enlisted man at the White House, regardless of what his previous duty was or what his schedule was, he went to the White House.

The same way with the Capitol building. At that time they had just assigned a young doctor up there, Commander George Calver.[*] George was setting up a clinic for the congressmen. When George Calver asked for a man, we gave it to him. There wasn't any argument about it. There was never any question about taking them away. So, a lot of those fellows just spent their whole career there. As long as they were satisfactory to Calver and didn't get into trouble, as far as we were concerned with them, we were through with them.

Q: And he spent his whole career . . .

Admiral Bieri: He spent his whole career there. He went from lieutenant to rear admiral.[†]

Q: He's retired now?

---

[*] Commander George W. Calver, Medical Corps, USN.
[†] Calver retired as a rear admiral in November 1947.

Admiral Bieri: Retired, yes. A very fine man; and a very good doctor, apparently, for that job.

Q: All the members like him. He took time with them, and listened to their minor ailments.

Admiral Bieri: When they got sick and went out to Bethesda, he always went out and held their hands. I got to know Admiral Calver very well, and like him very much.

I stayed in that duty for a little over two years. At the end of July in 1933, I was detached from the Navy Department and ordered to the USS Altair as the executive officer.* I drove to the West Coast with my family, reporting on the 31st of August. I stayed in that job two years. The Altair was a merchant ship that had been converted during the war as a tender for destroyers. She had a squadron of destroyers to take care of at San Diego.

Q: So that was actually your base, at San Diego?

Admiral Bieri: Yes. Personally, that was quite a pleasant duty. I was out there and never went to sea, except to go to the Navy yard. I got to see a great deal of my family.

Q: You took a house out there?

Admiral Bieri: Yes. At that time, my oldest son had entered the Naval Academy, so there were just four children at home.

Q: Was that Bernhard, Jr.?†

---

* The USS Altair (AD-11) had been built in World War I. She was commissioned as a Navy destroyer tender on 6 December 1921. She was 424 feet long, 54 feet in the beam, had a displacement of 13,925 tons, speed of 10.5 knots.
† Bernhard J. Bieri, Jr., graduated from the Naval Academy in the class of 1937. He retired from active duty in 1970 as a rear admiral in the Supply Corps.

Admiral Bieri: Yes.

I served on the Altair with two captains: Captain A. T. Beauregard and Captain Henry Gearing.* Beauregard had been my executive officer on part of my cruise on the Texas, when she was a flagship. Gearing was on duty with me in the Navy Department. He had charge of the recruiting division while I was on duty there. So I knew them both quite well. They gave me quite a free hand in running the ship. We had a good crew and some good officers aboard.

We did a lot of work for the destroyers. It was just an ordinary cruise, such as you'd expect to have on a ship of that type.

I left the Altair in June 1935.

Q: Was there, by that time, any concern for a possible adversary in the Japanese Navy? This was building up, wasn't it?

Admiral Bieri: Oh, yes. Of course, it was generally taken for granted in our Navy, I think, well before that time. If we did go to war, it would undoubtedly be with the Japanese. A lot of our training and work was pointed in that direction.

We hadn't much new construction at that time. We got a few new destroyers. Up to the time I left the Altair, I think probably four or five new destroyers had joined the Pacific Fleet. The rest of them were still the four-stack destroyers that were finished about the end of the war. They were getting pretty well along in years.

Q: Was there any noticeable increase in the interest of the Navy, due to FDR's coming into office?

Admiral Bieri: When did he come in?

Q: Nineteen thirty-three.

---

* Captain Augustin T. Beauregard, USN; Captain Henry C. Gearing, Jr., USN. The destroyer Gearing (DD-692) was named for Captain Gearing, his father, and his son.

Admiral Bieri: I think that everybody felt that President Roosevelt had great interest in the service. When any increases were made--of course, some of them were already under way--he would be very favorably inclined to them and push them along. In fact, he was instrumental in getting a lot of them started. He was never too much of a help, during this period, in attempting to build up the strength of the personnel. He was satisfied with the strength that we had.

To go on with my story, I reported to the Naval War College in June 1935 and spent a year there, until the following June, as a student. This I found an extremely interesting duty, and I considered it a great benefit.

Q: Did you have any difficulty in getting back into the routine as a student--I mean, applying yourself as a student?

Admiral Bieri: Not particularly, the way they handled students there. We were given plenty to read and certain courses to follow. There was no such thing as recitation or anything like that. We had lectures. After a few months, we had the war games. We had to make estimates. They would pick out certain officers, regardless of rank, to play the games with the estimate that they had made. They were given assistants from the rest of the class. They would divide the class up in two parts.

Q: That was the major focus of the course, was it, war games?

Admiral Bieri: Yes, and of course, a great deal of reading, history, lectures of various sorts by prominent scholars and naval authorities outside the college.

Q: Were you thrown in with a group of men who later became leaders in World War II?

Admiral Bieri: Oh, yes, many of them. During my time there as a student and member of the staff, we had two presidents: Admiral Kalbfus and Admiral Snyder.* Kalbfus was retired before the war. Snyder was also, but he came back to active duty and served as inspector general in the Navy under King.

The other officers, a great many of them, became leaders--Kelly Turner, for instance.† While I was on the staff, I was his assistant, which was a very valuable experience. Wilcox, who was on duty in the administrative part of the college, became a flag officer; and unfortunately, drowned early in the war.‡ Harry Hill was one of the classmates in my class.§ He became a flag officer. Aubrey Fitch came up there.**

I was there almost two years on the staff. Quite a number of officers went through there. I would have a hard time remembering who they were.

Q: How big would a class be?

Admiral Bieri: The class, at that time, was altogether about 40 or 50 officers.

Q: And you lived in residence, you had your family there?

Admiral Bieri: In Newport, yes.

You remember your own Naval Academy classmates better than most of the rest of them.

---

* Rear Admiral Edward C. Kalbfus, USN, served as president of the Naval War College from 15 June 1934 to 15 December 1936. Rear Admiral Charles P. Snyder, USN, served as president from 2 January 1937 to 27 May 1939.
† Captain Richmond Kelly Turner, USN.
‡ Captain John W. Wilcox, Jr., USN. As a rear admiral, Wilcox, Commander Battleship Division Six, was lost overboard from his flagship, the USS Washington (BB-56), on 26 March 1942, while she was en route to the British Isles. The circumstances of his death were never satisfactorily explained.
§ Commander Harry W. Hill, USN. His oral history is in the Columbia University collection.
** Captain Aubrey W. Fitch, USN.

Q: Was Admiral Spruance up there?

Admiral Bieri: Spruance was there and Theobald was there.*

Q: I guess Carl Moore was there too.

Admiral Bieri: Carl Moore was there.† Carlos Bailey and Bill Quigley became commodores; they were there.‡

It must have been a big bunch there, but I don't remember them all.

I got a great deal of good out of the two years that I spent on the staff. I thought that was quite as valuable to me, as the course at the college.

Q: What did you teach?

Admiral Bieri: I was in the strategy section, under Turner. When Turner and I were there as students, we were in the same class. The head of the strategy section was Theobald. Theobald and Turner got along like a cat and a dog in a cage. I was rather sympathetic to Turner's ideas. When they picked out the members of our class to stay on the staff, they kept me on and I was made an assistant to Turner.

We had to, of course, make up the strategy problems and comment on the estimates and so forth that were handed in by the students. We supervised the playing of the games. In addition to that, several of us in that department had to make lectures on certain subjects. I found that extremely challenging and interesting.

One thing that I resolved to do when I was put on the staff was that I was going to get away from this business of reading lectures. Lecture and speak.

---

* Captain Raymond A. Spruance, USN; Captain Robert A. Theobald, USN.
† Commander Charles J. Moore, USN. His oral history is in the Columbia University collection.
‡ Commander Carlos A. Bailey, USN; Commander William M. Quigley, USN.

Q: Look them in the eye.

Admiral Bieri: Look them in the eye. I was one of the first ones to do this at the college, at that time. Some of the chaps told me after my first lecture it was the first lecture they hadn't slept through in a long time. Nothing more monotonous than to hear a man read a paper. I got a great deal of experience.

Q: Was this a new technique for you, or was it something that came naturally?

Admiral Bieri: Yes, it was a new technique for me.

Q: You simply worked at it?

Admiral Bieri: Worked at it. I found it extremely useful to me in later years, when I became a flag officer and had to speak on various occasions, in different countries, and at different organizations in the United States, and so forth. I even got to the point where I had the temerity, at one time, to make a speech in French at Bone, North Africa. It apparently went over very well. In fact; it went over very well with George Dyer, who was my cruiser commander at that time.* He came up to me afterwards, and he said, "Admiral, that was a wonderful thing you did there and a fine speech. That was the first French I understood tonight!"

What caused me to make the talk in French was that preceding me on the speaking list was the mayor of the city, and the governor general of the province, Ano Prefect. They had a young woman who was interpreting the speeches as they went along. They were wonderful speeches in French. When the young lady put them into English, she did a murderous job of it.

---

* This was shortly after World War II, when Rear Admiral George C. Dyer, USN, was a cruiser division commander. The oral history of Dyer, who retired as a vice admiral, is in the Naval Institute collection.

Q: Took all of the electricity out of it.

Admiral Bieri: Took everything out of it. A lot of the facts, but nothing else, no sentiments. I thought to myself, if she's going to do that with my English speech in reverse, I might just as well talk French. So I spoke it in French. It wasn't too long, but it lasted quite long enough. I was very successful with it.

Q: Your method of lecturing, was it just scanty notes you had before you?

Admiral Bieri: Yes, I usually studied the subject very thoroughly and made notes. They had recorders there during the lecture, that took the lecture down and transcribed it for distribution later on. My method was to study the subject and to outline the talk as I was going to make it. As a matter of fact, after I did that, I seldom had to look even at my notes. I had enough interest in it and knew enough about the subject so I could go right on.

Q: I recognize that technique.

Admiral Bieri: It was very interesting. Some of the other members of the staff, following that, also did the same thing. It made quite a difference, I thought.

As I said, that was very interesting and a challenging duty for me. I got a great deal of professional good out of it. In fact, maybe it was not so good for my later assignments because when I left there, they put me on their staffs and I never got off of them. Except on one or two occasions.

I finally left the war college in January 1938. I'd been there two years and a half. I reported to Admiral Greenslade, Commander Battleship Division with the fleet, as operations officer, at San Pedro.*

Admiral Calhoun was the chief of staff, and we had a very good staff of able officers.† Admiral Greenslade was a fine officer to serve with. I knew him as a

---

* Vice Admiral John W. Greenslade, USN, Commander Battleships, Battle Force. The flagship was the USS West Virginia (BB-48).

midshipman. He was an instructor at the academy, but I hadn't served with him subsequent to that time. He was a very fine man, a very likable man, and a very smart man; a good naval officer.

Q: Up to this point, sir, you'd never been involved in any way with naval aviation, had you?

Admiral Bieri: No, but I learned that at the war college in handling ships and so forth, theoretically. I'd never been in submarines either. All my duty had been surface ships.

I was promoted to captain in June 1938. That was about seven years after I'd made commander. I stayed on that job with Admiral Greenslade for one year. Then they reorganized and sent new flag officers to the fleet. I was ordered as operations officer of the U.S. Fleet under Admiral J. O. Richardson.*

Q: What did that entail for you?

Admiral Bieri: It just involved moving to another ship. I moved to the California at that time and became operations officer for Admiral Richardson, of the U.S. Fleet.†

Q: Had you served with him in any way before?

Admiral Bieri: Yes, but I hadn't served with him for years. When I was a passed midshipman and ensign on the Delaware, Admiral Richardson was an engineer officer aboard. He was the first assistant engineer. I got to know him at that time.

He picked me out to be his operations officer when he picked out his fleet staff. He was a very remarkable man in many ways. One of them was the fact that he knew everybody, every officer in the Navy, practically. He not only knew the officers by name,

---

† Captain William L. Calhoun, USN, later a flag officer in World War II.
* Admiral James O. Richardson, USN, was Commander Battle Force from June 1939 to January 1940 and Commander in Chief U.S. Fleet from January 1940 to February 1941.
† The California (BB-44) was the Battle Force flagship. Richardson moved to the Pennsylvania (BB-38) when he took command of the U.S. Fleet.

but he knew their records. He made a study of that sort of thing. He also had duty in the Navy Department, and he kept himself well-informed about the officer personnel. He'd never forgotten it.

Q: In that sense, he shared this characteristic with Admiral Nimitz, too, didn't he.[*]

Admiral Bieri: I think Nimitz was much the same way. We had another officer one time in the service years ago as commander in chief, Admiral Coontz.[†] Harry Hill served as an aide to Admiral Coontz. He had the remarkable faculty of being able to remember the names of the enlisted men who served with him. Which was very remarkable because it's something I never could acquire.

After I'd been on the ship a couple of years, I could learn most of them, but I never got to the point where I knew them all by their names. Coontz was very remarkable that way.

Q: Tell me a little more about Admiral Richardson.

Admiral Bieri: Of course, he was one of our ablest officers. He had a great deal of experience as commander of destroyer squadrons. He came out there first as Commander Battle Force and then became commander in chief almost immediately.

He'd had a lot of service in foreign countries commanding ships. He was a very forceful man and a very likable man. He impressed people as being a very able fellow, and he could express himself extremely well. He not only impressed senior and junior naval officers, but he had great success with civilians.

---

[*] Fleet Admiral Chester W. Nimitz, USN, Commander in Chief Pacific Fleet and Pacific Ocean Areas during World War II. As a rear admiral, Nimitz served as Chief of the Bureau of Navigation from June 1939 to December 1941.
[†] Admiral Robert E. Coontz, USN, served as Commander in Chief U.S. Fleet, 1923-25.

As commander in chief of the fleet, I thought he did a very excellent job under very trying circumstances.* He had the fleet out there in this exposed position. He was not able to impress the Navy Department, nor the President, nor the State Department with the danger of this thing and with the need to do something about making it possible for him to protect the fleet. Also to fully man it, for the trouble that was evidently brewing and was quite possible to come along. He kept hammering at the Navy Department, particularly at the Secretary of the Navy, and the President to fully man the fleet. He kept after the bureau about furnishing him material for not only protecting and developing Pearl Harbor as a base, but also to develop the islands and the outlying bases which would be called for in war plans. He had, of course, when he went to Washington, frequent conferences with the President, the Secretary of the Navy, and the Far East man of the State Department.

Q: He was supposed to have had good rapport with President Roosevelt.

Admiral Bieri: He did in a way, until he wouldn't agree with the President.

Q: Until that decision . . .

Admiral Bieri: The President and the State Department refused to move the battleships out of Pearl Harbor.† Richardson, right up to the end, was very insistent that that was what they should do and that the fleet under the circumstances was not ready for war and could not get ready without more men and more material. Eventually, as I understand it, the President said, "We've got to get rid of that fellow." And so, they got rid of him. That was in February of 1941.

---

* For a detailed recounting of Admiral Richardson's difficulties, see his book, written in collaboration with George C. Dyer: <u>On the Treadmill to Pearl Harbor: The Memoirs of Admiral James O. Richardson, USN (Retired)</u> (Washington, D.C.: Naval History Division, 1973).
† Fleet Problem XXI took place in the Hawaiian area in the spring of 1940. When it was completed, President Franklin D. Roosevelt directed that the fleet remain at Pearl Harbor rather than return to its bases on the West Coast. The idea was that leaving the fleet in Hawaii would serve as a deterrent to Japanese aggression in the Far East.

Q: That was immediately after he had the understanding that he was going to stay on for another year.

Admiral Bieri: Yes, and he'd been there.

Just before that time, Secretary Knox, accompanied by Mr. Donovan, made a visit out to the fleet.*

Q: Wild Bill Donovan.

Admiral Bieri: He was the head of the OSS, Office of Strategic Services. Knox and Donovan visited the fleet. Just before they came out, Knox made a speech to some group in the United States which was widely reported to the press. In it he said, "Just let the Japs start anything, if they feel like it. We'll knock their ears back so quickly that they won't know what happened to them," or words to that effect.

This disturbed Admiral Richardson more than a bit, because he knew that we were not in a position to do anything of the sort as far as the Japs were concerned. So when Knox appeared out there in Pearl Harbor, he and Richardson apparently had quite a stormy session.

While Knox was out there, he had a dinner one night for the flag officers of the fleet. He invited all the flag officers, except the senior ones. He didn't invite Richardson or Pye, but he invited all the younger flag officers.† He made his talk to them. He said that what he found out there was a lack of fighting spirit, and what the Navy needed more than anything else was younger officers in charge of the fleet and in positions of responsibility. It was not

---

* William Franklin Knox served as Secretary of the Navy from 11 July 1940 until his death on 28 April 1944. William J. Donovan was appointed by President Roosevelt in 1941 to head the Office of the Coordinator of Information, which was soon renamed Office of Strategic Services.
† Vice Admiral William S. Pye, USN, served as Commander Battle Force from January to December of 1941.

too long after that that Admiral Richardson was detached from his job, and he was relieved by Kimmel.*

I found that duty a very excellent duty, of course. I apparently did my job to the complete satisfaction of the admiral and the chief of staff. We didn't know there was anything in the wind about relieving the admiral of his duty. One Sunday morning I was playing golf with the admiral and a couple other officers on one of the golf courses in Hawaii. George Dyer, who was flag secretary, came out and handed the admiral this message out of the clear blue sky that he was detached and being relieved by Admiral Kimmel.†

Q: Dyer reported the admiral said, "They can't do that to me."

Admiral Bieri: I forget just what he said, but I know it was a terrific shock to all of us at the time. That was the first of February 1941 when he was relieved by Admiral Kimmel.

I had been working on a plan for the fleet to protect itself with its own guns while it was in Pearl Harbor. Among other things, that was supposed to be a duty of the Army in general war plans. It was the responsibility of the Army to protect the base and the ships in the base. But the Army had nothing; they had no equipment for that purpose. Their biggest antiaircraft guns were some small 3-inch guns that they had out there. The Navy was able to mount some 5-inch guns, and of course, we had the guns on the ships and so forth. Still, that put us in a very vulnerable position. I was in the process of drawing up and revising the plan which we already had. So I was left there with special duty with Admiral Kimmel for about two months to work with Walter Delany, his new operations officer, on perfecting and developing this plan.‡

---

* Admiral Husband E. Kimmel, USN, relieved Richardson on 1 February 1941, becoming Commander in Chief Pacific Fleet, along with the title of Commander in Chief U.S. Fleet.
† Commander George C. Dyer, USN. For Dyer's recollection of the experience see Paul Stillwell, Air Raid: Pearl Harbor! Recollections of a Day of Infamy (Annapolis: Naval Institute Press, 1981), pages 43-48.
‡ Captain Walter S. Delany, USN.

I don't remember that we had included in that plan any plan to counter torpedo fire, because nobody thought that the Japs would fire torpedoes in that limited space and hit ships. But we did draw up a very comprehensive plan for the use of the ships' guns, at sectors of different ships, different positions that they were to cover, and that sort of business.

Q: Protect itself against aircraft too?

Admiral Bieri: Yes, aircraft. That was the principal danger at that time. Having finished this to Walter Delany's and the admiral's satisfaction, I was detached at the end of about a month and assumed command of the Chicago.* This was a great pleasure for me. I had looked forward to having a ship command. I hadn't had a command since I had command of the Corry.

I found a good ship, and a good group of officers on board. I think in the time I had her, we did quite a bit towards improving her efficiency. She was the flagship of Admiral John Henry Newton, who was the division commander.† I had never served with Newton before, but we became very good friends during my cruise there and worked together well.

Early in that period, early in 1941, Newton took his division and several destroyers on a trip to Australia. Two of the ships visited New Zealand, and two of the ships --one the Chicago--visited Australia. We went into the capitol, Sydney, the principal port, and Brisbane, and then joined up again. We had a very successful visit with the Australians.

Q: They were actually at war.

---

* The USS Chicago (CA-29) was commissioned 9 March 1931. She had a standard displacement of 9,300 tons, was 600 feet long and 66 feet in the beam. Her top speed was 32 knots. She was armed with nine 8-inch guns, and eight 5-inch guns. The USS Chicago sank in the Rennell Islands on 30 January 1943 as a result of attacks by Japanese aircraft.
† Rear Admiral John H. Newton, USN, was Commander Cruisers Scouting Force and Commander Cruiser Division Four.

Admiral Bieri: They were at war. It was just at the time that we had passed the aid bill, and we were very popular down there at that time.* And still are, I think, quite popular.

Q: There were units of the Royal Navy there, too, weren't there?

Admiral Bieri: No, they weren't. There weren't any units of the Royal Navy there. We didn't see too much of the Australian Navy while we were there. They were probably off on duty in the various places, but they weren't in port.

Q: Some of them were up at Singapore, I think.

Admiral Bieri: Our main contact in Australia was with the political people, government people, including the governors. We had social duties while we were there, very pleasant visits.

Q: What was the purpose of the cruise down there?

Admiral Bieri: I never could quite figure that out, unless they sort of timed it with the adoption of the signing of the Lend-Lease Act. They wanted to let the Australians know that they weren't being left out on the limb, I suppose.

Q: It was almost a forgone conclusion that we were going to be in this.

Admiral Bieri: Yes, we were running convoys at that time from the Philippines back to the east. We had some cruisers convoying with different merchant ships; also transports with materials.

---

* The Lend-Lease Act, passed by the U.S. Congress on 11 March 1941, was a device that enabled the United States to provide military aid--war materials--to Great Britain without intervening directly in the Eureopean war.

On the way down, we stopped at Samoa. We created quite a bit of commotion with that visit, because the governor of Samoa didn't know we were coming until we appeared off the harbor. On Sunday morning there, it was quite a shock to him.

Q: Why this lack of communication?

Admiral Bieri: I guess they just didn't want the word to get out that we were down that way. I didn't know that he hadn't been told, but it was deliberate. Captain Jasper Wild was the governor at that time.* We spent a couple of days there, and then went on to Australia and New Zealand. After our visits down there, we rejoined, and came north and stopped at Fiji. Then back to Pearl Harbor, where we continued to carry out training.

One of the things that the fleet was doing at that time was developing the bases on Johnston Island, Palmyra, and Midway. The fleet was backing up these operations.

Q: That operation, as it pertained to these islands, this was a part of the Hepburn Plan, wasn't it, for fortification.†

Admiral Bieri: I never heard it referred to as the Hepburn Plan. It was part of the Orange War Plan that existed at that time.‡

On Friday morning before Pearl Harbor, we sailed from the harbor with Admiral Newton on board our ship. We had his division of cruisers. They included the Portland, and one other. The Indianapolis went out with us. She had Admiral Wilson Brown, commander of cruisers aboard.§ And we had one squadron of destroyers.

---

* Captain Laurence Wild, USN, commandant of the naval station at Tutuila, American Samoa.
† In December 1938 a board headed by Rear Admiral Arthur J. Hepburn, USN (Ret.), submitted a report containing an extensive base-development plan for both the Atlantic and Pacific.
‡ See Edward S. Miller, War Plan Orange: The U.S. Strategy to Defeat Japan, 1897-1945 (Annapolis: Naval Institute Press, 1991).
§ Vice Admiral Wilson Brown, USN, Commander Scouting Force.

Q: George Hussey was involved in this, wasn't he?*

Admiral Bieri: He was, he must have had the squadron. We joined the Lexington. The object of this exercise was to put a group of fighter planes on Midway Island. We left on Friday about noon. Things were getting very tense about that time. The Japanese ambassadors had been going back and forth. It was quite evident that relations between the two countries were very badly strained.

We, for some time, had had orders to attack any submarine contacts we made in the vicinity of Pearl Harbor. The two admirals that went out with us had had a conference with Admiral Kimmel just before we left. When Newton came back aboard, I met him at the gangway, and as I walked with him I had a conversation with him.

I asked him what was new, if anything, and if he had any information about the Japanese situation other than what was in the local papers, which wasn't much. He said, "No." The order to fire on submarine contacts was still extant. We were going to escort the Lexington out to Midway, to put these planes on board Sunday. Also, that the Indianapolis would leave us as soon as we got outside and go down to Johnston Island. She was on a special mission down there--inspection, and so forth.

When Wilson Brown left, of course, that left Newton in command of the group. We headed out toward Midway, zigzagging during the day and carrying out certain exercises en route. Saturday was very peaceful. Sunday morning, I was up at the usual time, which was usually around half past 6:00. I'd had my breakfast. I was up on the bridge watching the operations as we were about to approach the launching point for the planes. They handed me this message from Pearl Harbor that said, "The Japanese are attacking Pearl Harbor."

So the landing of the planes on Midway was called off. There was quite a bit of confusion as to where the Japs came from, or where they were going, or what the force consisted of. It was quite evident that it was a pretty good force with all the planes they had. The first information that we had was that one carrier was sighted south and west of Pearl Harbor. So we started down in that direction. After steaming all day long, this was

---

* Captain George F. Hussey, Jr., USN, Commander Mine Squadron Two.

called off, was canceled. We were told that that was a drifting barge that some aviator had sighted and thought it was a carrier.

Then we found out that the Japs had finished their job and had apparently launched this from northwest of Pearl Harbor. They were in a position that we couldn't possibly reach or overhaul them. So we were told to remain at sea and await orders, which we did.

The next day, we were en route south with orders to make a raid on the Japanese-held island down there. They said they would have an oil tanker in a certain position to fuel the ships. We were told to run in and make the raid. We rendezvoused with this oil tanker and all took on oil. About the time we got the oil on, we got the word that the Japs were about to launch an attack against Wake. We were to proceed up there to support Wake. We were so badly out of position by that time that we couldn't get to Wake.

If the Japs started in the next day or so, which they did, and before we got anywhere near Wake, the Japs had it.

Q: That might be a good place to stop. We'll have a lot of questions about that whole phase. Even what you've told me so far shows the real confusion.

Bernhard H. Bieri #3 - 91

Interview Number 3 with Vice Admiral Bernhard H. Bieri, U.S. Navy (Retired)

Place: Bethesda, Maryland

Date: Thursday, 31 July 1969

Interviewer: John T. Mason, Jr.

Q: Admiral, it's good to be aboard again this morning and to meet the various members of your family. We're going to resume your biography this morning at the outbreak of World War II.

Admiral Bieri: At the time of Pearl Harbor, I had already received my orders detaching me from the Chicago and ordering me for duty to the Chief of Naval Operations in the Navy Department.

Q: Was this a surprise to you?

Admiral Bieri: No, I'd been as sea at that time in the neighborhood of four years. I was well due to go ashore. In fact, overdue. However, my relief didn't show up. He had been sent down to South America.

Q: Who was that, Captain Bode?[*]

Admiral Bieri: Admiral Deyo.[†] So, I wasn't relieved until after Pearl Harbor.

The trip that we made out of Pearl Harbor, just prior to the attack on Friday, was the last time that I went to sea on the Chicago. She didn't go to sea again before I left. I

---

[*] At the time of the attack on Pearl Harbor, Captain Howard D. Bode, USN, was commanding officer of the battleship Oklahoma (BB-37).
[†] Captain Morton L. Deyo, USN, was sent to Brazil in February 1942 to take temporary command of the transport Monticello (AP-61). In June 1942 he became commanding officer of the cruiser Indianapolis (CA-35).

was eventually detached and relieved by Captain Howard Bode on the seventh of January, 1942.

I proceeded to carry out my original orders, traveling to the West Coast with my family on the Navy transport Wharton.

Q: Did she sail with destroyer protection, that kind of thing, escort?

Admiral Bieri: I think she had some destroyer protection for a day or so, until we got out of the waters of the Hawaiian Islands. Then I think we proceeded on our own and picked up destroyers out of San Francisco. There were several other ships in company with us, transports and merchant ships. We landed at San Francisco. I proceeded across country and reported to Chief of Naval Operations on the 11th of February, 1942.

Q: Was it difficult to find living quarters in Washington at that point?

Admiral Bieri: I owned a house in Washington. I had a little difficulty with that. I couldn't get the man out of it, even though I'd given him over three months' notice. He'd agreed to get out with three months' notice, but he was very slow doing it. We had to live around in rooms for several months before we finally got settled.

At that time they were already reorganizing the command, following Pearl Harbor. As soon as I reported to the Chief of Naval Operations, I was assigned to duty with the Commander in Chief, U.S. Fleet, who had set up his headquarters in the Navy Department.

Q: That was Admiral King.

Admiral Bieri: Admiral King.[*]

---

[*] Admiral Ernest J. King, USN, served as Chief of Naval Operations from 26 March 1942 to 15 December 1945 and as Commander in Chief U.S. Fleet from 20 December 1941 to 2 September 1945; he was promoted to the rank of fleet admiral in December 1944.

Q: Had you known him prior to this or served with him?

Admiral Bieri: He was an instructor at the Naval Academy, as a disciplinary officer, when I was a midshipman. But I had never served with Admiral King. Naturally, I had met him a number of times. Most recently, when he came out to visit the Pacific Fleet when Admiral Richardson was still in command.

I think my assignment to his staff was made through Admiral Kelly Turner, who then was looking for an assistant.[*] Since I had served with Turner at the war college, he had me transferred over there when I came.

Q: This, indeed, was quite an honor, wasn't it? Because Admiral King had the reputation of being very selective.

Admiral Bieri: He left the selection of his people to a large degree to his top assistants. Any of them that didn't meet the requirements after they were selected, they got rid of.

I think I went down there because of Turner's recommendation. Turner was very anxious to get to sea, so he wanted me to relieve him.

At that time, the deputy commander was Admiral Willson.[†] He was looking for a relief for Turner. King picked out C. M. Cooke.[‡]

Q: Savvy Cooke?

Admiral Bieri: Yes, Savvy Cooke. He had served with King several times and had been on duty with him at the Naval War College. They knew each other very well. He was an excellent choice.

---

[*] Rear Admiral Richmond Kelly Turner, USN, was director of the War Plans Division in OpNav and had additional duty as assistant chief of staff for plans on Admiral King's U.S. Fleet staff.
[†] Rear Admiral Russell Willson, USN, was chief of staff to Admiral King on the U.S. Fleet staff.
[‡] Rear Admiral Charles M. Cooke, Jr., USN, became assistant chief of staff for plans.

Q: A very brilliant man, wasn't he?

Admiral Bieri: He was a brilliant man and a very practical man. I credit Cooke with being a very important factor in prosecuting the war. And because he was in the shadow of Admiral King, he was one person who never got his fair share of acknowledgement for what he really accomplished.

Q: Can you talk more about him?

Admiral Bieri: Yes. I had never served with Cooke. I knew him only as a midshipman. I found him a very fine man to work with. As you say, a very brilliant man. He was a man who had practical ideas and objectives and knew how to get them done. He was a far-seeing person. He looked into the future, made his plans accordingly, then followed them up. It's for that reason that I say a great deal of our success in the war was due to Cooke. He was also the important factor in getting along with the Army and setting up the different committees and staffs and so forth that we needed. Going out and inspecting the different commands, and that sort of business.

Q: Are you implying that he was more diplomatic than Admiral King, perhaps?

Admiral Bieri: I think he was, yes, more diplomatic than Admiral King. Of course, he had to be because he was a staff officer in a junior capacity. He got along very well with people. He knew a great many able officers and eventually brought them into the organization. I was a great admirer of Cooke.

As soon as I got to Washington, they were just in the process of setting up the joint planning staff. It was composed of an officer from the Army, one from the Army Air Forces, and one from the Navy. It was supposed to be Turner on the Navy side, but he was in the process of leaving. I went to only a couple of meetings with him. It was very evident from the start that it would not be a very workable organization with Turner and some of the men that the other services put in there.

Q: Who was the Army representative?

Admiral Bieri: The Army representative was still Gerow.* He and Turner got along all right together. The Air Force sent over a man named Orvil Anderson, who was a very argumentative fellow and a very opinionated chap.† Apparently, he and Turner couldn't hit it off at all. I went to one meeting with them as Turner's assistant. When we came out, Turner announced that that was the last meeting that he was going to with that fellow, and hereafter I would carry the ball. I carried the ball for the rest of the war.

Eventually Savvy Cooke came, and he started to go to these meetings. He ran into the same fellow at the first meeting we had. When we left, he said, "Well, Bieri, you're it. I go to no more planning meetings with that fellow."

Q: Did this General Anderson continue on?

Admiral Bieri: Oh, yes, he continued there during a large part of the war. In fact, just before the preparation for the landing in Europe, he was reassigned by the Air Force to a combat command in England.

Q: Why would the Air Force want to keep a man who rubbed people the wrong way?

Admiral Bieri: I don't know why they did. He not only rubbed the Navy people the wrong way, but he rubbed the Army people the wrong way. He had that general reputation to

---

* Brigadier General Leonard T. Gerow, USA, was chief of the Army's War Plans Division when the United States entered World War II.
† Colonel Orvil A. Anderson, USA.

everybody that knew him, even the Air Force people there. Why General Arnold kept him there, I don't know.*

I'm sure that if Admiral King had a naval officer of the same characteristics there, he would have yanked him out and put somebody else in. That was one thing that he insisted on: that we get along with our opposites.

As I said, I attended only one meeting with Turner. The rest of the short time that he was there, which was about two weeks, I took over those meetings.

Q: How did you react to General Anderson?

Admiral Bieri: He irritated me a great deal, but I never let him get my goat or anything like that. I just shrugged it off; I didn't pay any attention to it. Of course, the thing was that great many times we didn't come to any definite joint conclusion. We had separate opinions, which we had to send up to the Chiefs of Staff.

Q: What kind of problems did you wrestle with?

Admiral Bieri: We had all kinds of problems. In that early part of the war, one of the big problems was the procurement of equipment: ships and so forth, ammunition, aircraft, guns for the different services in the different theaters.

While there had been a great deal of experimenting and some pilot work in the building of amphibious craft, there had been no definite steps taken to set up a program for production for the future to meet the campaigns as we thought they were going to develop. The output of amphibious craft was very small, and everybody was yelling for more of them. MacArthur wanted hundreds of them down in the Southwest Pacific.† We just didn't have them to give them to him. They weren't being manufactured yet. The program had really not gotten started, so we had to set that up.

---

* Lieutenant General Henry H. Arnold, USA, was Commanding General of the Army Air Forces.
† General Douglas MacArthur, USA, was Commander Southwest Pacific Area and Force.

They were getting ready for the invasion of Africa, and there weren't enough landing craft to outfit the transports we were going to put in there. We had to use makeshift craft of various sorts. The British had no large program of amphibious craft production. In fact, we eventually had to supply them with a great many of them.

Cooke was far-sighted, as I said before, and we figured out the number of these different types of these craft that we had to get. We made a program which we submitted to the Chiefs of Staff, and they approved it. It became the Navy's job to get them. Cooke, by putting the pressure on the various parts of the Navy Department, particularly the Bureau of Ships, was able to get this program under way and effective in comparatively short order.

Then there was the question of transports. You probably recall that at the early part of the war the only transports we had were converted merchant ships. A great many of them were old ships. The few Navy transports that we had were built primarily for the purpose of carrying passengers between different outlying stations. We had practically no combat transports, except these converted ships. They were old merchant liners.

So we envisioned that to carry out the subsequent landings in Europe and far-flung landings that we expected to make in the Pacific, we would need a large number of military transports.

Q: And they had to be fast ones?

Admiral Bieri: We couldn't expect to have them very fast. They had to be built under the merchant shipping program. That was controlled, of course, by Mr. Douglas on the shipping board.[*] They laid down a very extensive program of building merchant ships. It seemed to us that the only way for us to get a combat fleet would be to get the hulls from that program and then have them built as combat transports.

---

[*] Lewis W. Douglas was the deputy administrator of the War Shipping Administration under the administrator, Rear Admiral Emory S. Land, USN (Ret.).

Q: You mean like the Kaiser Liberty ships they were turning out?*

Admiral Bieri: Yes, they were mostly of that kind.

We got up a program that called for about 450 transports of various kinds--personnel transports, command transports, and cargo transports. We immediately ran into a good deal of opposition on this, this time from the Army Quartermaster Corps. Also from the shipping board, Mr. Douglas's outfit, who didn't want to give up any of these hulls. They wanted them to carry cargoes. This resulted in quite a tussle between different services. That was the only time that I felt that the Joint Chiefs of Staff held up a program to any appreciable extent. As this thing was argued back and forth for at least a month, probably more . . .

Q: And the Joint Chiefs couldn't come to any . . .

Admiral Bieri: The Joint Chiefs didn't come to a decision on it for a long time, a couple of months.

It was pretty difficult, I guess for General Marshall to tell his supply outfit that he didn't agree with them.† He might have agreed with them when they started. Their thesis was that the Navy was going to entirely too much trouble to take these ships and make "men of war" out of them. In other words, give them certain factors of safety which you wouldn't find in a merchant ship. Give them certain armament, and put the proper boat-handling equipment on them and that sort of thing. Communications and whatnot too.

The Army quartermasters and the transportation outfit insisted that they just didn't see any reason why you couldn't take an ordinary merchant ship and make a transport out of

---

* The Liberty ship was a mass-produced cargo ship designed by the U.S. Maritime Commission for use by the Allies. All told, American shipyards built 2,770 Liberties. The standard Liberty was 442 feet long, 57 feet in the beam, and had a light displacement of 3,337 tons. It had a cargo capacity of 10,920 deadweight tons. Henry J. Kaiser's shipyards built many of the Liberties.

† General of the Army George C. Marshall, USA, served as Army Chief of Staff from 1 September 1939 to 18 November 1945. He was promoted to General of the Army in December 1944.

it without all the "folderol." Of course, the Navy had never agreed to that theory, and we didn't agree with it.

Q: You mean, you didn't agree in terms of safety?

Admiral Bieri: We didn't agree in terms of efficiency of handling a large Army overseas. It might be all right just to carry troops across the ocean, and land them something like we did in the First World War, or something like that. Where you are going to carry troops up to a hostile beach and then make a forced landing against opposition, you've got to have ships that can be handled, that can be protected, and have a certain degree of safety while they have the men on board. You need ships that can be loaded properly, so as to get the stuff off and to help carry the boats that will put the men on the beach. Also, they'd have to have communications so that the whole outfit could be handled as a unit.

Q: The whole aspect of antiaircraft guns was important, wasn't it, in this war?

Admiral Bieri: Yes. At that time, the Joint Chiefs of Staff was composed of four members; Admiral Leahy, who was the chairman of the Joint Chiefs of Staff, the President's aide; Admiral King, the Navy member; General Marshall, the Army member, and General Arnold, the Army Air Forces member.[*] The decisions that the Joint Chiefs of Staff made were always unanimous decisions by the time they reached the President. They knew that if they couldn't make a unanimous decision, the President would make the decision. So they would make a unanimous decision.

We couldn't get a unanimous decision out of them for quite a while. Eventually, General Marshall--and I always gave him great credit for it--decided the Navy was right on this thing, and he approved it. He went to the President, and we got our program of some 450 combat transports. This eventually proved to be a great help in the war, particularly in Europe and the Pacific.

---

[*] Admiral William D. Leahy, USN, was chief of staff to the Commander in Chief, President Franklin D. Roosevelt. As such he was de facto chairman of the Joint Chiefs of Staff.

Q: Admiral, may I interrupt for a moment. In connection with the simple task of ferrying troops across, largely to Europe but in some respects to the southwest Pacific, do you want to comment on the value of the Cunarders?

Admiral Bieri: No, I never had much to do with the Cunarders.* They were just transports for carrying large numbers of troops from one area to another. They were not combat transports. In other words, if the British wanted to shift a large number of men from Australia to the European theater, or up to the Near East, they were excellent ships for that purpose. But they were never intended to be used as combat transports.

Q: They depended largely on their speed, didn't they?

Admiral Bieri: They depended on their speed and their capacity to carry men.

Q: I was thinking in terms of ferrying U.S. troops, because they did a considerable amount of that.

Admiral Bieri: Oh, yes. For instance in the Atlantic we carried a great number of troops from the United States to England on the big ships, the Queen Elizabeth, Queen Mary, Aquitania, and those ships. Once they got to England, the troops were being organized into an amphibious force. Then you had to have a combat organization to carry them over to the beach. That's what we were working out.

In connection with that, several small incidents that came up were rather interesting. Very shortly after I reported, Turner sent for me one day, and he said, "We've got to go over to a meeting this afternoon at the Joint Chiefs of Staff." General Wedemeyer--I'm not sure if at that time he was a general or just a colonel--was one of Marshall's staff members

---

* The passenger ships Queen Mary and Queen Elizabeth of the British Cunard Line were used during World War II as troop transports.

and continued as such during the war.* He was going to talk to the Joint Chiefs of Staff and the staff planners on the question of the European invasion.

Turner and I went over. Wedemeyer was a very able talker; he apparently had a good military education in the Army, and he'd also attended the German War College prior to the war.† He was considered quite an able strategist by people in the Army. He talked to this group about the invasion of Europe. It was his idea that there was no reason in the world why we shouldn't even at that stage immediately invade Europe with a large force. He said the Army had the leadership. All it required was the will and desire to do it, and we could go in there. He belabored this thesis for an hour or so, and everybody listened to him very attentively. After the meeting broke up, as Turner and I were walking back to the Navy Department, he said, "Well, what did you think of that?"

I said, "I think that's a foolish sort of business. What are they going to do? How are they going to get the troops over there? They haven't got the troops trained. The Army hasn't got the material to stay in there, or even to put them ashore. It's just a foolhardy recommendation, as far as I'm concerned."

He said, "That's the way I look at it too." We never heard any more of that.

Q: In the light of the difficulties faced on the Normandy landings, I think your opinion certainly was borne out, wasn't it?‡

Admiral Bieri: Yes, and we would have taken a terrible beating. Of course, the British tried some raids in there, just some small raids.

Q: The Dieppe thing?

---

* In July 1942, Colonel Albert C. Wedemeyer, USA, was promoted to brigadier general.
† Wedemeyer had done so from 1936 to 1938.
‡ D-Day for the Allied invasion of France at Normandy was 6 June 1944.

Admiral Bieri: The Dieppe thing, and they took a terrific beating.[*]

Not too long after the African invasion, the British began to get itchy feet about going into the continent.[†] They were always ready to push into the continent, without considering what the cost was going to be, and what it was going to take to stay there, and eventually do the job.

Q: Was this Churchill's "soft under belly" theory?[‡]

Admiral Bieri: No, this was on the west coast.

They came up with the idea of gathering up all the old ferryboats, interior water steamboats--like the ones we used to use in the Chesapeake Bay and Long Island Sound, merchant ships, and that sort of thing--that could be scraped together, then sending them over to England and mounting an expedition to take people across the Channel to the continent. I think this was a brainstorm of Winston Churchill. He'd apparently sold the idea to the President Roosevelt.

The first thing we knew, we got orders to get all these various types of ships together. A great many of them were coal burners. A lot of the ferryboats had to have a deck load of coal to take them over there. We got together a very, very considerable armada of these ships. I don't recall just what the number was, but it was an enormous number. They started this thing across the North Atlantic. It was about the time that the Germans were operating their submarines in wolf packs.

This outfit ran afoul of one of these German wolf packs, and they were, I think, sunk to the last ship. It must have been the most marvelous pyrotechnic display that ever

---

[*] On 19 August 1942, in order to test their own tactics and the German defenses, the Allies staged an amphibious assault on Dieppe, a small French port on the English Channel. Within a few hours, three-quarters of the invaders were killed, wounded, or captured. For an excellent overall account of the operation, see Terence Robertson, Dieppe: The Same and the Glory (Boston: Little, Brown and Company, 1962).
[†] The Allies invaded Casablanca, Morocco, on 8 November 1942.
[‡] Winston S. Churchill was Prime Minister of the United Kingdom from 1940 to 1945.

was put on. They all burned up; they were all wooden ships and coal-burning ships. That was the end of that expedition.

Q: Isn't that interesting. I remember just a vague bit about that, about them going across. Do you think this was inspired in any way by the evacuation of the British troops from Holland, and Belgium, and so forth?*

Admiral Bieri: Oh, no, this was long after that.

Q: The fact that they were able to marshal this great assortment of ships and get these men out, did this in any way inspire Churchill to think of the reverse operation?

Admiral Bieri: I don't know what inspired Churchill to come up with these ideas that he had. Of course, he was a marvelous person. There wasn't any question about it. He came up with a great many harebrained ideas during the war. He never had too much trouble selling them to Roosevelt, because Roosevelt was an amateur warrior himself.

    The two to them would come to a conference--I never attended them. At these early conferences, a lot of things were hatched out. They had one or two of these ideas, and they just couldn't be talked out of them. The Chiefs of Staff couldn't even get them out of them; they just told them to go ahead and do it because they just thought it was a good idea. Almost invariably they were complete flops. They wasted a lot of money and a lot of time.

Q: Admiral, is this perhaps a commentary on the merits of amateur influence in time of war?

---

* As France neared defeat at the hands of Germany in the spring of 1940, a collection of small British naval vessels and private craft evacuated 338,226 British, French, and Belgian soldiers and delivered them safely to Britain. The operation, which took place in and near the English Channel port of Dunkirk, France, lasted from 26 May to 4 June.

Admiral Bieri: There isn't any question about it, in my mind. These amateur military strategists that are looking for a quick cure to fighting and to pushing through the war are just the same as people in other fields who are looking for shortcuts.

Q: What was the attitude of Admiral King on this particular thing?

Admiral Bieri: He was opposed to it, naturally. He was very much opposed to it, and Marshall was opposed to it. But it went through anyhow.

There was another harebrained idea that was brought up at one of the Quebec conferences.* I don't know how much support it got from our people, and whether the Air Force supported it or not. I really doubt that they did.

This one originated with Churchill also. It was the matter of getting aircraft across the Atlantic. At that time, there were not too many of the aircraft that had enough range-- none of them as a matter of fact--that had enough range to fly the complete distance across the Atlantic.

Q: The fighter planes?

Admiral Bieri: The fighter planes and the bombers. They had to stop up in Canada and then refuel, and take a short cut across to Scotland. Of course, the bombers could go further than the fighters. The fighters had to be pretty much escorted by the bombers, so if anything happened to them they could tell people where they were and so forth.

Churchill came up with the idea that what we ought to have was a series of floating islands in the North Atlantic that could be more or less moored there, or kept in a certain position by tugboats and so forth. These islands could be made by building frames, large

---

* Quebec was the site of two major Allied conferences during the war: Quadrant, which met 14-24 August 1943, and Octagon, which met 12-16 September 1944. The first reaffirmed the plan to invade continental Europe in the spring of 1944; the second dealt with plans for the postwar treatment of Germany.

frames or rafts, and freezing water on them; so that you'd have an ice island floating out there in the sea.

Q: Artificial iceberg?

Admiral Bieri: An artificial ice field that the planes could land on. They were to have fuel there, and then take off. They would have a series of these across the North Atlantic.

Q: Wouldn't they be vulnerable to torpedoes?

Admiral Bieri: Not too, I guess, because they weren't that deep. There might be some light shooting of torpedoes in the iceberg. They were more vulnerable, it later proved, to the sea itself. It's a bit hostile to that sort of thing.

That thing, at the insistence of Churchill and Roosevelt, was undertaken to the extent that the U.S. was given the job of building one of these up around Newport--an experimental one, equipping it, and freezing it, and setting it up. The first time it got out in the fairly rough water, it just broke up. And that was the end of that idea.

Q: Out of that did we have the Bluie bases, and so forth: Those bases in Greenland and Labrador.

Admiral Bieri: They were all ready. The Air Force developed those. They were used during the rest of the war.

Q: I got a comment recently from Admiral Oldendorf, I guess it was, on the impracticality of those bases too.[*] That they were so horribly expensive, and by that time we had begun to take them in transports anyway.

---

[*] Admiral Jesse B. Oldendorf, USN (Ret.).

Admiral Bieri: They flew quite a number across. I remember before the African invasion, I came back with Admiral Ramsay to Washington on the <u>Queen Mary</u>.* We were going to fly back, but we couldn't get out of England because of the weather. She was coming back empty to get a load of soldiers. I flew back when I went back to Europe right after the conference in Washington, by way of Gander.† I think we were flying in a converted merchant air transport.

When we got to Gander, a large group of U.S. Army Air Forces planes began landing there. I think there were several squadrons of fighters, and two squadrons of bombers. At that time, I think it was the B-24, and several squadrons of fighters. We had stopped there for fuel in the late afternoon, when these fellows came in. I was rather astounded when I saw these pilots come in. To me they looked like my young grandson out there. They were all nice young chaps, very eager, and terribly enthusiastic young fellows. You could see that they hadn't had any extensive experience, just their preliminary training. It was their plan that these squadrons would take off in turn and fly from there to Scotland.

Q: Not going by way of Iceland?

Admiral Bieri: No, Prestwick. We were to fly the same way. We left several hours before them, but they were supposed to get in there before we were. We got in there the next day, and it was still pretty bad around Prestwick when we got in there. We came down through a low overcast, generally foggy condition. When we landed, I inquired of the Americans there if these fellows had arrived. He said, "A few of them have arrived, but we don't know where the rest of them are. They've scattered all over the north of Scotland and flying around the North Sea, and we're trying to get them back."

Q: Just like a bunch of birds.

---

* Admiral Bertram H. Ramsay, RN, was the top planner for British naval forces in the Mediterranean.
† Gander, Newfoundland, Canada, was the takeoff point or landing point for many transatlantic flights.

Admiral Bieri: They were all over the place. They finally got them in all right, most of them, I think. They were having a lot of difficulty getting them over.

I think, later on, when the Air Force got settled up over there--of course, they improved the fighters, they could fly further. I think that a great many of the fighters were assembled over on the other side, taken over by ships.

Q: The real emergency was in that time of the Battle of Britain, wasn't it, the desperate need?

Admiral Bieri: Getting back to my staff work in Washington, I was quite surprised in the middle of the summer, '42, to receive orders to report to the Chief of Naval Operations for the Director of Naval Communications. I hardly had the orders in my hand when I got another set of orders canceling them and telling me to report on the first of August and to return those orders as they had been revoked. I was to report to Admiral Ingersoll, the Commander of the Atlantic Fleet, as Deputy Commander of the Atlantic Fleet.[*]

Q: What was the mystery back of this change of orders?

Admiral Bieri: I think they were looking for a Director of Naval Communications, and they had seen my previous duty in communications in the Navy Department. I was one of many they had available at that time, and somebody picked me out to go in there without apparently consulting the proper people on King's staff. That immediately brought King and Cooke into the picture, and they had my orders canceled. I, at that time, was attending all the meetings and doing all the Navy work on the joint staff planners.

Q: Before you take this North Atlantic assignment, may I ask, you intimated that there were trips to England during the time you were on duty with Savvy Cooke?

---

[*] Admiral Royal E. Ingersoll, USN, served as Commander in Chief Atlantic Fleet from 1 January 1942 to 15 November 1944. He was promoted to four-star rank in July 1942.

Admiral Bieri: Yes, this was in connection with this duty I'm just about to mention. I received these orders from Admiral King, issued by the Bureau of Personnel, assigning me to the Atlantic Fleet as Deputy Commander of the Atlantic Fleet. I was still a captain. I was sort of at a loss as to what this thing was all about, but I was finally called in and told that I was to report to Admiral Ingersoll for duty. Then I would be sent to Europe as liaison officer for the Atlantic Fleet with the European Theater of Operations headquarters in London.

Before I left, I was promoted to rear admiral. I carried out my orders early in August. I arrived in London and reported to Admiral Stark, who was commander of the U.S. Navy Forces in Europe, with these very indefinite orders to report to the Commanding General of the European Theater of Operations to which Eisenhower had just been appointed or designated.*

I reported there, and of course Eisenhower was in the process of making plans for the invasion of Africa. He had a naval group headed by Admiral Ramsay of the British Navy for his operating setup for planning purposes at Norfolk House. We had quite a number of American troops and transports and officers over there to head up certain parts of the amphibious forces.

Q: Was Admiral Hewitt designated yet?

Admiral Bieri: Admiral Hewitt had been designated and he was working out of Norfolk, Virginia, with Patton's divisions.†

---

* Admiral Harold R. Stark, USN, served as Commander U.S. Naval Forces Europe from April 1942 to August 1945. Major General Dwight D. Eisenhower, USA, appointed Commander United States Military Forces in Europe, arrived in London on 24 June 1942 to head the military buildup and planning.
† For the invasion of North Africa in November 1942, Rear Admiral H. Kent Hewitt, USN, was designated Commander Western Naval Task Force; Major General George S. Patton, Jr., USA, was Commanding General, Western Task Force, U.S. Army.

The people that were to go into the Mediterranean, with a contingent of American troops under General Fredenhall, were to land at Oran.* The naval commander of that outfit was Rear Admiral A. C. Bennett.†

Q: Where had plans for this been formulated--at Quebec?

Admiral Bieri: The original plans were formulated just as soon as the war started. We were working on this thing. There was, of course, considerable discussion at the high level as to whether we were to go right into Europe on the west coast, or were to go up under the "soft belly," or undertake some other operations. The American Chiefs of Staff apparently were not in favor of going into Europe at any place at that time, but they did agree to go into Africa. It started that way.

The planning for prosecuting the war in Europe started as soon as we got into the war. They finally concentrated on going into Africa about the middle of the summer of '42. Hewitt was set up down at Norfolk. I remember going down there to see him, before I went to Europe. The training of his group, and the organization was quite well along. They were carrying out landing exercises on the beaches inside the Chesapeake. The organization was well set up with the Army, and everybody was working together there.

Hewitt's outfit was to sail with Patton, directly from Norfolk to the west coast of Africa, entirely supported by American naval ships. What we had to go into North Africa with the British, was the one or two divisions under Fredenhall. As I said, the American naval commander of the expedition was Bennett. Bennett, before he went over there, was part of the Atlantic Fleet.

I received very indefinite instructions as to what I was to do when I got over there.

Q: Why, sir, were you under Royal Ingersoll?

---

* Major General Lloyd R. Fredenhall, USA, Commanding General Center Task Force United States Army.
† Rear Admiral Andrew C. Bennett, USN, Commander Advance Group Amphibious Force Atlantic Fleet.

Admiral Bieri: Because he had Bennett, and he had certain ships over there. I presume that King didn't want to send me over there as his representative.

Admiral King, I think, felt that in these operations where both the British Navy and the American Navy were involved, that neither our Army nor the British were very keen to have anybody around that represented him. I think he always felt that he ought to have somebody there that was directly responsible to him. He apparently couldn't sell that idea to Eisenhower or Marshall, nor the British. So, by making me Deputy Commander of the Atlantic Fleet, that was more or less my cover for going over there as representative for Admiral King.

Q: And you were well aware of your direct . . .

Admiral Bieri: However, it left me with a very indefinite status as far as any command authority was concerned. In fact, I had no command authority. There was no one that I could give orders to. If I saw anything that I didn't like, I couldn't change anything like that. It appeared to me that about the best I could do was to offer my good services to Eisenhower and the British as a friendly adviser about anything that concerned our troops.

Ramsay was--in our service, we'd call him a rather stiff-necked person. We got along very nicely together, and he was always very pleasant to me. But he was very jealous of anyone criticizing or commenting on things that they were about to do, or planning to do.

Eisenhower felt, naturally, that he had appointed this fellow as his naval commander, and he was obligated to take all his naval advice from this one man. I was a frequent visitor to Ramsay at Norfolk House but was given no office space or given access to the plans. My advice was not solicited and when given was not accepted. As I said, there wasn't too much for me to do.

While I was over there, just before we went into Africa, Stark received a letter from Bennett in which Bennett reported that the British were going to set up a project in connection with the landing. They would take two of the wooden Coast Guard ships, cutters which the Americans had given them, and they would load these down with raiding parties in the neighborhood of 400 or 500 men. One taken from the British forces and one taken from the American forces, about half Army and half Navy each. These two cutters were to accompany the amphibious forces. When the group arrived opposite Oran, they would split off, and at the moment the landing forces hit the beaches--which were at two places a considerable distance from Oran--these two cutters would make a dash for the harbor of Oran, cut it out, and prevent the French from doing any damage to the shipping or to the harbor.

Q: Was that where the Jean Bart was?*

Admiral Bieri: No, she was down at Casablanca. There was a good deal of merchant shipping in this place, and there were bound to be some light French craft in this place. Bennett took objection to this thing because he said, and quite rightly, he had come to the conclusion that it couldn't be a success. It would result in a heavy loss of American lives and a loss of both ships.

However, this operation had originated with the British and been sold to Ramsay. Of course, the British were always open to an operation of that sort. They had tried them out in the First World War, and had tried them out in the Second World War. Whether the results were commensurate with the cost has always been a question in my mind--that they never were. I so advised Ramsay.

Q: That one and other similar ones seemed to smack of a sort of 19th century approach to things.

Admiral Bieri: That's right. Stark sent for me; the letter was addressed to him. He handed me the letter, had me read it in his office, and he said, "What do you think of it?" I told him

---

* Jean Bart was a French battleship.

my opinion of it, the same as Bennett's. He said, "I wish you'd discuss this with Eisenhower."

The letter was addressed to him, but I said, "I'll be glad to discuss it with the general."

So I made an appointment to see the general. I went down armed with this letter to talk to him. He read the letter, and then he said, "I can't take your advice on this thing. I have to get my advice from Ramsay."

I said, "I realize that he's your naval commander, but I do think that the involvement of these American forces by the British requires that a lot of serious thought be given to it. I don't think, and none of my naval associates think, that this operation is going to be successful or give any returns." He said he couldn't go anything about it, and I could talk to Ramsay if I wanted to. Eisenhower didn't like it too much. He didn't like my bringing the subject up to him.

Q: Why didn't Stark do it himself?

Admiral Bieri: I don't know why Stark didn't do it.

Q: Didn't he have a good relationship with Eisenhower?

Admiral Bieri: Yes, he had a good relationship with Eisenhower. But he didn't like to go around getting into arguments about things.

Q: This was extracurricular, wasn't it?

Admiral Bieri: I had access to Ramsay's planning headquarters, and I used to go down there every day and talk about certain things. He never really took me into his complete confidence about what they were going to do, and how they were going to do it. He would talk, and listen, and tell me a few things. I brought this subject up. I told him that Bennett and I were both of the opinion that this thing would not pay proper dividends. He said, "If it doesn't do anything else, it's good for the spirit of the people to carry out one of these operations. If successful, it's a wonderful boost for morale." He was very peeved about this thing too, that we should question him on it.

Q: Was it generally known at that point, that you were kind of a representative for Admiral King?

Admiral Bieri: They knew I was over there for King.

There was nothing more I could do about this thing.

Q: Did you report it to King?

Admiral Bieri: No. I think the letter to Stark was sent on to King.

Of course, Bennett, while he was part of the Atlantic Fleet, was no longer in a military command in the Atlantic Fleet. He was administered by the Atlantic Fleet, but his command was the British over there in this task force. There was a British naval officer, Admiral Troubridge--a nice young fellow--in command of that group.* He was under command of Troubridge. So I had no command status as far as this thing was concerned.

It later developed that Bennett was of the opinion that I should have given orders to stop this thing, which of course I couldn't do.

The expedition went down, the landing on the beach was late being made, and the communications were poor. The two ships went in against the barrier, and by the time they broke the chains and started up the channel, two French destroyers came out of Oran and gunned them down. They sank both ships, with a terrific loss of life. The few men that got off were captured by the French and taken ashore. Nothing was accomplished.

Q: Was there any comment on this afterwards by Eisenhower and the others?

---

* Commodore Thomas Troubridge, RN, commanded the Center Naval Task Force for the attack on Oran-Arzeu, Algeria.

Admiral Bieri: Yes, there was; I'll come to that. The sequel to the thing was that Bennett, who was a headstrong young fellow and not too diplomatic, then sat down and wrote a letter to Admiral King, directly. He should have known that he was no longer in King's military command. If he wanted to comment about this thing, he should have commented to his military commander--Eisenhower--through his regular channels, but he didn't. He wrote a letter to King in which he said, "I told them that was going to happen, and nobody did anything about it." King sent this letter to Eisenhower.

By that time we were in Algiers, and Eisenhower sent for me, and he was mad as the dickens. He was just terrifically furious.

Q: With you or with Bennett?

Admiral Bieri: With Bennett. That Bennett had the audacity to report this thing directly to Admiral King instead of reporting through the naval command to him. There wasn't much argument about that. He said he was going to get that fellow out of there immediately, no matter what had happened.

I said, "Look, General, these young fellows have never worked in anything except a naval command. They've never worked on these unified commands, so to speak. I don't think there was any intention of Bennett to go over your head and report to Admiral King. I think that he just felt that here is a part of the U.S. Navy, and he was reporting it to the U.S. naval headquarters."

I was about to leave there at that time to come home. I'd finished my usefulness over there. By that time Bennett was ashore in Oran.

I said, "I'm going back and I'll stop in Oran and tell Bennett that he made this mistake. And that he ought to admit it and recall his letter and put it through in the proper way." So Eisenhower agreed that they'd handle it that way.

I stopped at Oran, and spent the night there. I talked to Bennett about this thing, and he said, "Well, I'll be damned if I do." The result was that Bennett was back in the United States almost by the time I was. That was part of the end of that affair.

The next part was the reaction on me. A couple of years later, there were four officers recommended for advancement to vice admiral. I was one of them. There was Jimmy Hall, Harry Hill, myself, and one other officer.* Harry Hill was the senior one, and I was next. I knew that this recommendation had gone up from the commander in chief's headquarters. The other three officers were promoted, and I wasn't.

About two weeks later than that, still nothing came through, and I ran into Randall Jacobs one day.† I said, "Randall, what ever became of that recommendation that I'd be promoted to vice admiral? I haven't seen anything of it."

He said, "President Truman refuses to promote you."‡

I said, "What's the idea?"

He said, "I don't know."

So I went in to see Admiral Edwards, who then was the Deputy Commander in Chief.§ Apparently Jacobs spoke to him about me, and Edwards sent for me. I sat in his office, and he said to me, "Do you know a fellow named Bieri who was responsible for the loss of lives of about 500 or 600 men at the invasion of Oran?"

I said, "No. The only other 'Bieri' I know is Don Beary, and I know he didn't have anything to do with it."**

He said, "This guy's name was B. H. Bieri."

I said, "What do you mean?"

He said, "The aide to President Truman, Commodore Vardaman, Naval Reserve, when these names came up, took the list in to the President.†† He said, 'Here's a list of the officers to be promoted to vice admiral. This guy here shouldn't be promoted under any

---

* Rear Admiral John L. Hall, Jr., USN; Rear Admiral Harry W. Hill, USN.
† Vice Admiral Randall Jacobs, USN, served as Chief of the Bureau of Navigation/Personnel from 19 December 1941 to 15 September 1945. He was promoted to vice admiral in February 1944.
‡ Harry S Truman became President of the United States following the death on 12 April 1945 of President Franklin D. Roosevelt.
§ Admiral Richard S. Edwards, USN, Deputy Commander in Chief U.S. Fleet.
** Rear Admiral Donald B. Beary, USN.
†† Commodore James K. Vardaman, Jr., USNR, served as naval aide to the President from May 1945 to April 1946.

circumstances. He was responsible for the loss of 500 or 600 men at the battle of Oran.' Then he told him about this incident." Then he said that I had knowledge that this thing was going to happen, and I should have stopped it--given an order to stop it.

It developed that Vardaman was Bennett's intelligence officer, and he'd picked up some of this information when he was over there at that time. This is the story he told Truman.

Q: Who had succeeded Roosevelt.

Admiral Bieri: Yes, succeeded Roosevelt. So I wasn't to be promoted.

At that time Eisenhower had gotten back from Europe, after the surrender. Admiral King and Eisenhower, and I think it was Jacobs, went up to see the President. Edwards told me later, "By the combined efforts of Admiral King, Eisenhower, and Jacobs [it might have been General Marshall there]; you are now to be promoted to vice admiral."

Q: They corrected the record.

Admiral Bieri: They persuaded the President that he had acted on faulty information. I was made a vice admiral, junior to all the other chaps on the list, but that didn't make much difference.

Q: What happened to the career of Bennett?

Admiral Bieri: Bennett was given a shore assignment, some training unit in the United States, and retired right after the war. He was a very able officer, but he certainly made a mistake that time.

I stayed in London during the planning stage of this operation. Eventually it was decided that Admiral Andrew Cunningham, RN, not Ramsay, would command the British and be the naval commander going into North Africa. I think this was made by the Combined Chiefs of Staff in deference to the fact that Cunningham had fought the entire war down there in the Mediterranean. The British wanted him to finish the business up.

I moved down to Gibraltar when Eisenhower's headquarters moved down, just before the invasion. I flew down in an Army B-24, in company with a British general. We sat up in the nose of this thing to look out on the water. We flew down from Bournemouth directly to Gibraltar. We flew in the daytime unescorted.

Q: This is the time when the Bay of Biscay was a dangerous place.

Admiral Bieri: Yes, we flew down unescorted, very close to the water. You could see the direction of the sea and the wind. I got into a conversation with a young Army chap, who was navigator of this flight.

I said, "It looks like we've got a westerly wind that will carry us in toward the beach, toward the Bay of Biscay." He said, "Oh, no, we've got a tail wind." I didn't argue with him.

Then I said to him, "Don't you fellows ever load these guns you've got here?" They were .50-caliber machine guns, but they weren't loaded. They had the belt hanging over a hook and the guns were just set up.

He said, "Oh, no, we don't bother about loading those. The Germans have got a few Messerschmitts out here. We fly right down close to the water. If we see one of them coming, we just give her the gun, and we just lose them. They can't catch us." I didn't say anything, but I was still kind of dubious about this whole business. The next thing we knew, we sighted land, not only dead ahead, but also on the port hand.

We'd been blown clear over into the Gulf of Biscay, almost to the boundary of France and Spain.

Q: Awful good target, weren't you?

Admiral Bieri: We had to head west to beat the band to get around the point and steer south again. We eventually got to Gibraltar, with a sigh of relief.

I was assigned to the general officers' mess at the Fortress. The next day, General Jimmy Doolittle of the Air Force flew in on one of these things.[*] He got in just at dinner time. I was sitting alongside of him.

He said, "Boy, we had an experience coming down here today. One of those Messerschmitts jumped us. These guys weren't ready for them. They poured a bunch of bullets into us, and hit the pilot and second pilot. I had to get in and do the flying."

I said, "I came down yesterday. I wondered why these guys didn't have their guns loaded."

He said, "They're going to have them loaded from now on."

Q: So many planes had been lost on that same route.

Admiral Bieri: So that was the way that we got to Gibraltar. The headquarters stayed at Gibraltar until the forces were all landed in Africa. My relations with Andrew Cunningham were excellent. He was a wonderful man and, of course, a great naval commander. He took me into his complete confidence as far as all the operations were concerned. I attended all his staff meetings. If he felt like it, he'd ask me questions about things, and ask me what my opinion was and so forth. I had a very fine relationship with Andrew Cunningham.

Q: He was far more pleasing to the Americans than Admiral Ramsay was.

---

[*] Major General James H. Doolittle, USA, Commanding General, XII Air Force. Earlier in the year, Doolittle had commanded the successful raid against Japanese cities with B-25 bombers flown from the USS Hornet (CV-8).

Admiral Bieri: Oh, yes. He was a born leader of men, Cunningham was. Ramsay, I would say, was more or less a martinet type and didn't give too much consideration to the feelings of his subordinates or other people. What he did was right, and that was it.

There wasn't too much for me to do, but I did contact all the American ships that came in. In particular the merchants ships that were damaged, and so forth.

One day, about three days after the landings were made at Casablanca, Cunningham sent for me and he said, "Bieri, we haven't been able to get any information out of Patton or Hewitt down there. Eisenhower wants to get some information. We've been sending down our mosquito planes, but every time we send one down there, they are shot down. We don't know who shoots them down, unless the Americans are shooting them down. There aren't any other planes around there to touch them. Eisenhower wants to send a staff group down there to interview Patton and Hewitt and find out what's going on down there in the way of fighting and what progress they're making. We'd like you to go down on one of the British fast mine layers." They were capable of going about 30 odd knots--4,000- or 5,000-ton ship.

So this party of staff officers and myself got on the ship at Gibraltar and headed down for Casablanca with a young British captain named Freiberg in command of her. We would arrive off Casablanca sometime after dark. Hewitt had been notified that we were on our way. I don't know whether he got the message or not.

On the way down, I remarked to Freiberg, who was making about 30 knots, I said, "Don't you fellows ever zigzag?"

He said, "Oh, no, we don't worry about zigzagging. I was a submarine skipper. I never could hit anything going faster than 10 knots, and I don't think they can now." The sequel to that was, about two months later, he was sunk by a submarine in the Mediterranean.

We got through in a rather peculiar way. It turned dark, and just before we got to Casablanca, the entire naval contingent for landing troops and supplies on the west coast was there with their escorts; they got under way and stood out to sea. We steamed right through this whole group of naval ships to the entrance of Casablanca. We managed to make ourselves known, and keep from getting fired on. Captain Freiberg took us down to the entrance buoy at Casablanca, put us in a power boat, and let us go in. He stood off to sea and we made a rendezvous to be back there at a certain time in the morning, while it was still dark.

We went ashore, and after some difficulty we located the Augusta, which was Hewitt's flagship, and Hewitt. We told Hewitt what we were there for. I got all the naval dope from Hewitt without any difficulty, of course. But Patton was up someplace in the country with his troops. They had communication with him and sent word that this group was there to get information from him. He said, "I'm too damn busy for that sort of stuff. Tell them to go to hell."

Q: Send that back to General Eisenhower?

Admiral Bieri: They sent that back to me. I sent him another message, and I said to him, "That's fine, General, that's all I wanted to know. I'll go back and report it to Eisenhower."

In about five minutes another message came through and said, "Patton will be right down."

He showed up in about half an hour with a couple of aides. They all had helmets on, a carbine over their shoulder, and a big pistol on each hip.

Q: Fighting men.

Admiral Bieri: He was very genial toward me, shook hands, was glad to see me, and was in a very jovial mood. Then he went to work on these Army files that we had brought down from the staff. He gave them a real working over. He didn't mince any words about any information they brought down there. I don't think he gave them too much information, but I had gotten enough from Hewitt, so we were pretty well armed and satisfied. That was my last encounter with Patton. I never ran in to him again during the rest of the war.

Q: Were you making regular reports to Admiral King on all of this?

Admiral Bieri: No, I made no reports to Admiral King. He knew I was over there. I did report to him that I thought that my usefulness about this time--

Very shortly after that, we moved the headquarters to Algiers at St. George's Hotel. I had only one Navy enlisted man with me. He was a chief yeoman. We set up office in this hotel in the part that was assigned to us. We had a very adequate big suite, very adequate living quarters, and the mess was right down below. So we decided to live and work in this place they gave us. Then they advised us that we couldn't live there. The enlisted man had to live in a certain place, and I would have to have a billet as signed to me. The quartermaster of headquarters came around and wanted me to go out with him and pick out a house. I said I didn't want a house.

He said, "Maybe you'd like to live in a mess."

I said, "That would suit me fine." So I moved in with a bunch of British officers and Jerry Wright.* The rest of the stay in Algiers, we lived in this mess.

My usefulness there had come to an end, practically. I still went to all of Cunningham's meetings, went out on his inspections with him, and so forth. I accomplished one thing while I was there.

There were a great many merchant ships being damaged. The British had very inadequate facilities or personnel to repair these ships, even enough to get them back to England for repairs. We were very much in need of merchant ships.

Q: Where were they repaired in Britain?

Admiral Bieri: They weren't being repaired too much, but at least they got them back there. Some of them could be repaired. Some of them could also be repaired at Gibraltar.

They would just bring them in when they got a big torpedo hole in them, tie them up to a dock if they still floated, and let them stay there.

---

* Captain Jerauld Wright, USN.

We were walking around one day inspecting the waterfront and things. I said to Cunningham, "Why don't they patch these things and get them out of here, and get them over where they can fix them up?"

He said, "I wish I could, Bieri, but we just haven't got the personnel who know how to do it or can do it. I can't get them. We're that short of people."

I said, "I'll tell you what I can do. I can get you a man over here who will get all these ships moving. They've got him over there at the Italian port on the east coast of Africa, trying to raise a bunch of sunken merchant ships, which won't be any good when they get them up."

Q: Was this Sullivan?

Admiral Bieri: No this was Captain Ellsberg.[*]

I said, "You get him over here, and he'll get these ships fixed up for you. He'll get the ships out of Oran, and get this thing started."

He said, "Okay, let's go back to headquarters and get Ike to send a message to Admiral King, and see if we can get an order started." So, we did. We got him.

He was a naval constructor, class of 1914, very smart chap. When he came over there, he was a ghost of his old self. He'd been working over there in that hot climate. He'd been working very hard, he was just a shadow of a man, but he was full of pep. He went to work and started this thing. But it was too much for him physically, and he had to be relieved.

Then they sent Sullivan out there, and he was also a very excellent man.[†] I didn't know at that time that Sullivan was available, but he came over and finished up the job.

Q: He came over from New York.

---

[*] Captain Edward Ellsberg, USN, a Navy salvage expert.
[†] Captain William A. Sullivan, USN. The oral history of Sullivan, who retired as a rear admiral, is in the Columbia University collection.

Admiral Bieri: He came over from New York, sent over by Admiral King.

By that time, I figured that I wasn't contributing too much any more. Admiral King ordered me back to headquarters in Washington.

I departed Algiers, by Casablanca and Oran. That's when I had the conference with Bennett, and I saw Jimmy Hall at Casablanca. An Army transport flew us across the desert down to Accra, and back to the United States.

We left Algiers on the 15th of December, and got back Christmas Eve. Much to the surprise of my family, I played Santa Claus and walked in Christmas Eve. Nobody expected me.

I got very commendatory letters from Admiral Cunningham and General Eisenhower. I reported again for duty to the Commander in Chief U.S. Fleet on the 20th of January.

At that time King was out in Hawaii, and Cooke was out there with him. The Chiefs of Staff were all out there, I think. I reported to Edwards, and I said, "I'm back now, and I've got a man doing that job over there in the planning place. I'm ready to go out to the Pacific. I've got my bags packed, and I can get right on the train."

Edwards said that he was to talk with the admiral that evening on the phone, and he would let me know in the morning. He called me in the next morning and told me that he had spoken with King, who had replied, "Tell Bieri to keep his shirt on. They have more people out here now than they can use, and I still need a few in Washington."

So on January 20, 1943, I resumed my job with the joint planners, which I continued until the following October, when I was appointed as assistant chief of staff. In addition to taking up some of the administrative duties from Cooke, I continued on with the planners as we were making preparations for the forthcoming conference which was to be held in Cairo.

The U.S. group that was to attend this left the Chesapeake in the USS Iowa on the 11th of November and proceeded across the south Atlantic with two destroyer escorts.* In addition to President Roosevelt and his party, there were the four Chiefs of Staff, each of

---

* The battleship Iowa (BB-61) was commanded during this voyage by Captain John L. McCrea, USN. The oral history of McCrea, who retired as a vice admiral, is in the Naval Institute collection.

those heading one of the forces and being accompanied by their assistant chief of staff, two or three strategic planners, and a group of logistic planners. Work was continued on the way over as the Chiefs of Staff held daily meetings.

The Iowa arrived at Mers-el-Kebir (Oran) on the 20th of November, and the President and the Chiefs of Staff were flown immediately to Cairo with a heavy escort of fighters. The transports not being able to take all, the planners were left at Oran until the night of the following day, when we left by air under cover of darkness.

The meetings of the Combined Chiefs of Staff began at once in the Mena House, where the British has set up the facilities for the Chiefs' meetings and working spaces for the different committees of the British and Americans. Appropriate billets had also been arranged outside the Mena for the Prime Minister and President, and for the others. Noon and evening meals were taken by the staff at the Mena, but we had our breakfasts and slept in commandeered houses near the Mena.

The planners' work continued late into the nights in order to have the position papers ready to present to the Combined Chiefs for their meetings on the following days. The conference was completed on the afternoon of the eighth of December '43. Each day the Joint Chiefs would meet in the forenoon, and then the Combined Chiefs would meet in the afternoon. The demands of each theater were taken up in turn, beginning with the European, then the Pacific, Southwest Pacific, and finally Southeast Asia. The Mediterranean needs were considered at the same time as the European.

I did not see the President after he left the Iowa but understood that he and Mr. Churchill were billeted nearby, as were the Chiefs of Staff. Chiang Kai-shek was present for several days, but Stalin said he could not attend due to his pressing duties of personally commanding the fighting in Russia.[*] The meeting with him was at Teheran and is discussed later.

---

[*] Generalissimo Chiang Kai-shek served as President of Nationalist China on the mainland from 1943 to 1949 and as President of the Republic of China on Taiwan from 1950 until his death in 1975. Joseph Stalin ran the Soviet Union essentially as a dictatorship from the late 1920s to his death in 1953.

We made the allocation of forces and material to the theaters. Of course, the European theater had the priority. We finally got down to Southeast Asia. By the time we got to Southeast Asia, there wasn't much left to give to Mountbatten.[*]

Q: Was he present at this conference?

Admiral Bieri: Yes, he was present. He had his staff there. The way the Combined Chiefs conducted their meeting was they first heard from the theater commander or his representative what he planned to do for the coming year and what he needed. Then the planners would come in knowing beforehand what his plans were. We would come in with what we recommended they be given from what was available.

Q: They weren't all there--these commanders. MacArthur wasn't there, was he?[†]

Admiral Bieri: No, MacArthur's chief of staff was there.

Q: Who was that?

Admiral Bieri: Nimitz wasn't there, he was represented by Admiral King. The rest of them were there--Eisenhower, Wilson in the Mediterranean, Mountbatten was there.

Q: That was Maitland Wilson?[‡]

Admiral Bieri: Yes. Sutherland, who represented MacArthur, was there.[§]

---

[*] Admiral Louis Mountbatten, RN, Supreme Allied Commander Southeast Asia, 1943-46.
[†] General Douglas MacArthur, USA, Commander Southwest Pacific Area and Force.
[‡] General Henry Maitland Wilson of the British Army was Middle East Commander in Chief.
[§] Major General Richard K. Sutherland, USA, was MacArthur's chief of staff.

As I said, the Chiefs of Staff turned down the operation against Rabaul, and choose instead to carry out the campaign simultaneously with the Central Pacific and Manus and then on to the Philippines.

When we got to the Southeast Asia, there was very little left to give to Mountbatten. The Chiefs of Staff heard his proposed plans, which were quite ambitious. They realized there wasn't much left to give him, but they told the planners to adjourn to see what they could do for him. And come back the next day with it.

Q: What was the scope of his plan?

Admiral Bieri: He was making landings in various places.

Q: In Indonesia, and that area?

Admiral Bieri: Indonesia, Malaya, and around in there.

Q: Amphibious landings?

Admiral Bieri: Amphibious landings. He commanded the whole thing. He wore out three hats down there.

The combined planners adjourned to the planning room with Mountbatten's staff. His staff was headed by Admiral Troubridge, the chap that was formerly in North Africa. They were an old British Navy family--the Troubridges. This fellow was a big, fat, jolly sort of a chap. They had a one-armed Army officer, and an Air Force officer.

I was the senior member of the planning group. When we got in the room, I said, "Admiral, you know what we've got left to give to you fellows. Now, what do you suggest we do out there? What can you do?"

He said, "I'll tell you, Admiral. If we can find a place where there aren't any Japs, we can probably give it a hell of a good shaking up." That was just about the gist, in a few other words, of our recommendation to the Chief of Staff--I think poor old Mountbatten got a half a dozen LSTs and a few extra landing craft.[*] He didn't get much.

Q: Kind of a holding operation.

Was there strong protest from somebody like General MacArthur, demanding more material than you were willing to give?

Admiral Bieri: There was always that from MacArthur. In this particular case, MacArthur wasn't about to give up his project of taking Rabaul. Which, if you may recall, was a very heavily fortified and manned Japanese base. But it was being completely cut off by the American Navy and would eventually die on the vine, as it turned out. So he sent Sutherland back to Washington to get the Chiefs of Staff to reconsider their decision on Rabaul.

After the conference, we flew back across Africa, then across South America, to Washington. After five days of flying, we arrived back in Washington in early December.

At a subsequent meeting with the Chiefs of Staff, Sutherland appeared to make his plan for a change of decision. He was a rather unusual character. He didn't seem to have too many supporters or friends around the Army part of the place. In presenting his case, he was much of the prosecuting attorney type. He was quite an orator. He got up at the end of the table and made a very impassioned presentation of his Chiefs' point of view. He wound up by saying, "In the eyes of my Commander in Chief, the failure to take Rabaul will go down in history as one of the greatest military errors that had ever been made." Having finished with these wise words, the Chiefs of Staff asked the planners to present their arguments, which I did for them. The decision was to stick to the plan. That was all we heard of that.

Q: I suppose this whole episode is a commentary on the wisdom of having central planning for a worldwide war.

---

[*] LSTs--tank landing ships.

Admiral Bieri: No question about it.

Q: Before you leave the Cairo conference, tell me a little about the activities which centered around it. Perhaps the social activities, were there any of the planners?

Admiral Bieri: No social activities at all.

Q: There weren't any?

Admiral Bieri: There weren't any. We worked from early morning, except for mealtimes, until bedtime. The whole time I was there, the planners got off one afternoon. We made an automobile trip down to see the pyramids, down around Memphis, and then came back on up.

We finally completed on the eighth of December at noon. I had anticipated being able to go over and see a little of Cairo in the afternoon along with my confederates. Admiral King sent for me just at lunchtime.

He said, "Bieri, the British want to discuss with us the matter of sending their forces into the Pacific as soon as this thing is finished up over here and they can get ships available. You know my policy in that regard. I want you to meet with Admiral Lamb [who was the top British planner] and discuss it with him this afternoon. See what they want and tell them what they can have."

So my sightseeing tour went by the board, and I spent the afternoon talking to Lamb.

Q: That provokes a question from me, sir. Admiral King has always been credited with being somewhat anti-British in his bias, and there probably is enough evidence to support this. What was it based on, why was he so?

Admiral Bieri: I don't think that King was anti-British. I think that King didn't have as much confidence in the British as they had in themselves. He didn't want the British to run his show; he was going to run it himself, wherever it was. He was not about to let the British take advantage of him any place. He was perfectly willing to accept them, if they played the game all the way through according to the rules.

For instance, in connection with this business of sending ships out to the Pacific, it was a very easy thing to send a couple of men-of-war out there and get credit for sending forces into the Pacific. He felt that if the British were going to send task forces into the Pacific, it should be a complete task force with the proper maintenance facilities, support facilities, as well as the combat ships.

Q: Of course, there was some problem there, wasn't it? I mean, maintaining the British units in the Pacific.

Admiral Bieri: Of course, they would eventually have to draw their material from us. We had plenty of combat ships out there at that time. There was no occasion for us to have a lot of combat ships out there that really weren't needed and to have us support them. Repair them, supply them with tankers, and all that sort of stuff.

So he was perfectly willing to accept a British task force out there, but it had to be a complete task force. The British didn't want to do that. They just wanted to send some men-of-war. Of course, this was largely a political move, so that they would be on hand with their ships when the final date came.

Q: This was a very important factor in a global war. The political motivation had to be considered along with the military, didn't it?

Admiral Bieri: Oh, yes. He was willing to consider that too. Later, he did accept token forces out there.

Q: I suppose the most flagrant example of that is the Russian insistence in getting in on the final coup in Japan.

Admiral Bieri: I had a long talk with Lamb, and the British, I think, were a little disappointed that we wouldn't take their ships without supporting forces. But we did take a few ships out there that were on hand, when we went back to Shanghai and other British places. Hong Kong.

Q: Under Admiral Fraser?*

Admiral Bieri: Yes, he was out there at that time.

Q: What was King's attitude toward the Australian naval forces and the New Zealand ones?

Admiral Bieri: He was very favorably disposed toward those people. He knew what their limitations were. They operated with our people. They usually operated just in their own area. They didn't go very far in the Pacific. They operated in the Solomons and up through there. So whenever they got into real difficulty they'd go back to their home bases for their work. Their demands on us for logistic support were not too great.

Q: You said that you and the planners certainly weren't involved and didn't have time for social activities. Yet there were some centered around the principles in the conference, were there?

Admiral Bieri: I think there were; I've heard there were. The Prime Minister and the President were over there. They had some dinners or luncheons with the Chiefs of Staff. I know they had frequent meetings with the Chiefs of Staff. Then Chiang Kai-shek came there, and they had meetings with him.

---

* Admiral Sir Bruce Fraser, RN, Commander in Chief British Pacific Fleet.

Bernhard H. Bieri #3 - 131

It was during the Cairo conference that the Chiefs of Staff went and met Stalin in Teheran. That meeting was finally arranged. At first Stalin said he was too busy and would send a substitute. Our Chiefs of Staff refused to go until he agreed to come himself. Stalin was at Teheran, but he wouldn't come to Cairo.[*]

The conditions for setting up that meeting were that only the Chiefs of Staff, each accompanied by one assistant, could go up there. King and Cooke went up there for our Navy. Marshall and Handy; and one of Arnold's assistants went with him.[†]

Q: How often did you see King, as planners, in Cairo? You say you saw him every day?

Admiral Bieri: Yes, we saw him every day. As a general rule, we didn't have very much to take up with him except at the meetings themselves. Cooke was there, of course, and he was in constant touch with the top echelon. He kept the planners informed as to what was going on, what would be taken up, and what our position was.

Q: I suppose, Admiral, even though you had the agenda for the day, and had your planning all in hand as it pertained to the agenda, there were still rush jobs, last-minute additions, and all that kind of thing, weren't there?

Admiral Bieri: Oh, yes.

Q: Can you recall any of them that they threw in?

Admiral Bieri: None particularly, because there was always something. For instance, with the American planners, we always had to resolve these differences of opinion about the campaign in the Pacific and such things as the Rabaul question and the assignment of the

---

[*] The first meeting of the big three--Roosevelt, Churchill, and Stalin, was in the conference at Teheran, Iran, from 28 November to 1 December 1943. It was an interruption of the Cairo meetings.

[†] Major General Thomas Handy, USA, was Assistant Chief of Staff, Operations Division. In 1944 he became a lieutenant general and Deputy Chief of Staff.

naval forces. MacArthur wanted to take all the naval forces under his own wing out there at that time.

We had a very good group of planners at the time, all of them younger than I was. General Roberts was the Army planner, and General Smith the Air Force planner. Each of us had an assistant; Edmund Burrough was my assistant.[*] This group of planners worked together very well.

We had some questions come up on the way over that we got resolved, not too much to our satisfaction. The Army was eventually taking delivery on their final bomber, B-29s.[†] The Army Air Forces would have a group of these planes ready to use before we captured Guam and the islands from which they could operate up there.

Q: Were you already planning your raids on Tokyo?

Admiral Bieri: Yes, they were planning for that. That's one reason they had the support of the Army Air Forces through the central Pacific, because they had to have bases from which to fly these B-29s against Japan.

The Air Force had gone ahead and made arrangements with the Chinese to develop some airfields in the eastern part of China, from which they could fly these B-29s. As they said--"into the back door of Japan," and bomb the Japanese coke ovens in Formosa and Manchuria. They had a large group of Chinese working on these airfields. The idea was to fly the B-29s up there from bases in India and then take off there for the bombing raids.

Q: This was the "Flying Tigers?"

---

[*] Rear Admiral Edmund W. Burrough, USN, served on the Joint War Plans Committee of the JCS, 1943-45.

[†] The Boeing B-29 Superfortress was the most advanced bomber of World War II. It had four 2,220-horsepower engines that gave it a top speed of 365 miles per hour at 25,000 feet. It had a maximum range of 5,830 miles. It was armed with eight .50-caliber machine guns, a 20-millimeter cannon, and could carry a bomb load of up to ten tons.

Admiral Bieri: No, this had nothing to do with the "Flying Tigers." This was Arnold's own Strategic Air Command, and he was going to do this thing.

We didn't know anything about this plan--at least I didn't and I don't think the men in the Navy knew anything about it--until they brought it up on the way over to Cairo on the Iowa.

We got to thinking about this thing, and we said, "That seems a foolish use of these big B-29s at this time. Why don't they station some of them in the northwest corner of Australia, up around Perth, and bomb the Japanese oil fields in Sumatra, and Java?" The Japanese fleet at that time was based in Sumatra. The reason that they were based there was because they didn't have to carry the oil from all the way down there up to Japan to support the fleet. Which was getting to be pretty difficult, on account of our submarines. These B-29s were made to order to chase them out of this place and get them out on the water, where they could be gotten at.

The minute we presented this opposite plan, the coke oven plan, which we said wouldn't amount to anything if the Japanese didn't have the oil to take up there to keep up their industry, and didn't have the fleet to support the merchant ships (they were losing an awful lot of ships, anyhow) that we didn't think there was any comparability of the two plans.

It was quite practical for the B-29s to fly from Perth up to Balikpapan, Borneo, Sumatra, and Java, to do the bombing job. It was very evident that the Air Force knew that they couldn't put any planes in Australia without turning them over to MacArthur and Kenney.* They were not about to do that.

So they went into a huddle, and they came back with an alternate plan which they presented to the Chiefs of Staff. It was to set up the main base for the B-29s in Ceylon, from which place they could fly both against the coke ovens, and against the oilfields. We questioned that plan on the grounds that Ceylon didn't have an airfield that could support the B-29s. It would take too long to build one to be effective.

---

* Lieutenant General George C. Kenney, USA, Commanding General, Far East Air Forces.

Q: They had one in Kandy, didn't they?

Admiral Bieri: Yes, there's an air base there but not big enough to handle B-29s. The Air Force said they'd discuss this with the British. The British were willing to extend that field to take the B-29.

Q: And Mountbatten wouldn't want them under him command?

Admiral Bieri: No, he wouldn't. The result was that the Chiefs of Staff accepted this plan of the Air Force of basing them at Ceylon and flying both ways. They never did get the planes into Ceylon, because they were never able to get the British to extend the airfield. I don't know whether there wasn't enough room or what.

I don't believe they had much success against the coke ovens anyhow. We finally got Guam, and they put them all out on Guam.

Q: I don't ever remember the coke operation as being reported.

Admiral Bieri: That was a harebrain scheme.
We returned from Cairo in December.

Q: May I ask one other question, because he occupied such a unique position, that of General MacArthur? What was the attitude of the Chiefs of Staff toward him?

Admiral Bieri: They realized that they had a very difficult problem on their hands with MacArthur, who had formerly been the Chief of Staff in the Army.[*] He had a lot of political prestige. The Army men were very loath to ever say "no" to anything MacArthur wanted. If they could possibly give it to him, they gave it to him, even in the early part of the war, when it wasn't advisable to assign landing craft, for instance, to that area, because we didn't

---

[*] MacArthur had served as the Army's Chief of Staff from 21 November 1930 to 1 October 1935.

have the transports to carry them down there. But we gave him a lot of landing craft, because he said that his engineers could train these people in Brisbane and go by small boat from Brisbane up around New Guinea and start their campaign.

We sent them a lot of landing craft. They set them up out there, and they trained them. They never got off of home base, because they found out that you couldn't go to sea in a ship that couldn't carry fresh water or food or that sort of thing. They had to wait for their transports.

He was very impatient. When he realized he couldn't get any transports, he went out and bought up all the old merchant ships that he could find anywhere in the East Indies, Australia, and New Zealand. He got together a very sizable armada of broken-down antiquated ships that he was going to use to carry his boats on his amphibious expedition. Then he ran into the question of manning these ships. He said he needed 5,000 naval men to man these ships. King said, "Give him 5,000 Coast Guard men." So we gave him 5,000 Coast Guard men.

Then it developed that most of these ships had broken down, and he couldn't get spare parts for them. There was no place out there that manufactured parts for them. They were picked up all over the world originally, and most of them were too antiquated to have spare parts. So the result was that armada never got off first base either.

King played ball with him all the time. As far as I could see, he was very respectful and considerate of everything that MacArthur asked, except he wouldn't let him command the fleet. He gave him an able commander and certain naval ships.

Q: That was Admiral Kinkaid?

Admiral Bieri: Yes, Kinkaid. They had Leary down there first.[*] Then they had Carpender,

---

[*] Vice Admiral H. Fairfax Leary, USN, served as Commander U.S. Southwest Pacific Force from 20 April 1942 to 11 September 1942.

and then Kinkaid.*

He furnished him naval officers for the staff and the amphibious eventually with naval crews and so forth. But we would never agree to put the Pacific Fleet under MacArthur, as he wanted. He always wanted to get command of the Pacific Fleet. He would send any number of ships down there that MacArthur needed for his operations and always under the Pacific Fleet Commander, but that's as far as he'd go.

I remember one time, MacArthur said he had to have command ships for all his division commanders who were taking these divisions up around New Guinea. All the other places where we had Army people going to sea with troops, the Army commanders always rode with the naval commanders in the command ships. We younger fellows didn't see any reason why we should change the rule down there, but when we took that up with King, he said, "Give him the ships." So we gave him a ship for each one of his Army commanders to have a command ship to ride around on.

Q: Was that a practical thing, or just vanity?

Admiral Bieri: There wasn't any advantage to it, because it just separated the naval commander from the Army commander. They had to get together anyhow, there was plenty of room on . . .

Q: So, in essence, it was vanity, wasn't it?

Admiral Bieri: It was vanity, yes.

King never crossed him, except he was adamant on the policy that a competent fleet in the Pacific would remain under command of Admiral Nimitz. If any naval task forces were required in the Southwest Pacific for operations, they were turned over for the

---

* Vice Admiral Arthur S. Carpender, USN, served as Commander Southwest Pacific Force from 11 September 1942 to 19 February 1943 and as Commander Seventh Fleet from 19 February 1943 to 26 November 1943. Vice Admiral Thomas C. Kinkaid, USN, served as Commander Seventh Fleet from 26 November 1943 to November 1945.

operation to either the South Pacific commander or Kinkaid. When they finished the job, they'd go back to the Pacific Fleet.

There's no doubt that MacArthur did a good job, but he was in a world by himself. He had ideas, and some of them would have been pretty costly if they had been carried out, especially that Rabaul operation.

Q: You say he had strong political backing. Was this centered in the White House?

Admiral Bieri: I think so, yes. In the White House and in Congress.

Very early in the war, when he was out in the Philippines, just as I relieved Turner, there was the business going on of defending the fort out there and getting people out.[*] MacArthur couldn't see any reason why we couldn't support him logistically with submarines. The Army was inclined to back him up on it. It took an awful lot of persuasion and instruction on our part to show him that it was impossible to support an operation like that logistically--to carry food, ammunition, replacements, and that sort of stuff in there in submarines. We not only did not have enough submarines, but no submarine could carry a big enough load to make any contribution to the thing.

Q: That's where he tangled with Admiral Hart.[†]

Admiral Bieri: Yes.

Q: On that question, I think. I wonder in speculating on MacArthur, if one couldn't say that some of his strength lies in his histrionics--his ability to make headlines and to be dramatic?

---

[*] This is a reference to the heavily fortified island Corregidor at the entrance to Manila Bay. Its American defenders surrendered to the Japanese on 6 May 1942.
[†] Admiral Thomas C. Hart, USN, served as Commander in Chief U.S. Asiatic Fleet from 25 July 1939 to 4 February 1942.

Admiral Bieri: Oh, yes. Of course, he knew that he couldn't be removed from command. There was no place to send him. He's been an Army Chief of Staff, and there was no place to send him. He would have to be shelved. To shelve MacArthur was impossible. It would have the whole country up in arms, with his publicity and all that sort of stuff. So that was the best place to keep him. I don't think he would have fitted in anywhere else. He would have been a terrific liability in Europe, trying to deal with the British and the Allies over there.

Q: It had to be his show completely, didn't it?

Admiral Bieri: He couldn't have taken Leahy's place in the White House, because that would have had him too close to the seat of power in this country. I don't think that Roosevelt was the kind of man that would go too far with him, because he would like to dominate him and Roosevelt wasn't about to be dominated.

Q: Is that a good stopping place?

Admiral Bieri: I think we might stop here if it's all right with you.

Bernhard H. Bieri #4 - 139

Interview Number 4 with Vice Admiral Bernhard H. Bieri, U.S. Navy (Retired)

Place: Bethesda, Maryland

Date: Thursday, 4 September 1969

Interviewer: John T. Mason, Jr.

Q: Admiral, today we begin chapter four of your very fascinating story. The last time you had told me about the Cairo conference and gave me a very good insight into how such top level conferences operated. Today I expect you'll go on with . . .

Admiral Bieri: I spent from the 9th of November, 1943 to the 11th of December, 1943 at Cairo. Then I returned to Washington to resume my duties at fleet Headquarters.

Q: Again in planning, was it?

Admiral Bieri: No, I had been relieved as planning officer by that time, on my return, by Admiral Duncan.* I had been placed in the upper half of the list of rear admirals and was assigned as assistant chief of staff on the staff of the Commander in Chief. The chief of staff was Admiral C. M. Cooke. He had relieved Admiral R. S. Edwards, who had been made the Deputy Commander in Chief. I still attended quite a number of the planning meetings, but I had from then on largely administrative duties on the staff.

Q: Such as what, sir?

Admiral Bieri: Presiding at the daily meetings of the heads of the different sections and divisions and performing various odd tasks. For instance, one of the things I remember doing was to go to Minneapolis for the Secretary of the Navy and presenting an award to

---

* Rear Admiral Donald B. Duncan, USN.

the Brown and Bigelow Company. The company was engaged in manufacturing material for the armed forces.

Q: That was the Navy E program, was it?

Admiral Bieri: Yes. Then, I made a trip to the war college to address one of the graduating classes.

Q: Up in Newport?

Admiral Bieri: In Newport. I generally handled the interior working of the staff.

Q: Were there any particular problems that you had to wrestle with at that time?

Admiral Bieri: No. There were a great many different things that came up. Questions that had to be answered and decisions to be made, as much as I could without bothering the three higher ups. Admiral King, Admiral Edwards, and Admiral Cooke were engrossed with the higher aspects to the war, the strategic situation and so forth.

Of course, in a job like the assistant chief of staff there was always a lot of work to do, answering inquiries from people in the field and that sort of thing.

Q: Did you have daily access to Admiral King?

Admiral Bieri: No, I had very little reason to have access to Admiral King. I would see him occasionally at the meetings of the planners, when I attended as an observer. I also lunched in his mess. My dealings were mostly with Cooke and Edwards.

On the sixth of May, 1944 I was detached as assistant chief of staff and other duties that had been assigned to me. I had orders to proceed to London to report to the Commander U.S. Naval Forces, Europe. That was Admiral Stark.

The idea was that I would report to the Supreme Commander of the Allied Expeditionary Force, General Eisenhower, for duty on his staff, which I did on the 16th of May, 1944.

Prior to my going over there, and one of the reasons apparently for sending me over there, was that Admiral King was not entirely satisfied with the questions that concerned the use of our naval forces. They were not being handled entirely to his satisfaction.

The U.S. naval forces that were over there at that time getting ready for the invasion of France were all operating under the British Naval Commander in Chief, Admiral Ramsay.* They were, of course, preparing for landing the American forces in the northern part of Europe, according to plans that had been made. There were questions that came up from time to time. A rather very serious question came up a month or two before I went over.

Admiral King and General Marshall were accustomed to send some of their staff out from time to time to visit the various theaters and see what could be done to help them. About three months before I went over there, they had sent General Handy of the Army and Admiral Cooke of King's staff, who were opposites on the respective commands.

They flew to Europe to have a look around and see what was going on. They looked over the naval plans for the landing. They became convinced at that time that the naval plans did not provide adequate fire support for the troops that would land.

In talking this over with Admiral Ramsay, they got no place, because Ramsay was very set in his ideas. He and his staff had figured out what they needed and what they were going to use. Both Cooke and Handy, being strong-minded men, took this matter up with Eisenhower and the chief of staff. The latter supported Ramsay.

Ramsay was the Naval Commander in Chief, and if he was satisfied, it was his responsibility. This didn't satisfy Cooke and Handy, and they came back and made their personal reports to their Chiefs. Admiral King and the Joint Chiefs of Staff took the matter up with Eisenhower. They demanded that there be more fire support furnished for these forces.

---

* The official title of Admiral Sir Bertram Ramsay, RN, was Allied Naval Commander Expeditionary Force.

Q: This meant more vessels?

Admiral Bieri: Competent vessels. Now, of course, the British had plenty of ships, if they wanted to use them for that purpose. We, of course, were engaged in the Pacific quite heavily. We were also, as far as our destroyers were concerned, were very heavily engaged in the Atlantic, in convoy duty and antisubmarine work.

However, our Navy scraped together another division of cruisers and another division of battleships, and a destroyer squadron or two. The British came through with some more ships. All of which, as later events proved, was very fortunate.

Q: All of these arrangements were accomplished before you went over?

Admiral Bieri: Yes. But this had created a rather ill feeling, especially toward our Navy, on the part of Eisenhower's staff. When I reported, my orders were rather definite. I was supposed to report to Commander Allied Expeditionary Force, General Eisenhower, for purposes of answering questions of that sort as far as our forces were concerned.

Q: This was a somewhat similar assignment to the one you had previously, before the North African campaign.

Admiral Bieri: Yes. In this particular case, I reported to General Bedell Smith, who was the chief of staff.* he greeted me in a very friendly sort of a way. Then he said to me, "I don't know when General Eisenhower will be able to see you. It will be in the next day or so. To be very frank with you, Bieri, if Admiral King had sent over anyone else but you, we've have to put him on the next boat and sent him home." Of course, I was aware of why this was so.

---

* Lieutenant General Walter Bedell Smith, USA.

Bernhard H. Bieri #4 - 143

Q: Did they deem this interference?

Admiral Bieri: Who?

Q: Eisenhower and his staff. Was this interference on the part of Admiral King, sending a special emissary?

Admiral Bieri: No, but I'd like, after I get finished with this story, to talk with you a minute about the command setup.

Q: All right, fine.

Admiral Bieri: After a day or so, I was informed that General Eisenhower would see me. Of course, I'd known him before. I went in and reported for duty. He said very frankly to me, "I don't know what I'm going to do with you, Bieri, because I have a naval commander in chief. I have an idea that Savvy Cooke was back of this business of sending you over here. My commander of naval forces is Admiral Ramsay. The only thing that you can do is become a member of his staff."

I told him that I was unaware of why I was sent, that Admiral King had told me personally that I was to go over there and look out for the interest of our ships and to be of every possible assistance to General Eisenhower and the naval people. And that was what I was over there for.

He made it quite clear that I was to be a member of Admiral Ramsay's staff and, by that fact, a member of his headquarters. Admiral Ramsay was personally pleased to see me. We had a long talk. He was very much of the opinion, and he expressed it very strongly, that any naval officer over there had to be on his staff. In other words, he would be assigned certain tasks, and that was his job and that was what he did. Not necessarily for the purpose of giving any advice or assistance along that line. I explained to him the method in our service, but he was adamant. He said, "It wouldn't work in our navy. We tried it out with Mountbatten, and we had trouble out there."

I was advised that I would only function as a member of staff of the Allied Naval Commander of the Allied Expeditionary Force. In this capacity he would expect me to visit him frequently and advise him regarding operations of the U.S. naval forces.

At that stage of the plans, we had Admiral Kirk, who was the senior one in the American side of the Naval Expeditionary Force. Of course, I was in not position to do that without consulting Kirk.[*]

Q: You mean report to Ramsay?

Admiral Bieri: On the operation of our forces.

Things stayed in this situation more or less for several days. I was sort of a fifth wheel around that place.

Q: That must have been a very awkward situation.

Admiral Bieri: Yes, it was not a very pleasant situation. I, for instance, was never given an opportunity to talk with Ramsay's chief of staff. I met the other members of his staff casually at lunch once or twice.

Finally, I was told by Admiral Ramsay that he was going to make me a deputy chief of staff to work on postwar plans.

Q: Postwar plans?

Admiral Bieri: Postwar plans. Of course, I hadn't come prepared for that. I had no guidance in the way of any policy statements by either our Navy Department or State Department or from the Commander in Chief.

---

[*] Rear Admiral Alan G. Kirk, USN, who eventually became Commander Western Naval Task Force for the landing at Normandy on 6 June 1944. The oral history of Kirk, who retired as a four-star admiral, is in the Columbia University collection.

So I was moved over away from the command center and worked with a very junior group of British and American naval officers who were struggling with the postwar plans.

Q: Did you protest that assignment?

Admiral Bieri: I protested in this way, that I wrote this whole thing out to Admiral King to tell him what was going on.

I spent my time at this business the best I could. In the first place, I had to get some policy directives. Apparently nobody in our service had been working on this thing.

Q: That's rather understandable, isn't it.

Admiral Bieri: It was and it wasn't. Because the British, in those sort of things, are fighting a war for a purpose, and they want to know what they're going to get when they get through. The British, of course, were always very anxious to reestablish their status at sea. They had some pretty definite statements of policy which had been gotten out by their government. Their people had that to work on. Our people didn't.

I presented this whole picture to Admiral King. I had very little contact with the operations that were going on. I did make one trip with Ramsay on a destroyer over to the beach in France, after they landed over there. I think that was all.

As soon as the landings were made, Admiral King, General Marshall, and General Arnold--accompanied by their next senior assistants--arrived over there. I discussed this matter with Admiral King, and he said, "If they're not going to use you for anything else, I'll see that you get back."

As soon as he got back, I received a set of orders to return to Washington headquarters of the Commander in Chief.

Q: May I ask you a couple of questions about that period? Did you call on Admiral Kirk and make known to him your predicament?

Admiral Bieri: I saw Admiral Kirk only once. He was operating with his forces quite some distance from London. I made on trip up there and talked to him about the situation.

Q: And what about Admiral Stark? What part did he play in this picture?

Admiral Bieri: Let me hold that for a few minutes, until we get to the command part of this thing.

I went back to Washington sometime after the landing, about the 26th of June. The minute the orders came through from the headquarters of the Commander in Chief for me to return to Washington, I got a series of letters issued by Admiral Stark, Admiral Ramsay, and Bedell Smith. All of which were very complimentary, and indicated that my departure would create a great vacuum in the organization. However, it was all very nice, but I went home.

Q: But actually they hadn't permitted you to do anything.

Admiral Bieri: I hadn't done anything.

Q: So they were just saying these things.

Admiral Bieri: They were just saying things.

Smith put it this way: "More important than ever, however, are the tangible dividends we have obtained from his assignment. Already several senior air officers have been assigned here and made an integral part of this headquarters, a measure which was violently opposed until recently. Further reorganization of the air command side will undoubtedly take place in the near future which will result in SHAEF becoming more of a combined operational headquarters than we had ever hoped for. Admiral Ramsay is not only quite reconciled to Bieri's presence, but now ill be very loath to see him go. He has made a very definite place for himself here, and I strongly recommend that he be allowed to remain, at least until the operational echelon of this headquarters is well established on the continent."

I was ordered by Admiral King and assigned to duty again as deputy chief of staff.

Q: I wonder if you couldn't tell me more about that period, because I think you've skimmed over it. It was such a terribly important period in the history of the war. I think maybe you have some other observations to add.

Admiral Bieri: My observations are in the nature of my comments on the command structure in the various theaters of the war.

There's a great deal of wordage in history and dispatches and so forth about supreme commanders and that sort of thing, the unified commands, and the importance of various commands. As far as I could ever make out, the only supreme commands that existed were the Russian command and the German command. The rest of them were more or less misnomers.

The command setups in the various theaters of wars in which we were engaged were very interesting. For instance--in the Pacific, Admiral Nimitz was in command of the Pacific Ocean areas, which were very well delineated as far as he and MacArthur were concerned. All the major naval forces in the Pacific were under the operational control and command of Admiral Nimitz.

When MacArthur required any naval forces to carry out his larger operations, those naval forces were assigned to him by the Joint Chiefs of Staff through Admiral Nimitz. The regular naval commanders in Admiral Nimitz's command took them down there and operated them to a very large extent.

General MacArthur did have a staff in which he had a naval commander who was a United States naval officer, finally Admiral Kinkaid; and he had an air officer, Kenney. He himself was Commander in Chief. He had an Army officer, I think it was General Krueger, who commanded all his Army forces. There you have a well-defined command situation.*

---

* Lieutenant General Walter Krueger, USA.

In accordance with the strategy which was developed by the Chiefs of Staff, MacArthur knew what he had to do each year. He made the plans for doing this. When he didn't have the adequate forces, he called on the Joint Chiefs of Staff, and they furnished him the necessary naval forces from the Central Pacific.

Nimitz had much a similar command, although there never was an air officer attached to his staff. The air, of course, was naval air and depended on naval people. Early in the war, there was one Army air officer attached to his staff, and there may have been one later. If there was, he had little to do because they had no control over the Army air operations.

The Army was thrown in with the naval groups that were operating in the different sections of the Pacific. For instance, those that were operating in the South Pacific came under Halsey, of course commanded by their own officers. Sometimes they commanded American Marines as well as American Army. The same thing was true up in Alaska.

The Army Air Forces in the Southwest Pacific was entirely commanded by MacArthur, through Kenney. They did all the tactical work that these forces were required to do down there.

The Army Air Forces in Washington and in all theaters always maintained command of what they called the Strategic Air Force, the big heavy planes. In the Pacific, they did this, just as they did in England or Europe.

They had never turned any of these planes, even for operational purposes, over to either MacArthur or Nimitz. The only planes that could really carry out long-distance missions were just coming out about the time of the Cairo conference, the B-29. There were enough of those planes finished at that time, so the Air Force had to begin giving consideration to finding bases for them in the Pacific so that they could be employed.

At that time, there were only two places which were available. I've spoken of this before. One was Western Australia, from which they could reach the oil fields of Sumatra and Borneo. The other one was from the mainland of China, from which they could reach certain installations in western Japan, such as Formosa, and other places that Japan held on the continent.

In other words, they were waiting for the Americans to capture adequate territory, like Guam and other islands in the Western Pacific, so that they would have air fields from which to operate the Strategic Air Forces. Until they had that, they were not going to disperse any of this force and turn it over to any other purpose than to bombing the mainland of Japan.

I believe I mentioned before that en route to the Cairo conference, the planners suggested to the Chiefs of Staff that these planes, which were finished and had a considerable number to work, be based in Western Australia, to be used against the oil ports and the anchorages which the main Japanese fleet were then using down in Sumatra. The Air Force, under General Arnold, did not receive this suggestion very favorably; but they couldn't deny the logic of the thing. They finally said that they would operate against these objectives from Ceylon. And at the same time, operate as they planned to do against the Japanese coke ovens from the airfields that the Chinese were building for them in China. As a matter of fact, they never got around to doing anything about the oil ports. We had captured Guam. They set up their big airfields on Guam and started bombing Japan.

Now in Europe, you had this so-called supreme command of General Eisenhower. His mission, of course, was to defeat the German Army on the continent of Europe. He was given what they called an Allied Expeditionary Force composed principally of British soldiers and American soldiers--the British Army and the American Army.

The command setup was British, in each instance, except in the case of the Army. The forces were assigned to his expeditionary force. They were commanded by a senior British officer. For instance, he had a senior naval officer, Admiral Ramsay, who was the naval commander in chief. He had an air officer on his staff, General Tedder who was the commander of the air.* The Army command was vested in Eisenhower himself. The American Army was never assigned to the command of Montgomery, the British commander.† They had Bradley in charge of the American troops, so Eisenhower directly commanded the two armies, the British Army and the American Army.‡

---

* General Arthur W. Tedder, RAF.
† Field Marshal Bernard L. Montgomery, British Army.
‡ Lieutenant General Omar N. Bradley, USA.

Q: What was the reason for that?

Admiral Bieri: The reason for that was the Army's experience in the First World War had led them to the conclusion that if we ever got into another war in Europe or anywhere else connected with a foreign country, that nobody was going to command our armed forces but the Americans themselves.

In Europe, this didn't apply to the Navy.

Q: Because World War I experience there had been different.

Admiral Bieri: In World War I, we had naval forces in Europe who were commanded by British naval officers. For instance, the battleships were sent to the North Sea under an American rear admiral, and they were formed as an integral part of the British fleet, and operated under British orders. Our destroyers in Ireland were nominally under the commander of the U.S. naval forces in Europe, who was Admiral Sims, and had headquarters in London.[*] They were commanded by the British admiral, Admiral Bayly.[†] So our naval forces during the First World War were directly under the command of the English, the operating forces. As I said, they did the same thing in Europe with our naval forces during the war. They put them under the direct command of the English naval commander.

The Strategic Air Forces upheld themselves in Europe. They were never placed under the complete command of Eisenhower. He only got those forces when he needed certain parts of them to carry out an operation. As soon as the operation was completed, they went back to the command of Spaatz, who was the Strategic Air Forces commander in Europe.[‡] He operated the bombing command, they called it, in cooperation with the British bombing command. The British did the same thing with their Air Force.

---

[*] Vice Admiral/Admiral William S. Sims, USN, served as Commander U.S. Naval Forces Operating in European Waters from 1917 to 1919.
[†] Admiral Sir Lewis Bayly, RN.
[‡] Lieutenant General Carl Spaatz, USA, Commanding General, U.S. Strategic Air Forces in Europe.

There were certain tactical groups that were assigned for a considerable length of time, a period off and on, to Eisenhower's command. They were operated while they were down there by the senior British air officer on the staff.

Neither the British naval forces or the American naval forces in the Atlantic were ever under the complete command of Eisenhower. He got command of the ships that were to be involved in the operations, and he had them for the period that they were in the operations. The plans for the use of the ships were made and carried out during the invasions, by the British naval commander in chief.

A very large part of the naval forces in the Atlantic were directly operated from America and from London. They had to continue the antisubmarine war, and they had to be operated from there. As soon as the naval forces finished their jobs for the landing of the invasion forces and that sort of thing, they reverted back to command of the Admiralty and Commander in Chief U.S. Fleet.

That was the situation that existed. While Ramsay, who was a very pleasant fellow as far as I was concerned, was a very stubborn man and was very loath to accept advice from other people, Andrew Cunningham, who was the naval commander under Eisenhower in the Mediterranean, was an entirely different type. He was most cooperative, and if he didn't use you, at least he gave a very good impression that he was using you. He listened to advice and frequently took it, if it was any good, and was glad to have it.

I spoke last time of the problem they had in the Mediterranean of getting the damaged merchant ships out and clearing the ports. Admiral Cunningham had an entirely inadequate salvage force, and he had no salvage officers with experience. So I finally suggested to him that we get Captain Ellsberg, later Admiral Ellsberg, class of 1914 Naval Academy, who was engaged at the time in raising some Italian and Ethiopian ships that had been sunk on the east coast of Africa. We brought him over and put him to work. He got the job going, set up the organization, and so forth. He had been working very hard in this hot climate over in the east, he became ill and had to go home. He was relieved by Sullivan, and he did the rest of the work over there.

My relationship with Admiral Cunningham and my relationship with Admiral Ramsay were two entirely different things. I always had the feeling in working with Ramsay that if I tried to offer any advice or suggest anything, he felt that I was interfering. I never asked to attend one of those staff conferences. On the other hand, in working with Admiral Cunningham; I attended every one of his staff meetings. I sat alongside of the admiral and his chief of staff. I participated in the staff discussions, or whatever they were having, whenever I felt like it. I was frequently asked for my opinion on various things. So it was a lot of difference.

When we were at Gibraltar, he sent for me one day. He said, "We've been fighting down here in Africa now for about a week. We know what's going on in the Mediterranean. We're getting daily reports from all our commanders here in the Mediterranean. But we have no idea what's going on down at Casablanca on the west coast." The operation down there was being run by Hewitt and Patton, and it was entirely an American operation. They were just failing to make any reports to either Cunningham or to Eisenhower.

Eisenhower suggested that we send a naval vessel down there to see what was going on. The group of staff officers and Cunningham suggested that I go along as the head naval staff officer. So I went down on that trip and got in touch with Hewitt and Patton. Between myself and the Army staff officers that went along, we came back with a pretty good story of how affairs had been going down that way.

This was sort of a diversion from what I was supposed to have been doing over in Europe. I was ordered back to Washington. Duncan had taken my place as a planner, and I had fully expected to be ordered out to the Pacific, but Admiral King said they had plenty of people out there, and he needed me more, so I stayed there.

Q: Sir, would you revert back to that European situation, and discuss Admiral Stark's position and all of that? It's not clear to me.

Admiral Bieri: Admiral Stark had the title of Commander, Naval Forces, Europe. He had headquarters at Grosvenor Square in London. He had a complete staff. The chief of staff when I first went over there was Admiral Kirk. He had all the other usual staff members; operations, intelligence, and so forth. They occupied a large building. As far as I could make out, their function was to maintain liaison with the British Admiralty and to look out for the general housekeeping affairs of the American Navy in Britain. He had no forces under his command, no operational command whatsoever. It was purely a political job, as far as he was concerned.

It later developed that he had a very excellent officer on his staff. He was a Naval Academy graduate who'd resigned and come back into the service named Captain Pat Flanigan, who was a logistics man.* Flanigan was a very aggressive and very able fellow, who took it on himself, more or less, to see that any of the American naval forces in and around Britain that needed anything got it. In that respect, Stark's staff, through Flanigan, did a very good job.

Q: They were operational, in that sense.

Admiral Bieri: In that respect, they were operational. It was entirely due to the personality and drive of Flanigan himself. He, of course, developed very good relations with the British. He had been a businessman in New York for a good many years. He was also engaged in the shipping business. He was able to get a great deal done and do a great deal for the American forces over there logistically. That was their only operational function.

Q: Did Stark have any relationship with Eisenhower?

Admiral Bieri: Purely social, I would say. They were always on very fine personal terms. When Eisenhower's headquarters was in London and there was a luncheon meeting of high officials, the First Lord of the Admiralty, some of the high fleet officers, and others, they always included Stark. I went to quite a few of them myself with Admiral Kirk.

---

* Captain Howard A. Flanigan, USN (Ret.), who had graduated from the Naval Academy in the class of 1910, a year before Bieri. Flanigan retired as a commander in 1936 and subsequently worked on the New York World's Fair of 1939-40. He was recalled to active duty from 15 May 1941 to 3 February 1946, eventually being promoted to rear admiral on the retired list.

Stark was not involved in the actual planning or the training for any of the troops that were over in England, except for Flanigan, who looked out for their logistic needs.

Q: In one sense, sir, it doesn't seem that there was any great need for that particular command over there in the midst of war.

Admiral Bieri: I never saw anything that came out of that command that amounted to anything, except for Flanigan's part of it. They maintained personal and social relations with the British and the American high command.

All the questions in relation to the use of forces--the distributions of forces, the operations of forces, and so forth--were all taken up directly with the American Joint Chiefs of Staff. Eisenhower, for instance--all his business was with the Joint Chiefs of Staff as far as American forces were concerned.

When they needed more naval forces, they didn't go to Stark about it. They went directly to the Joint Chiefs of Staff for an opinion. So Stark was not an operational commander. He was a "spare wheel."

Q: To be frank, was it kind of a made job?

Admiral Bieri: It was a place to put him, after his job as Chief of Naval Operations was over.[*] We did have, prior to our entry to the war, over there a group of officers composed of Admiral Ghormley, an Air Force officer, and an Army officer.[†] They did some preliminary discussions and planning with the British. Ghormley eventually--this was established as we got into the war--was designated as Commander Naval Forces Europe. I doubt that he had much of a staff at that time, or was given any particular duties except to

---

[*] Admiral Ernest J. King, USN, relieved Admiral Harold R. Stark, USN, as Chief of Naval Operations on 26 March 1942.
[†] Vice Admiral Robert L. Ghormley, USN, served as Special Naval Observer in London from August 1940 to April 1942.

continue these so-called strategic talks that he was engaged in. As soon as King took over, he was relieved. That's where they sent Stark, as Commander Naval Forces Europe.

Q: Filling that same title?

Admiral Bieri: To fill the title. This so-called "triumvirate" of three officers who had been discussing strategy and so forth was dissolved. Their duties went over to the Joint Chiefs of Staff.

Q: Where did the naval attaché and his large staff fit into this picture?

Admiral Bieri: The naval attaché was Admiral Kirk, and he was the chief of staff to Admiral Stark. They all had quarters together at Grosvenor Square. Kirk was the attaché.

Q: Then Kirk later came under Eisenhower.

Admiral Bieri: Kirk, later on, very shortly before the invasion was designated as commander of the U.S. naval forces engaged in the operation. However, he flew his flag on the Augusta, and he had Bradley on board with him. They were off Omaha Beach.

Q: The Utah was.

Admiral Bieri: Yes, the Utah was north.
He carried Bradley on the Augusta, and he was supposed to command all the American ships that were engaged on both Omaha and Utah.* Naturally, that carried with it the authority to shift ships from one sector to the other. As a matter of fact, the Augusta did not take a very active part in the fire support of the operation. She was really only a

---

* Omaha and Utah were the code names assigned to the two landing beaches on the Normandy coast for American soldiers.

headquarters ship. In my opinion, that was a mistake. With her guns and everything, she should have been used as a fire support ship.

Over on Utah, Moon commanded the landing, and Hall commanded on Omaha.* I forgot what Hall's flagship was, but he was embroiled in the operation. Moon was also. They may have had command ships; I don't recall.†

On Omaha, we had a division of battleships, the Texas and the Arkansas. We also had a division of cruisers over there. At Omaha, the principal fire support came from destroyers. They had various makeshift ideas which were conceived for the need of adding to the fire support, which amounted to having Army guns mounted on personnel carriers, not LSTs but small craft. Most of those swamped. The fire support at Omaha was not adequate, in my opinion. The British fire support was furnished by its own battleships, destroyers, or cruisers.

The scheme of this landing was that it was a surprise landing, so they couldn't make any advance use of fire support to drive out any Germans that might be in the vicinity. As far as the American troops were concerned, except for the bunch they ran into out in Omaha, they really didn't need it.

They had set up an air plan in which the British air bombers were to make their strikes at daylight in the area around the bend of the two beaches. They missed the target. They dropped all their bombs on pastures and farms way inside the shore line. They didn't have the modern facilities we have now. So that was just wasted. All the fire support they got was from the naval ships.

Does that answer your questions about Admiral Stark's headquarters?

Q: Yes. So then you became the special emissary for Admiral King.

Admiral Bieri: Admiral King, yes.

---

* Rear Admiral Don P. Moon, USN, commanded Assault Force "U," and Rear Admiral John L. Hall, USN, commanded Assault Force "O."
† Moon was in the USS Bayfield (APA-33); Hall was in the USS Ancon (AGC-4).

Q: You were going directly from King to Eisenhower.

Admiral Bieri: I reported to Stark, apparently purely for administrative purposes, to get my pay and so forth.

Q: You were under no illusions as to your assignment, were you?

Admiral Bieri: I was ordered to duty with SHAEF, which was the supreme Allied command in France.

Q: May I ask you, where were you during the actual landings? Where were you on D-Day? What were you doing, what was your function?

Admiral Bieri: I was down below Portsmouth, where they had their naval headquarters. Ramsay had his headquarters down there south of Portsmouth. Eisenhower had moved down there in the woods. We were camping out. General Eisenhower lived in a trailer, and there were trailers for officers and some of the seniors. There was an Army officers' mess which I joined. I never left there.

I don't think that Ramsay ever moved his headquarters across. I think he continued operating from there. The one trip that I made with Ramsay to the landing area was about a week later. I went with Admiral Ramsay on a destroyer, and we went over to see how things were going. The troops had been landed, and they had already gone inland, away from the coast. They were landing stores on the beaches to be picked up with various small craft. They were in the process of building the two big artificial ports. These ports were very ingenious things; they were conceived by the British. You've heard of those?

Q: Yes.

Admiral Bieri: We went over one afternoon, and we landed on the beach. The troops had gone a considerable distance on the shore by that time. We walked around through the area where the heavy fighting or the landing, along the beach, had taken place. There was quite a pileup of stores and so forth. They were beginning to get trucks down there to move the supplies up to the armies. They were well on the way to completing these two artificial ports. At sea it was a beautiful day.

We were returning to Portsmouth by destroyer, we met a continuous stream of supplies coming across the channel--small tugs, merchant ships, and material in barges and so forth, to the landing area. At that time the sea was absolutely calm and continued so. We debarked at Portsmouth and went back to our headquarters. During the night was when that storm came in and wrecked the American port.

Q: It was an unpredicted storm, was it?

Admiral Bieri: It was unpredicted, yes.

Q: It wrecked the artificial port on the American beach, but it didn't wreck the British?

Admiral Bieri: It wrecked the American port, but it didn't wreck the British.
    I continued over there at headquarters for some time.

Q: What were you doing?

Admiral Bieri: After my arrival in May, I reported to General Eisenhower's headquarters. I was received by General Bedell Smith, chief of staff, who said that it was only because of my personality that it was acceptable to receive a rear admiral and had anybody else been nominated the answer would have been a flat "no."

Q: Now, what did he mean by that?

Admiral Bieri: They didn't want any American naval officer over there.

He said that I could serve only as a member of Admiral Ramsay's staff. I had been sent over by Admiral King to report to Eisenhower to be on his staff. He said, "I think this whole thing was instigated by Savvy Cooke."

Q: Bedell Smith said this to you?

Admiral Bieri: Yes.

I told him that my understanding was that Admiral King thought that all the services should be represented on the staff of the Supreme Commander, according to the Combined Chiefs of Staff's agreement under the organization of the combined command.

He said that wasn't their idea and that I would have to serve on Ramsay's staff, who was naval Commander in Chief. So they game me orders to report to Ramsay.

Ramsay made me what he called assistant chief of staff. I was to work under him directly on a planning team for postwar affairs and postwar settling.

Q: While you were in the midst of the greatest offensive?

Admiral Bieri: Yes. I called this to the attention of Admiral King. I told him I had no objection to working on this business, but if I was going to work on it I wanted some instructions from our government because there weren't any over there. No one seemed to have any instructions on what we were to do after the fighting was over, except that the British had their own instructions. They had four or five captains and colonels, Air Force and Army, working on this problem according to their instructions.

When King came over subsequently, we discussed it, and he decided to recall me. He recalled me when he returned.

Q: How much time had elapsed before he came over there?

Admiral Bieri: This was after the landing, about a week after, when he and General Marshall and several other assistants came over there. Then on the 26th of June, word got out that I was going to leave the staff and be sent home.

Q: Then you'd only been there a little over a month.

Admiral Bieri: Yes. Then they started a lot of correspondence about this thing. Of course, Stark wrote and said I shouldn't be detached, that I was too valuable to be detached. Smith wrote a memorandum in which he said, "It is true that when Admiral Bieri was assigned here there was considerable question in our minds whether the duties which could be given him were commensurate with his rank and experience. It may be that even now an officer with less rank could carry on, but Bieri's position and personality have made him ideal for service in this headquarters. At the present time, with the naval craft situation so obscure accompanied with bad weather, Bieri has acted as the personal representative to General Eisenhower and this staff in dealing with Admiral Ramsay's headquarters and various British naval commanders."

Q: Was that true?

Admiral Bieri: No, not at all.
"Nor would we have left it to him to thrash out important questions of what shipping and craft can be used for Anvil and so forth." Which is another thing, that if they did, they never told me anything about it.

Q: Anvil being landing in Marseilles?[*]

Admiral Bieri: Yes.

---

[*] The Allied invasion of Southern France was on 15 August 1944.

Then he went on to say, "More important to me, however, are the tangible dividends we have obtained from his assignment. Already several senior air officers have been assigned here and made an integral part of this headquarters, a measure which was violently opposed up until recently. Further reorganization on the air command side of Anvil will take place in the near future, which will result in SHAEF becoming more of a combined operational headquarters than we had hoped for."

Q: In other words, your appointment to the staff precipitated something. And was that true?

Admiral Bieri: No. If they were there, I never met them. I suppose they were there, but as far as I know they were attached to SHAEF. But by that time, I had been detached from SHAEF and put on Ramsay's staff. I didn't have too much contact with SHAEF, except I had access to their chart room and went over there every day to see how things seemed to be progressing, particularly from the naval point of view.

Q: That was a very awkward position for you, wasn't it?

Admiral Bieri: Yes, it was quite an awkward position.

Q: You were kind of a pawn between King and Eisenhower.

Admiral Bieri: That's right.
On the 28th of August, eventually, they issued me orders to return to Washington. In the meantime, I had been working in this project over there as best I could. I had one or two younger naval officers who had been connected with the thing before I came.

Q: What did you actually see your job as being?

Admiral Bieri: We were supposed, I presumed, to decide what German naval facilities we'd take over, what ships we'd take over, what stations we'd take over, and that sort of thing, in setting up the war.

Q: This postwar business?

Admiral Bieri: Postwar business. But we had absolutely no instructions from our own Navy Department or from the State Department about any of their ideas or any of their policies as to what the Navy might want in the way of Germany naval material or what particular things they were interested in. Of course, we were lacking in intelligence, except for what we could get out of the British.

Q: So it was only through the British that you knew what would be available?

Admiral Bieri: That's right. We were just a part of the British section, of which I was nominally the senior one, the head. But that was it.

Q: Did the British understand the peculiar situation under which you found yourself?

Admiral Bieri: I think they did, yes.

Q: Why did Admiral King put you in this position?

Admiral Bieri: As I said, he felt that there ought to be a United States naval officer at the headquarters of the Supreme Commander to advise if he wanted advice and to act as contact between our own forces and headquarters on things that came up.

Q: But this could only be effective if the Supreme Commander was in agreement and he wasn't, in this case.

Admiral Bieri: Yes, and he wasn't.

Q: Why didn't Admiral King iron this out in advance of the assignment?

Admiral Bieri: I don't know. I had no advance notice that I was going over there until practically the time I went. And no instructions, except that I would be attached to Supreme Allied Headquarters.

Q: When you went, were you equipped with any special means of communication with Admiral King other than the normal naval channel?

Admiral Bieri: No, and not even those. I could take my messages up to London and have them sent by Stark. But I had no communications of my own, especially when we moved down to Portsmouth. The only way I could communicate with Stark was to go up personally, or I'd use the scrambled telephone which wasn't too good, to say anything I might want to say just between King and myself.

During my time over there during this particular duty, I did make another trip of my own over to the continent. At that time, General Eisenhower had established his own personal headquarters in a camp over in Normandy. Our forces had taken St. Lo and were well on their way to Paris. At that time, I visited Cherbourg and had a look at the submarine pens and that sort of thing around Cherbourg. Then I went on down the coast to take a look at the ports, just below St. Lo, to see what we might expect to get out of those ports in the future.

Q: Did you have any difficulty in going to these various areas?

Admiral Bieri: No. Presumably, it was quite safe to travel around there. A week before I went over there, one of our young officers was shot by some German snipers while he was nosing around the submarine pens.

We had taken all the country down through St. Lo and presumably cleared it out. Occasionally somebody got killed down in that direction. Travel was comparatively safe. We went down by car, and a young naval officer was with me. My main object in going down at that time was also to pay my respects to Eisenhower and say good-bye to him, because I had my orders to go home.

Q: Had you seen him frequently in the interim?

Admiral Bieri: No, not very frequently. I would occasionally run into him. I had access to the operations room in the headquarters near Portsmouth. I used to go over there daily and listen in at the meetings and so forth. I would see him just to say good morning to him, or something like that, at some of these meetings. The meetings were generally supervised by the operations officer or the chief of staff. Smith was usually there.

Then I returned to Washington in August 1944 by air to resume my duties as deputy chief of staff.

Q: What did that entail on this occasion, when you went back?

Admiral Bieri: The same as before.

Q: Administrative function?

Admiral Bieri: Administrative function.

When the war in Europe was over, in October 1945, I was detached from Admiral King's staff and ordered to be the Chief of Naval Operations as Assistant Chief of Naval Operations for Administration. I was appointed a vice admiral.

Several months later, at the end of the year, I was detached from that job and ordered to report to the Commander of the Atlantic Fleet as Commander of the Tenth Fleet.

Bernhard H. Bieri #4 - 165

Q: Is there anything that you can tell me about that period, which is almost a year, in the Department in Washington, during the war? There must have been something of importance to relate about that.

Admiral Bieri: There were many meetings with our own planners and with the joint planners, and frequent attendance at the meetings of the Joint Chiefs of Staff. We were being given various instructions and orders to look into, such as the postwar organization of our own naval forces and the unified Department of Defense. There were questions in regard to what to do with the Pacific Islands that we had taken back and acquired. Then also the continual planning for the defeat of the Japanese by an invasion of Japan.

There were certain of us that felt that was never going to be undertaken or necessary.

Q: You mean the invasion of Japan?

Admiral Bieri: The invasion of Japan.

Q: Why did you feel this way?

Admiral Bieri: We felt that once the Japanese fleet was defeated, that they were unable to get material from overseas, maintain their industry, maintain their shipbuilding, and carry on their commercial life such as it had. Their connection to the continent was broken; there'd be nothing left for them to do but call it off, especially if their principal ally, Germany, had been defeated. I was quite sure that they wouldn't want to get mixed up with the Russians at that stage of the game.

Q: Did Admiral King share this point of view?

Admiral Bieri: I think he did feel that to a very large extent, but it wasn't the agreed position on the Chiefs of Staff. Of course, MacArthur was convinced that we were going to have to land in Japan with a large military force to subdue the Japanese. That, of course, changed very rapidly.

A great many of the plans that we made for moving forces into that area--we were getting more forces in the way of landing craft, landing facilities, and that sort of thing--were called off as soon as it became evident that the Japs were going to have to surrender. (We had the atomic bomb.)[*]

Two other little interesting events in my career--when I returned from Europe the second time . . .

Q: You mean, after the Normandy landing?

Admiral Bieri: After the Normandy landing. Admiral King was out in the Pacific. They were having a conference out there. Cooke was with him.[†] I got back and was without a job, so I went in to see Edwards. I said, "Look, Admiral, I've been here ever since the war started. Somebody else has taken over my planning job. I'm ready to go out and help finish this war in the Pacific. I've got all my stuff packed and I'm ready to go, tomorrow morning."

He said, "I'm going to talk to the boss tonight. He's out in Honolulu. I'll talk to him on the telephone. I'll tell him about it and that you want to come out."

The next morning he sent for me and said, "I talked to the admiral last night." He sort of grinned and he said, "He said to me, you tell Bieri to keep his shirt on and stay where he is. They've plenty of people out here to fight this war, and I need a few of the good ones left in Washington." So I stayed there. Then he said to me, "I've got a thing here I want you to look out for."

---

[*] In the first combat use of atomic bombs, U.S. B-29 bombers hit Hiroshima, on the island of Honshu, on 6 August 1945 and Nagasaki, on Kyushu, on 9 August.
[†] Cooke by this time was a rear admiral.

Q: Edwards said that?

Admiral Bieri: Yes. I said, "What's that?"

He said, "It's this 'Nemo' business."

I said, "'Nemo?' What do you mean 'Nemo?'"

He looked at me and said, "You're probably the only person in Washington that doesn't know what 'Nemo' is." He laughed.

I said, "I never heard of it."

He said, "'Nemo' is the code name for that German submarine that Gallery has just captured out in the Atlantic. I've been handling all the correspondence and stuff about that. It's supposed to be top secret. You take it over from now on."[*]

I apparently was the only one in Washington that didn't know what "Nemo" was, because I'd just gotten back.

Then some weeks or months later, he sent for me one day and said, "I've got another job for you."

I said, "What is it?"

He said, "King has gone out in the Pacific, and Cooke has gone out in the Pacific, and Purnell has gone out in the Pacific."[†] He named off a whole new list of people in operations. Apparently he and I were the only two they were going to leave in Washington. He said, "I want you to look out for the Manhattan Project business while they are gone."

I said, "What's the Manhattan Project?"[‡]

Q: You had not heard of this?

---

[*] Captain Daniel V. Gallery, Jr., USN. While in command of the USS Guadalcanal (CVE-60) in June 1944, his forces captured the German submarine U-505. Gallery eventually became a rear admiral and wrote a number of popular books about the Navy. His oral history is in the Naval Institute collection.
[†] Rear Admiral William R. Purnell, USN.
[‡] Manhattan Project was the code name for the U.S. effort to create an atomic bomb in World War II.

Admiral Bieri: Here I was sitting number-four man on the staff, all the time this thing was going on, and none of that business ever went through my hands. I had no excuse for inquiring into it, or sticking my nose in other people's business. It never came up in the planners. As far as the Navy was concerned, it was one of the most hushed-up affairs I ever heard of.

Q: The knowledge confined to whom?

Admiral Bieri: The knowledge of it was confined to the people who were actually working on it. One of them was Purnell down in operations; Admiral King and Admiral Cooke and Admiral Edwards in the fleet side; the operations side was Horne and Farber, his assistant; and Purnell, and Parsons, the man who actually was doing the work on it.* Nobody had ever discussed it.

Q: Admiral Nimitz didn't know about it either.

Admiral Bieri: I don't know. I didn't know anything about it--the Manhattan Project.

He said, "That's the atomic bomb they're going to explode over Japan in a couple of days."

I said, "I don't know anything about it. What am I supposed to do about it?"

He said, "Oh, you won't have anything to do about it. If anything comes up, if you can't handle it, come to see me about it."

Q: What had you been doing?

---

* Vice Admiral William S. Farber, USN, was Sub-Chief of Naval Operations. Captain William S. Parsons, USN, was involved in the development of the atomic bomb in New Mexico. During the mission of 6 August 1945, Parsons was the weaponeer on board the B-29 named "Enola Gay" that dropped the bomb on Hiroshima, Japan.

Admiral Bieri: I'd been handling a bunch of details--the reassignment of new forces, and old forces from the Atlantic and so forth.

Q: You mean fighting warships?

Admiral Bieri: Yes. The regular daily routine that you have on a large staff; different things have to be coordinated between the section heads. I presided every morning for about an hour on the staff meeting in which practically all the number-two men brought in all their problems and questions which they wanted taken care of.

I had a lot of outside duties, such as going around making speeches and doing things that the boss-man didn't want to do himself. It really was a very interesting period of my time on the staff with Admiral King. Although I was busy with household chores, I kept <u>au courant</u> on the situation.

I had access to the chart room and knew what was going on in different areas. If I had any suggestions, I could present them to the chief of staff or the deputy. I kept an eye on the planners, on what was going on with the planning committee and the problems that they had to take up. Admiral Duncan was the chairman, so I didn't have to worry too much about that. He was a very able fellow and knew what was going on. There were personnel problems to handle.

Q: To what extent did you make use of the WAVES in that high echelon?[*]

Admiral Bieri: We had quite a few WAVES working for us. For instance, all during the war my secretary was a WAVE. I had a very good secretary and a very reliable one.
There were quite a number of WAVES in Admiral King's flag secretary's office, for instance. King and Edwards and Cooke had principally chief petty officers. That was a very interesting thing, because when we set up the headquarters at the beginning of the war, Admiral King came there. One of his first directions to the staff was that all the secretarial

---

[*] WAVES--Women accepted for Voluntary Emergency Service.

personnel were to be senior enlisted men, particularly chief petty officers. He sent out an order to the fleets to send a large number of qualified CPOs, yeoman stenographers, to headquarters for duty. We got these chaps over there, and in nothing flat we were bogged down.

They were great fellows aboard ship when they had to write just a few letters a day probably and had plenty of time to do it, but when they got into that mill, they were lost. The next thing we knew, we had a big influx of WAVES, yeoman WAVES. Business began to hum. It was very interesting.

Q: So these senior officers where convinced of the merits of the women in the service?

Admiral Bieri: Yes, we were very convinced. I had a lot of business at that time, and I had about three or four of these girls working for me. They were all stenotypists. We were having a lot of conferences and things. The girls would come in there, one at a time, and record the proceedings for half an hour or three quarters of an hour. The next one would come in and take over, the first would go out and write it up. By the time we got through the conference, we had the whole works. If we'd been waiting for the other chiefs, we'd have been waiting about four days.

So the number of enlisted people who worked in that sort of thing in the headquarters--Admiral Cooke had one excellent one that he had all during the war; he eventually was promoted to lieutenant commander. He was very able as a stenographer, turned out a lot of correspondence. In our lower echelon, we used WAVES a great deal and they were very, very satisfactory, and very reliable.

I don't believe, with one or two exceptions, that any of those girls were taken out of the headquarters for committing any sort of indiscretions.

Q: Would you talk a little, Admiral, about the security precautions and arrangements at that echelon in the Navy?

Admiral Bieri: The prime instruction was that nobody was supposed to seek any information that they didn't need to carry out their job.

Q: Witness your lack of knowledge about the Manhattan Project.

Admiral Bieri: Yes. If you needed some information to carry out your job, you could go anywhere you wanted to get it. If you didn't need the information, or were just curious about something, you let it alone. Or if you heard rumors about something, you just let it alone. I think that was very generally observed. In the first place, everybody was kept very busy all the time all during the week, even on Saturdays and Sundays. You just didn't have time to go around and try to gather up information. I drove to work with four or five officers.

Q: Car-pool type thing?

Admiral Bieri: Car pool. All of them were in headquarters in one capacity or another. We never discussed any business affairs riding in or coming from work.

The only people that I ever saw around the Navy Department who seemed to have time enough to come around and try to get information were some old friends of mine. I never could quite find out what their jobs were. One of them was Paul Foster, who was working first in the Bureau of Ordnance and then down in the Secretary's office. That guy was always around trying to find out what you were doing, what you were working on.

Another one was Oscar Badger.[*] He seemed to have a lot of time to come around and pass the time of day and hope to get some conversation. Another one was a classmate of mine named Hanson; Admiral Hanson who has since died.[†] He wasn't around very much. He didn't stay there very long because he didn't have much of a job.

---

[*] Rear Admiral Oscar C. Badger, USN.
[†] Rear Admiral Edward W. Hanson, USN.

Foster had more time than anybody else I knew in the Navy Department to come around and get the dope. He was a very smart fellow. I have no doubt that he knew all about the Manhattan Project and everything else. He'd get it somehow.

Q: He seemed to have a particular entree to FDR.*

Admiral Bieri: As a general rule, there were places in the organization where only certain people were allowed to go. One of them was the so-called Commander in Chief's chart room, where they got all reports of all the operations of all the places all over the world. These things were posted immediately when they came in. We had three reserve officers on duty in there. They knew that if anything leaked out of that place, or if anybody got into that place that wasn't supposed to, they'd get their heads chopped off. They watched that place like hawks. They were on duty night and day in this place all during the war.

There were just a very limited number of people on the staff who were allowed to go in the chart room. One of them was Admiral King; and Edwards, Cooke and myself. I think later on, Duncan. I never had occasion to take anybody else in there. I would go in there and check up, maybe in the morning when I first arrived if I had time. I went in to check on what had occurred during the night.

Q: Did Admiral King have a briefing in the chart room?

Admiral Bieri: Yes, he came in every day. He would occasionally bring in with him somebody like the Major General Commandant of the Marine Corps or some chief of bureau or somebody like that. None of those people had free entry into that place. The names of those that could go in were posted on the door. They were the ones that went in, unless others were taken in by the authority of the Commander in Chief. Very much the same situation existed as far as the antisubmarine business was concerned. George Dyer and people around there had very tight security over it.

---

* FDR--Franklin D. Roosevelt.

Q: Admiral King occasionally came down to the Secretary's chart room, which was a similar chart room, for the briefing.

Admiral Bieri: Oh, yes. He came down for briefings down there. There were a lot of things that came into the Commander in Chief's chart room that didn't get down to the Secretary's place either.

Q: No, I'm sure of that.

Admiral Bieri: And there probably were some things that went to the Secretary's place that didn't get up in the other room. I don't know if it was generally known about the Manhattan Project down there.

Q: I don't think it was. I contributed to the Secretary's chart room, so I was in and out of there quite often.

Admiral Bieri: Of course, it was understood by all the staff and personnel in the headquarters that no one communicated with the press. That was strictly Admiral King's business, and he was forever limited at that.

Q: You mean, in terms of operations?

Admiral Bieri: Yes.

Q: Now when you went out on a speechmaking tour awarding Navy E's, you communicated with the press.

Admiral Bieri: Oh, yes. I talked to them about generalities. For instance, out in Minneapolis they had several dinner meetings for me. One of them was attended by not a very large group but well-informed, a group of businessmen and politicians. I read the papers about the Combined Chiefs of Staff and the Joint Chiefs of Staff.

Naturally they wanted to know what it was. It's very easy to talk to people about a thing like that without giving them any information that needs to be withheld from the public. They all seemed to enjoy it.

Speaking at the Naval War College was not very difficult, because the questions that were asked by the students were usually relative to the subject we were discussing and pretty much kept in bounds.

Q: You'd be at greater liberty to tell them that this was a classified subject.

Admiral Bieri: Oh, yes. Any real news that ever came out of the Commander in Chief's headquarters was either given out by Admiral King or Admiral Edwards. There wasn't any such thing as a press officer.

Q: I don't think you've told me about Admiral King, the man.

Admiral Bieri: I had never served with Admiral King, except as a midshipman, when he was a discipline officer at the Naval Academy during the first two years I was there. He was a very strict disciplinary officer. I never served under him again, until I served on his staff. I never knew him personally. I never knew his family. He never knew mine.

Just before Admiral Richardson was relieved as the Commander in Chief in the Pacific Fleet, Admiral King came out there one time. He was Commander in Chief of the Atlantic Fleet at that time.[*] He spent several days with us. Admiral Taffinder and I messed with Admiral Richardson.[†] Of course, Admiral King was his guest while he was there, and he also was the admiral's guest in the mess.

---

[*] King did not become CinCLantFlt until 1 February 1941, the same day Richardson was relieved as CinCUS. On 17 December 1940, as a rear admiral, King became Commander Patrol Force U.S. Fleet in the Atlantic. On 1 February 1941, the billet was upgraded to Commander in Chief Atlantic Fleet with the rank of full admiral.
[†] Captain Sherwoode A. Taffinder, USN, was Admiral Richardson's chief of staff.

The discussions never got down to anything personal; it was usual business and what we thought of various things. I remember one of the subjects which we were very much concerned with, and he was too, was the lack of antiaircraft protection on the bigger ships.

I talked with him several times while he was there, while we were up on the bridge during maneuvers of one thing and another.

My acquaintance with King was very limited. Of course, after I joined his staff, he knew who I was. I had almost daily association with him when we went to the Joint Chiefs of Staff meetings. As the senior planner, I had generally the task of presenting the planners' position on the particular problem they were taking up. So he knew who I was, and he knew what I was doing.

I must say, he never seemed to object if I brought up an idea that hadn't been discussed with him or the rest of his staff. He accepted it for whatever it was worth.

As I said, I was promoted a couple of times while I was on his staff. As far as I knew, I got good fitness reports. I was given assignments that he felt like giving to me. When I finally left the staff when the war was over, I went in to say good-bye to him. I was going to sea. We got into a personal conversation.

I'll tell you about another time that we had a little personal contact. We were flying back from the Cairo conference in an Army plane. It was pretty well loaded. A couple of us were playing cribbage. He came down the aisle and said, "You fellows know anything about that game?"

We kind of laughed and said, "Oh yes, sir."

He said, "I'll be down to play with you in a little while." He came around and sat down and played with me. He beat me about four or five games in a row. That satisfied him, and he went about his business.

When I went in to pay my respects and say good-bye to him, he said to me, "Are you married?"

Q: "Are you married?"

Admiral Bieri: I said, "Oh, yes. I've been married many years."

He said, "Have you got a family?"

I said, "Yes, I have five sons. They're all in the service."

He said, "Well, I never knew that." That's as far as our personal acquaintance ever went.

Q: Curious, wasn't it?

Admiral Bieri: I went to a number of social affairs with him during the war. They were usually official affairs ashore.

One job while I was assistant chief of staff--he put me on the committee that undertook the job of raising a memorial to Sir John Dill in Arlington.* You've seen that, I suppose?

Q: No, I haven't.

Admiral Bieri: You should see it some time. It's a wonderful thing.

Of course, Sir John Dill was very much liked by all the Americans that came in contact with him. He was the epitome of an English gentleman. He was the representative of the British Chief of Staff on the Washington Combined Chiefs of Staff.

I think he had died in England, but he became ill over in this country and went back. I'm not sure, maybe he's buried out there in Arlington. The memorial to him is out there in Washington.

The question came up of a memorial to Sir John Dill. The President was very interested in it and decided that it ought to be placed in Arlington. We had a large

---

* Field Marshal Sir John Dill served as Chief of the Imperial General Staff in 1940-41. He was subsequently head of the British Joint Staff Mission to the United States. Following his death in 1944 he was buried in the Arlington National Cemetery, a notable honor for a foreign officer.

committee to work in this thing. Admiral King was one of the members, and I was; also General Marshall and several Army officers, some aviation officers, and a group of civilians including Mr. Bliss.

Q: Robert Woods Bliss.[*]

Admiral Bieri: We got this famous sculptor, Davidson, as I recall, the man who was a great horse sculptor. He produced the statue of Sir John Dill on this charger. It's a beautiful piece of sculpture. It stands in the Arlington Cemetery on the side of a knoll, not too far removed from the Tomb of the Unknown Soldier.

Drive around there and you just happen on it. Very few people know what it is when they see it, except these people who are associated with Sir John during the war. Some time when you're over there, ask about it, and look for it.

Q: I will.

Admiral Bieri: Then they had some fine dedication services when it was finally unveiled. The British sent over some very excellent men to represent their Chiefs of Staff. The British Chiefs of Staff were like our Chiefs of Staff; they were in London.

Q: That was called the Imperial General Staff, wasn't it?

Admiral Bieri: Yes. Our Chiefs of Staff were naturally in Washington. Most of the Combined Chiefs of Staff business was done in Washington.

They had some very good and some high-powered representatives over here to be with our people. I was always very much impressed by these fellows, particularly the naval

---

[*] Bliss, a long-time American diplomat, retired in 1933 after a 30-year career. Then, in November 1942, he was appointed a consultant to the Division of Cultural Relations, State Department.

men and their army men. The naval men were usually either ex-First Lords of the Admiralty, or they were men that had had very high naval commands at sea.

Q: Was Sir Dudley Pound over here?

Admiral Bieri: No. He may have come over on a trip. Sir Dudley Pound was First Lord of the Admiralty when I went to London the first time.* Sir Percy Noble was the first naval representative over here. I think probably Pound may have relieved Noble, but I'm trying to think who relieved him in London. Then Admiral Cunningham came over, but he was only here a short time. He was only here about six months or so.

Q: Mountbatten came over occasionally, didn't he?

Admiral Bieri: He was never over here as one of the Chiefs of Staff representatives. He made frequent trips over here as consultant for various things. He had too many hats; he'd have to represent everybody.

When Cunningham left, Admiral Harwood, who fought the Battle of Plate, came over.† He was a very fine fellow. I think he stayed over here pretty much toward the end of the war. Sir John Dill was over here a long time as the army representative. Maitland Wilson was over for a while. I don't remember who the other chap was; they had three.

They always had a high-ranking quartermaster that sat in at the meetings. Also the air force chaps, whom I didn't get to know very well.

Q: On the subject of the British, would you say something about the sharing of intelligence, sharing of ordnance, and that kind of interchange?

---

* Actually, Admiral of the Fleet Sir Dudley Pound, RN, was First Sea Lord, serving in that post from June 1939 until his death on 21 October 1943.
† In 1942 Admiral Sir Henry Harwood, RN, became Commander in Chief Mediterranean. In December 1939, as a commodore, his division of three cruisers defeated the German pocket battleship Admiral Graf Spee off Uruguay's River Plate.

Admiral Bieri: As far as I know, there was a complete exchange of information. I don't think there was any exchange of information on the Manhattan Project, unless it was on the very, very highest level. As a general rule, we exchanged technical information quite freely with the British. In fact, we also exchanged a lot of technical information with the Russians, on the ships and things which were geared toward the enemy.

Q: Oh, we did? Tell me about that.

Admiral Bieri: After the Yalta Conference that was another job I had as assistant chief of staff.* Through Averell Harriman, we had agreed to furnish them with certain munitions of war.† The Army munitions and those that they could carry by rail went up through Teheran from the south. We, of course, lost a great many men and ships delivering supplies to the Russians around Murmansk.

In addition to that, at the Yalta Conference we agreed to give them a very considerable number of ships, principally minelayers, minesweepers, escorts, and that sort of thing. We were to deliver them on schedule to the Russians at a port in Alaska. We were supposed to take them up there and then tell these fellows how they worked, show them how they worked, and turn them over to them. They got a lot of information from us on those ships.

There were a lot of us that didn't feel very kindly about this business. I remember after the thing had been going on for quite some time, we were having a little difficulty finding the ships and equipment to give to them. The next thing we knew, we got a message from the White House which said, "Stop dragging your feet. Furnish the Russians with the stuff," or words to that effect. We had to build a little fire under them and get it started again.

---

* Yalta, a resort city on the Crimea in the Black Sea, was the site of a meeting of the Allied Big Three--Roosevelt, Churchill, and Stalin--in February 1945. The conference reaffirmed the principle of seeking unconditional surrender by Japan and plans for the postwar division of territory.
† W. Averell Harriman served as U.S. ambassador to the Soviet Union, 1943-46.

Q: This decision was made entirely by FDR then?

Admiral Bieri: Yes, the arrangements were made at Yalta by Roosevelt. I know King wasn't very keen about it, and I know Leahy wasn't very keen about it. It had the wholehearted concurrence of the President and also Averell Harriman, who was ambassador at that time.

So we had a fire built under us to get some ships out there and speeded the delivery up pretty good. We completed the program which was promised to them. They got various ships. They must have gotten quite a lot of technical information from them.

Q: From the equipment?

Admiral Bieri: The equipment on the ships.

Q: From the perspective of time, do you think that was an error or not?

Admiral Bieri: I don't think so because I think they would have gotten it eventually anyhow. They were supposed to return these ships after the war was over.

Q: This was that lease-lend arrangement?

Admiral Bieri: Yes, but they never did. They never returned anything and they never paid for anything. That's the way it was scheduled.

There was one thing that we had no great trouble in keeping secret during a good part of the war. That was the electronic fuze.[*] The electronic fuze was a very touchy subject with the Air Force. They just didn't want anybody in Europe, especially the

---

[*] The proximity fuze for 5-inch antiaircraft projectiles had a small radio transmitter in the nose that caused a projectile to explode when in the vicinity of an enemy plane. It was also known as the VT, or variable time fuze.

Germans, to find out about this fuse. On the other hand, the Army people were anxious to use it. They finally did use it in the Battle of the Bulge.

The main reason that we were able to keep the thing secret so long and use it to our advantage for so long in the Pacific was that the Air Force had a very high respect for the fuze and they didn't want it to get in the hands of the enemy or anybody that was going to use it against them.

Interview Number 5 with Vice Admiral Bernhard H. Bieri, U.S. Navy (Retired)

Place: Bethesda, Maryland

Date: Thursday, 10 September 1969

Interviewer: John T. Mason, Jr.

Q: Admiral, before you tell me about your sea duty following your service in the Navy Department during the war, would you tell me about the aftermath to the Yalta Conference? You intimated that some of the decisions taken at Yalta by the President and his advisers were then handed to you for implementation. I wonder if you'd tell me what they were and what you did?

Admiral Bieri: The Yalta Conference was early in February 1945. I'm not certain about the details, but at that conference it was agreed that we would turn over to the Russians a certain number of new type small auxiliary vessels in the Pacific. Principally, I think they were patrol vessels, minesweepers, and perhaps some minelayers--that general type.

A base was set up under a Russian-speaking American naval officer who'd been in Russia. I think his name was Franko. He was set up in Alaska; I don't remember what the name of the port was.

Q: But that was the area where they were being turned over?

Admiral Bieri: Yes. The ships were prepared on the West Coast, principally at Seattle at Puget Sound. Then sent with American crews up to Alaska, where Franko then turned them over to the Russians, who brought their crews over to man them at that place.

Q: Were these an outright gift or what?

Admiral Bieri: They were, I think, supposed to be on loan. Such of them as were fit were to be returned after the war, just like the other ships we gave the Russians. Of course, we never got any of them back, any of these or any of the others. And they never paid for any of them.

The decision to turn these vessels over was one of the tasks that was given to me in my capacity as deputy chief of staff to supervise. We picked out the ships and sent them over. At that time, there was still a great demand for ships of that type in our own fleet. We were also losing a great many ships at that time of various types in operations in the Western Pacific--Japan, Okinawa, and those places.

Our natural tendency was to give our own people the first consideration for ships of that type that were needed.

Q: In other words, you're saying it wasn't a very popular decision with the Navy Department.

Admiral Bieri: It wasn't a very popular decision with the naval officers that had to do this thing.

Apparently the word got through to the Russians and to the President and Mr. Averell Harriman that we were dragging our feet on this proposition. So we got great big orders from the White House to get busy and get the ships over there. So we went ahead and filled out the order. I think this thing kept up right up until the end of the war before we finally got them all over there.

Q: Was this truly at the expense of our own need?

Admiral Bieri: Yes, I think it was, at least the needs as we looked forward to needing them. One of the things we knew we'd have to have if we ever became involved in an invasion of the Japanese islands was craft of that sort.

Q: Why did the Russians at that point have such need for these smaller vessels?

Admiral Bieri: That's the question. The Russians always seemed to have a need for anything they could get from us. They were never too anxious to reciprocate.

I recall that very early in the war the Army was attempting to find ways of getting aircraft from Europe into Southeast Asia and China. In order to do that, they would have to overfly Russian territory, and they would have to have certain bases and fields in Russia where they could land, to refuel and so forth.

An Army Air Forces officer named Follett Bradley, who was a graduate of the Naval Academy in the class of 1910, was in charge of this project.[*] They had worked out quite a scheme, but every time they approached the Russians on the matter, the Russians had some objection. They wouldn't let us fly through there. The whole thing finally just died down. They never got anywhere on it.

It was typical of the Russians not to reciprocate in any of these things. They were perfectly willing to receive material; they probably needed it. But things that they might have helped out on, they just flatly refused to help on.

Q: In the case of these vessels, what was your task involving the implementation of the order?

Admiral Bieri: Our task was, when we were informed that a certain number of these vessels were ready for delivery and were manned, to determine which ones we were going to send up to Alaska and which ones we were going to send out to our own fleet. We would then issue the necessary directive to the bureaus that were handling the ships for the disposition they were to make of them.

Q: Were efforts made to remove from the ships some of the equipment which was perhaps still in a secret category?

---

[*] Major General Follett Bradley, USA.

Admiral Bieri: As far as I know, they were not. I don't think there were too many super-secret things on them. They were improving them some, a great many of the mechanical things and so forth. I'm quite sure they must have been given some ammunition, but never included any of the electronic fuzes which were still classified at that time. They were mostly minelayers and minesweepers, so I don't think there were any antisubmarine weapons in them, outside the sonar. That was just one of the many jobs we had to do about that time.

Q: Can you cite any others that were of interest and should be part of the record?

Admiral Bieri: Not particularly, because my duties at that time were very largely routine administrative duties of that type. While I didn't attend planning meetings and matters of that sort, there were no events of any great outstanding importance. That planning on that level, the Commander in Chief's level, had largely to do with what was going to happen in the future. To lay out the strategic plans for the future. They were at that time pretty well developed.

We were in the process of getting ready to go into the Philippines. As you recall, once Germany was defeated, the Japs began to fold up pretty fast, especially after we got rid of all their air and immobilized the fleet around the Philippines. But there was always the expectation and probability that we might have to land in Japan. Of course, plans were going ahead for that probability or possibility, with the idea that MacArthur would be the commander, and Nimitz the naval commander. There were plans for the assembly of forces from the Atlantic and other places for use in connection with such an operation if it came up.

One of the things that was always a big problem was shipping. Of course that was handled by the logistic people.

I don't recall any other particular things that we were involved in at that time.

Q: Your administrative duties, did they involve you with the Secretary's administrative secretary?

Admiral Bieri: No, very seldom. I had very little contact with the Secretary.

I had contact with all the members of the Commander in Chief's staff and quite a few of the people in the staff of the Deputy Chief of Naval Operations through Admiral Horne.[*] I occasionally had business with some of the bureaus.

As I said, we always had daily staff meetings at which either Cooke or I presided. I handled the questions that the other members of the staff brought up. At the same time, we were kept informed and briefed as to what was happening in the various departments.

As the war progressed also, more and more problems came up in connection with the reorganization of the military forces after the war--the problem of combining the three different forces under one roof in the Pentagon.

One problem that I recall that I was handed by Admiral King was to make a survey of the room the Navy would require if we moved into the Pentagon in entirety and how much the Army would give us. And if they didn't have enough room, where would we go; particularly if they eventually disposed of the old Navy building?[†] That study was still going on when I left.

Of course, they never got too much of the Navy in there. The administrative Navy found itself around other parts of town. Just the top echelon got in--the Secretary and Joint Chiefs of Staff.

There were a lot of questions that came up about the unification of the forces and that sort of thing, which were discussed and studied by the planners.

Q: How did Admiral King feel about this whole development?

---

[*] Admiral Frederick J. Horne, USN, served as Vice Chief of Naval Operations from 26 March 1942 to 10 October 1945.
[†] The Navy Department building was at 17th Street and Constitution Avenue in Washington, D.C. The building remained in use until the early 1970s, when President Richard Nixon directed that it be demolished.

Admiral Bieri: I never talked to him personally much about it. I never heard him say too much about it, but I'm quite sure that he felt that there had to be the continuation of an organization such as we had during the war. Just what form it could take was another matter.

Q: Who gave this whole idea its main impetus?

Admiral Bieri: I think the main impetus for continuing it after the war probably came from the Army. The Army had operated under the general staff system for quite a number of years. The Air Force had a similar organization. The Navy system was somewhat different, though it was brought gradually in line with the Army system during the war.

The Navy, I don't believe, has ever gone quite as far in developing its staff system in giving authority to staff officers as the Army and Air Force have. In other words, the commanders in the fleet in the Navy look to the Navy Department and the Chief of Naval Operations and his staff for instructions and orders that emanate usually from Washington. It's not customary for subordinates in that organization to go out into these fleets and issue orders on the spot, for instance.

In general, I think Admiral King believed that we would have to have some sort of combined organization or joint organization after the war was over.

Q: Was that your feeling too, Admiral?

Admiral Bieri: Yes, I felt we did too. The Army brought this up. There were a lot of people in the Army who wanted to have a very active hand in this thing. They wanted to do it while we were still fighting the war, especially in the early part of the war.

The Navy was not in a position at that time to change the practices that it had over the years or swing its organization completely around with the general staff system. In order to make our cooperation with the Army easier and more facile, we did name the different things like Operations, Plans, and so forth with numbers and letters that corresponded with the Army's.

There were many questions of that sort that took up a great deal of time, particularly with the planners. I'd left the planners by this time. I think Duncan would know more about that.

Q: You said last time, when it came to the release of information to the press on war operations, this was entirely in the hands of Admiral King. But in a larger sense in terms of public relations in the Navy's growing facility in this area, did you have responsibilities?

Admiral Bieri: No, I had none. As far as the headquarters of the fleet was concerned in Washington, the Commander in Chief's field, there was no press officer--as they used to be known in the service and I think they still have a press officer. Admiral King himself met certain people of responsibility in the press. One of them was David Lawrence, who had frequent contact with him, I know.* There may have been others.

The general publicity emanated from the Secretary's office. As to the day-to-day operations and important things that happened in the fleet, that came directly to King. He was the man that advised the Secretary what to release and what not to release. Edwards was the deputy commander and he was involved in this to a certain extent. The rest of us were strictly out of it.

Q: The whole Navy relationship with industry, the Navy E program, that was under the Secretary?

Admiral Bieri: That was under the Secretary, yes. I think it was handled for the Secretary by Admiral Woodward.† He was in the Secretary's office, and I presume he got his information from the bureaus that were responsible for getting material.

I have, as I said, not too many recollections of things that they did about that time because they were getting pretty well routine. It was a question of supplying the forces in

---

* David Lawrence was president and editor of the magazine U.S. News.
† Rear Admiral Clark H. Woodward, USN (Ret.), was recalled to active duty in June 1941. In June 1942 he became Chief of the Navy Industrial Incentive Division.

the field, reallocating forces as they weren't needed in one theater and were needed in another. This became very active, as soon as the war in Europe was over. By that time, we had most of our ships, except the antisubmarine, in the Pacific, anyhow.

Q: Admiral, thinking in terms of the cooperation lent by the Royal Navy in the Pacific in those later days of the war, were such matters as pertained to the two fleets handled in the Pacific or was some of it done in Admiral King's office?

Admiral Bieri: The question of what ships the British were to send over and when was handled by Admiral King and the British First Lord or his representative. Up to the time I left, there weren't too many of them that had arrived over there. There were a few fast minelayers. I think one carrier group about '45 was operating under Halsey.*

Q: I think it was the Victorious.
   Did you have any contact with Admiral Nimitz during those years?

Admiral Bieri: No personal contact. The last time I saw Admiral Nimitz was when I was detached from the fleet after Pearl Harbor, a few months after that. He had just reported for duty. He, at that time, very kindly expressed the willingness to have me stay on out there, but I already had my orders and there wasn't any particular reason for the Navy to change them, so I kept on.

Q: Had you known him prior to that time?

Admiral Bieri: I had never served with Admiral Nimitz, but I had known him for quite a number of years. When I was the executive officer of a destroyer tender in San Diego Bay in 1933 to '36, he had command of the reserve destroyer force down there over at the

---

* Admiral William F. Halsey, Jr., USN, Commander Third Fleet.

destroyer base, where they kept the reserve destroyers. I occasionally saw him in connection with repairs we had encountered.

Q: Can you remember, in connection with Admiral Nimitz, any incidents of any significance? My reason for asking this, is that we have been collecting data on him.

Admiral Bieri: No, I don't. He was always most pleasant to deal with. Of course, he was a very impressive person.

Q: In what sense, sir?

Admiral Bieri: Impressive in the sense that he dealt with you more or less as an equal. If he had something to ask of you or your opinion on something, you felt that he really wanted to know it, and if it was any good, he would give it consideration. He was very well liked by everyone. I know that he was very highly thought of by his superiors. I think either the captain or the admiral on one of his ships, while he was still quite a young officer, made the remark on one of his fitness reports that he was at that time qualified to be an admiral. I don't think there was ever any question in the minds of most of the people that knew Admiral Nimitz, that he would one day be one of the outstanding flag officers of the fleet.

When I knew him down in San Diego, he was still a captain. I don't remember Admiral Nimitz serving in the fleet while I was in it. For instance, when I was in the fleet as a navigator back in '33, he was, I believe, out in the Asiatic.

Q: He was with the Augusta.[*]

Admiral Bieri: Yes. I don't recall if he ever commanded battleships. I think he commanded cruisers. Originally, he was a submarine officer. He had very considerable to do with the

---

[*] Captain Chester W. Nimitz, USN, commanded the heavy cruiser Augusta (CA-31) from 16 October 1933 to 12 April 1935.

early development of submarines and submarine forces. I think he on several occasions commanded parts of all the submarine force.

As you grow up in the Navy, if you didn't serve directly with these people, or people that you were senior to, you got a pretty good general idea of who they were and what they were capable of doing, or how they were looked upon by their juniors and seniors. You more or less make up your mind about which ones are eventually going to be flag officers and which ones weren't.

Q: This was possible because of the size of the Navy, wasn't it?

Admiral Bieri: It was probably possible because of the size of the Navy. You got to know these individuals and their reputations over a good many years. You could observe the type of duty they were getting and the positions they were filling in the service, and the people who chose them for those positions. There were always some surprises--people who became flag officers who you didn't think would ever get there. On the other hand, there were always a number who seemed to be working very hard to become flag officers, who became quite sure that when the time came, they would become flag officers.

Nimitz was one of these people that took things in stride. He didn't seem to go after publicity and that sort of thing. He did a good job wherever they sent him, and he always had important duties. Everybody was quite sure that he was one of the men that eventually would come up on top.

Those conditions have changed a whole lot in recent years.

Q: Yes, it's a much bigger outfit now.

Admiral Bieri: A much bigger outfit and a more varied outfit.

During this time that I was deputy chief of staff, one of the assignments that I got was to serve on the first selection board that they had had since the beginning of the war. I suppose you've had information on the manner of selecting flag officers during the war. At the end of the war, they discarded that system.

They had sent out to all the fleet commanders and gotten their recommendations on the captains that these people thought should be promoted to flag rank for performance of duty at sea during the past year. Before they acted on this thing, I think Admiral King and the Chief of the Bureau of Personnel, Admiral Jacobs, and Edwards and Horne would take this list; they were very largely influenced in their selection of the people they took from the lists which they got back from the fleet commanders.

Q: This was only natural.

Admiral Bieri: Yes, also what they knew about them. They were, in fact, acting as a selection board all during the war for flag officers. Occasionally, they would reach out when they needed a flag officer for a particular job, they'd take somebody that was on the list or recommended and make him flag officer. They didn't make flag officers just once a year or something like that.

Q: It was kind of an open season?

Admiral Bieri: Yes. They were making flag officers from these lists all the time. During this period when I was deputy chief of staff, they suddenly stopped that. They ordered a selection board. This was not a statutory selection board in that the board was not ordered by the Secretary of the Navy, but it was going to be given to him for approval.

I was one of the flag officers that was available, and I was made a member of this board. Admiral Bellinger was the senior member of the board and the president of the board. We had people on it such as Mitscher, Kitts, and myself. It was quite a good-sized board. We were ordered to select a certain number of flag officers, both line and EDOs, and to submit the selectees.*

We were given the recommendations which came in from the fleet commanders. I think that they expected that we would largely be governed by these lists. We began by

---

* Vice Admiral Patrick N. L. Bellinger, USN; Vice Admiral Marc A. Mitscher, USN; Rear Admiral Willard A. Kitts III, USN; EDOs--engineering duty officers.

being given these popularity polls which we got in from the fleet. This board sat down and made a very thorough study of the records and wartime careers of all the officers that were eligible to be flag officers, and those who were still of the proper age and hadn't made it during the war, right down to the bottom where we would naturally go to get them. We came out with a list that differed quite a bit from the so-called popularity polls that had come in from the fleet.

I resumed my regular duties, and I didn't hear anymore about this for a long time. We selected some very fine officers on that slate.

Q: How many were you selecting?

Admiral Bieri: I think we were selecting about 50. Of course, quite a number of officers on the board who had been in the fleet, had particular officers that served with them that they were keen about; and they were good officers. We finally got down to the point where we said they had to be within a reasonable age bracket and had to have had combat duty in the war--satisfactory combat duty. It should be an officer that the government could look forward for considerable service after he was selected. We made up a list and sent it in. The discussion was very complete in each of these cases. We arrived at that list with the very minimum amount of voting. I think the rule was that he had to get three-quarters of the votes of the members. By the end of the second ballot, we had them all selected. This list was turned in, and nothing developed on it for quite a while.

I saw Jacobs one day, and I said, "Randall, whatever became of that selection list we worked on?"

He said, "The President refused to approve it." It did go to the Secretary first.

I said, "Why not?"

He said, "You fellows didn't select any reserve officers."

I said, "We had no orders to select any reserve officers. We were selecting regular line officers for flag rank in the Navy."

He said, "The President wouldn't sign it because there weren't any reserve officers."

Before this thing came out, I left Washington, being reassigned new duty. Then the list came out. There were quite a number of changes made in the list.

Q: By whom?

Admiral Bieri: By the Secretary or the President or whoever handled it. It was not a statutory board, so they didn't have to refer it back to the selection board.

Q: I see. They could act as a board themselves.

Admiral Bieri: They could act as they did during the war.
 They took off several very fine young officers who were later selected. They added on some Naval Reserve admirals, which we had not had any orders to pick up, and put those in. They added in some officers that most of us agreed on were not equal to the ones we had picked up. Anyhow, that was the list.
 The next board that was formed and convened to select flag officers, selected all the officers that we had selected and that had been taken off the list.

Q: This next board was a statutory board?

Admiral Bieri: The next one was a statutory board. Personally, I always thought that we did a pretty good job.

Q: None of the men really lost out then, they were just delayed in the transfer?

Admiral Bieri: A year. I served on two more selection boards. The last one, I was the president of the board. It was very interesting to me, the things that were gone into. The officers that were on the board did a very thorough job, a very conscientious job. We discussed all these officers at great length. We knew that there were many of them that were--one just about as good as the other. You had to make a choice. Then there entered into this selection too something which had not entered into it before the war so much. That was the need of certain types of officers, specialists.

For instance, the Navy had an admiral who was a communication fellow, like Admiral Redman who had been running communications for a long time.

Q: Jack Redman?

Admiral Bieri: No, the older brother, Joseph.*

There weren't any other admirals on the Navy list that were really communications officers trained in that sort of thing. The board felt that there ought to be at least one or two officers that had had a lot of experience in communications. So, naturally, we had to take a choice between this officer and that officer. We picked up the fellow that had the speciality experience because there were plenty of them that didn't have speciality experience.

Q: This is an indication of the new Navy.

Admiral Bieri: An indication of the new Navy.

Of those two boards that I served on, the first one was quite promptly approved. I forget who was the senior member of that board.

The second one, I was president of the board. We worked more than two weeks. We had on the board the commanders of a great many important units in the fleet. The report wasn't approved.

Q: Truman was President then?

Admiral Bieri: Truman was President, but I found later it hadn't gotten to him yet.

---

* Rear Admiral Joseph R. Redman, USN.

These officers that were serving on the board had to get back to their jobs. They were getting rather restless after waiting a week for some action on this thing. I went one day to see the Chief of Naval Operations. I told him that we had this report in for well over a week and the officers were anxious to get back. Most of them had approached me to see what I could do about it.

Q: Who was CNO then?

Admiral Bieri: Sherman.[*] He said, "The Secretary, Matthews, got the report. Go and speak to him."[†]

So I asked to speak to the Secretary, went in, and presented the case to him. He opened the top drawer of his desk and he had the list there. He said, "You've left an awful lot of good officers off this list." It was apparent that he was interested in one or two that weren't on the list.

I said, "Mr. Secretary, I think all the members of the board are convinced that we left an awful lot of good officers off the list. We've selected the officers that we thought were all excellent officers and qualified for flag duty and would fit the needs of the Navy in the way of experience and specialities and so forth. As a matter of fact, I didn't find a single one of my captains on this list. I had several of these people serve me as chiefs of staff, captains of ships, and chiefs in the Navy Department under me. Not one of them was selected; as a matter of fact, I didn't vote for them. Not because they weren't qualified, but we thought the other people were better qualified."

He pulled the list out and signed it and sent it on.

Q: That raises a question about selection boards and favoritism. As you describe it, there isn't much possibility of this.

---

[*] Admiral Forrest P. Sherman, USN, served as Chief of Naval Operations from 2 November 1949 to 22 July 1951.
[†] Francis P. Matthews served as Secretary of the Navy from 25 May 1949 to 30 July 1951.

Admiral Bieri: I found none at all on the boards that I was on.

The first board that I was on, which was not the statutory board--I wouldn't call it favoritism, but one of the members of that board has as a chief of staff during the war a man who was undoubtedly one of the outstanding young officers in the Navy. He put up a very valiant fight and argument to select this young man as an admiral. It would have meant moving him way up over many other officers.

Maybe we were a little bit conservative in those days. Most of us said, "That's fine, we recognize that this man is an excellent officer. Personally we think that we'll do him an injustice, because he will undoubtedly be selected in a couple of years or more. Then he'll have a chance to have a very distinguished career, particularly with people of his own time and not have to serve as a subordinate." That was actually what happened.

I found that working in these boards that there was never any pressing for individuals because you knew them personally. As I said, I passed over and when I finally voted, I didn't vote for several officers that served under me that I was confident would have made good flag officers, probably as good as the ones we selected.

Q: In other words, like a judge, you disqualified yourself from that?

Admiral Bieri: No, I didn't disqualify myself, but I wouldn't hold up the vote. I remember nobody else would. After everybody read a certain group of records, at least two officers looked at every record in the group that he was given. You could take and make a resume of any record that you wanted to. The resumes of the records that were made were then read by everybody, and they could check back against the records themselves. These resumes of the records were discussed amongst the officers, members of the selection boards.

Q: The records comprised the total record of the man?

Admiral Bieri: The total record of the man.

I ran into no favoritism. At that time, we had on us no pressure from above as to whom we should select.

I understand that subsequently in some of the selection boards, the board was actually told by the Secretary that they would select certain officers that had qualifications which pinpointed the man so well that we was one that the higher officials wanted selected.

Q: Is this an example of politics entering into the picture?

Admiral Bieri: Yes, an example of politics entering into the picture. I found none of that in my time. I was always very happy to see it that way.

So many other factors have come in recently that I just don't know how it's working. That was a long time ago, '45, when I was on the boards a quarter of a century ago.

Q: Is it a similar system which still prevails?

Admiral Bieri: They have a similar statutory board system of selection. Of course, what they have to do now is select officers who are qualified. They have to have a certain number of officers who qualify for submarines. They have to have a large number of officers who qualify in aviation. They have to have officers who qualify for specialities, like mine work, antisubmarine work, destroyers, cruisers, and surface ships.

Q: Oceanography too.

Admiral Bieri: And oceanographers and that sort of thing.

I believe now that when the selection board gets their instructions, they also get instructions from the Chief of the Bureau of Personnel or the Secretary--or whoever signs the order--that certain types of officers will be required. To select on that basis, as well as on the basis of fitness. I believe naturally with the large air predominance that we now have, the air officers get a slightly better chance of getting selected than the others; unless they're submariners.

That's sort of getting away from . . .

Q: An interesting digression however.

Admiral Bieri: I was in that job as deputy chief of staff until October 1945. I received orders as Deputy Chief of Naval Operations for Administration. That meant that I moved down the corridor in the group that was under Admiral Horne, up to that time known as the Chief of Naval Operations Group. I had there very strictly an administrative job.

I was on a number of boards that considered some of the questions that were coming up with the disposition of the Pacific Islands, which probably was one of the most important ones I served on.

Q: That must have been an interesting assignment. Tell me about it.

Admiral Bieri: It was interesting, as far as I was concerned, and I only stayed in this job about three months. We never got very far in the way of making any decisions. We had a great deal of discussion about it. We brought in to the group that discussed it quite a diverse representation of government. Mr. Sullivan, the Assistant Secretary, was the head of the group that discussed it.[*] We had people from the Interior Department, other people from the Navy Department, people from the War Department, from the Air Force.

At the time I left, I think the services were pretty well in agreement that the islands ought to be administered by the services, instead of being turned over to one of the civilian agencies.

Q: You mean similar to the way Guam had been administered prior to the war?

---

[*] John L. Sullivan served as Assistant Secretary of the Navy for Air from 1 July 1945 to 17 June 1946.

Admiral Bieri: Yes. Of course, there were a lot of things that we hadn't considered at that time. One of them was what would happen and did happen when the United Nations was formed.

Our principal argument was that we would have to service these people. That is, we would have to furnish the ships and material to keep these people going. They had all been under, in one form or another, military government for a long time. The units were so small that it didn't seem possible to make one big state or unit out of them. The most expeditious way to handle them was the way we had handled Guam, Samoa, and those places.

Q: Admiral, before a real final decision could be made, was it not a determination by the Allied group in terms of peace and disposition of the conquered areas?

Admiral Bieri: Yes, while we had them all pretty well under our military control at that time, we realized that we really weren't going to have the final say as to how they were going to be disposed of anyhow. There were other people that were going to come in on it. The question of course was finally settled in the United Nations, when they set up the Trust Territory. The control of the islands, as far as the United States was concerned, was turned over to the Department of Interior.

Q: Who had taken the initiative in terms of this board?

Admiral Bieri: I think the Secretary of the Navy started it. It might have been the Joint Chiefs of Staff, I'm not sure. As I said, Mr. Sullivan was on the board as the president, and I was one of the members. That took up quite a lot of time.

While I was in this administrative job, it was not too exciting a job, I attended to the retirement of officers and the interior working of the Navy Department. That is, the part of the Navy Department that was under the Chief of Naval Operations. I got orders to be detached from this job in December of 1945. I had been made a vice admiral at that time.

Q: Admiral King was retiring about that time, wasn't he?

Admiral Bieri: Yes, he was retiring and we were about to get Admiral Nimitz as the Chief of Naval Operations.*

Q: Do you know anything about that appointment?

Admiral Bieri: No, I don't. As I said, I was detached from this job in December and ordered to duty to the Atlantic Fleet to command the Tenth Fleet. Under Admiral King's plan at that time, it was to consist, and had consisted of for some time, of forces in the South Atlantic. In addition, when I took it, it was also to include the naval forces on the west coast of South America.

Q: And the Caribbean?

Admiral Bieri: No, it wasn't in the Caribbean. It started out with Brazil and just the other South American countries; also the west coast of Africa and the west coast of South America.

I was finally assigned a flagship, the Fargo, in March of 1946.† I joined her in Philadelphia and she was fitted out for duty. We left the following month, April, to look over the territory. Among my orders at that time was to stop at Bermuda and Trinidad on the way down, then visit various ports on the east coast of South America, except Buenos Aires.

Q: Why was that eliminated?

---

* Fleet Admiral Chester W. Nimitz, USN, relieved Fleet Admiral Ernest J. King, USN, as Chief of Naval Operations on 15 December 1945.
† USS Fargo (CL-106) was commissioned 9 December 1945. She had a standard displacement of 10,000 tons, was 611 feet long, 66 feet in the beam, and had a draft of 20 feet. Her top speed was 33 knots. She was armed with twelve 6-inch guns and twelve 5-inch guns.

Admiral Bieri: That was because they were still having trouble there with Peron*.

Then I was to go the African coast and visit several ports there, including being present at the inauguration of President Tubman in Liberia.†

When I arrived at Montevideo, after visiting several ports, I received orders detaching my flagship and myself from the 10th Fleet and to proceed to the Mediterranean and report to the commander of the 12th Fleet, the Commander Naval Forces Europe, Admiral Hewitt, for duty in command of the U.S. Naval Forces in the Mediterranean as a relief for Rear Admiral Jules James.‡

Q: Before you comment on that, may I ask a question about the Tenth Fleet. In the light of our recent difficulties on the western coast of Latin America with Peru and Ecuador, and their claims of sovereignty over the first 200 miles of waters off the coast--were any issues of that sort alive in that time?

Admiral Bieri: No, I had no orders or instructions in connection with any of these things. I'll come to this a little later about orders and policies issued to fleet commanders.

I then proceeded to Gibraltar and I finally made contact with Admiral James at Naples. Admiral James's force in the Mediterranean consisted of one cruiser, one destroyer, and a lot of skeleton naval bases that were left over from the war.

Q: Which we were continuing to maintain?

---

* Juan D. Peron became President of Argentina on 4 June 1946.
† In January 1944 William V. S. Tubman was inaugurated as President for a term of eight years. Admiral Bieri may have been recalling ceremonies in early 1946 in connection with the opening of Liberia's first railroad and U.S. Navy supervision of port construction at Monrovia.
‡ Admiral H. Kent Hewitt, USN, served as Commander U.S. Naval Forces Europe/Commander 12th Fleet from August 1945 to September 1946. Rear Admiral Jules James, USN, served as Commander U.S. Naval Forces Mediterranean, 1945-46.

Admiral Bieri: Which were being maintained. He furnished me with an airplane to take me from Gibraltar to Paris, where I met with Admiral Hewitt. Hewitt had no definite orders for me, except that I was to return to Naples, relieve Jules James as commander, and carry out my basic orders.

Q: Why was Hewitt stationed in Paris? This was before NATO was set up.*

Admiral Bieri: He was over there attending some sort of a meeting. It might have been in connection with postwar affairs, but his headquarters were in London. He was at that time staying at a hotel in Paris, where I met him. He had quarters there.

    I returned to Naples and relieved Jules James, who was due for retirement. I took over the so-called fleet, which at that time consisted of my flagship. The other two ships went home.

    I received an order then from Admiral Nimitz in which he said, that he wanted me to close out all these bases in the Mediterranean. I was to get the personnel off the beach and get them to sea.

Q: What about the material?

Admiral Bieri: And to dispose of the material there.

Q: Dispose, in what way?

Admiral Bieri: We sold a lot of it eventually and shipped some of it back to the United States. We salvaged a little, gave some to our allies over there, and kept some for our own use. We had no base, and we had only one ship.

Q: Were some of the installations turned over to Allied governments?

---

* NATO--North Atlantic Treaty Organization, which was established in 1949.

Admiral Bieri: The land belonged to the Allied governments. In some of the places, we did give some of the material to the Allied governments. For instance, in Naples we turned over practically all the target practice material and that sort of stuff to the Italian Government, on the condition that they would let us use it when we wanted to have target practice.

I had these orders from Nimitz. I told him that I would go right ahead with it, but what I needed was some ships to get these people to sea on. He sent me some ships. He sent me about a squadron of destroyers, an additional cruiser, and a destroyer tender.

In the course of June to October, with the able assistance of Captain Fitzgerald, my chief of staff, we closed all these bases in the Mediterranean and got the people off the beach.*

Q: How many people were involved? How many people were on the beach?

Admiral Bieri: It was surprising the number of people that were on the beach. For instance, in Naples there were about 300 people on the beach, presumably looking out for naval material and so forth but principally taking care of themselves.

Q: Having nothing to do?

Admiral Bieri: Having nothing to do. In addition to the 300 people, there was at least one and a half pieces of motor equipment for each person. They had been living in a large number of commandeered houses in various places around. They had officers' clubs and enlisted men's clubs, which had been established during the war, which still were operating. They had a dispensary ashore for the men--quite an establishment.

---

* Captain William F. Fitzgerald, Jr., USN. During World War II, Fitzgerald was a member of the Joint War Plans Committee of the Joint Chiefs of Staff; one of his assignments was as a member of the U.S. delegation to the Cairo-Teheran Conference in late 1943.

There was a smaller establishment at Algiers. There was an establishment down at Palermo, where we had a large number of motor torpedo boats, which proved to be the greatest problem we had in getting rid of material.

There were people, extra small contingents in various ports in various cities. We had some extras up at Rome, over at Bari. Most of them were in Algiers, Naples, and Palermo. Especially at Naples, there were a large number of buildings which were filled up with material that had been left over there and men all over the place. We got them all off and home or at sea by the end of October. I had left my chief of staff with a contingent of officers and men in Naples, and they had operated from there in closing places up. I took the ships that I had and started cruising around the Mediterranean.

We had, of course, still a large Army contingent in Italy and over on the Yugoslavia border. In fact, we had a division over there with General Bryant Moore.*

Q: Was this on the Adriatic coast or up around Trieste?

Admiral Bieri: This was north of Trieste. Our troops were facing a considerable group of Yugoslavs. The British had a near division of troops that were down at Trieste. There was a little disturbance up there of some sort, very shortly after I took command. I decided that I'd better go up and see if there was anything that I could do. So I took the _Fargo_ and the other cruiser which I had and a couple of destroyers--I think the other cruiser at that time was the _Portsmouth_--and we went up and moored at Trieste and contacted the Army and established relations with Moore and his staff. I spent some time there.

On the way up, I had a message from the Chief of Naval Operations saying he thought it would be a good idea if I went to Trieste. I was able to send him back a reply and tell him that I was already on my way.

Q: Anticipated?

---

* Major General Bryant E. Moore, USA.

Admiral Bieri: That brings up the question of orders that were issued to me as a commander of a fleet unit operating in foreign waters. The only orders that I had were to proceed to the Mediterranean with my flagship and relieve Admiral James as Commander of the U.S. Naval Forces in the Mediterranean.

James had no orders to give me or to turn over to me. I had no statement of policy from anyone in the government as to what our relations with the different nations was supposed to be or what they wanted us to develop. I had no instructions about what operations I should carry out, which ports I should visit, or anything of that sort.

It later developed that I made out schedules about what I was going to do and what I expected to do and submitted them to Commander Naval Forces Europe and to the Chief of Naval Operations. They were generally approved, with the exception of certain ports which we were forbidden to visit. Principally, we were not permitted to visit any ports in Spain or in Egypt or in Palestine, which at that time was still a mandate of the British.

Q: Political considerations determined this in all three cases.

Admiral Bieri: The way I got that was by making out a schedule indicating that I might visit these places. I was told that I couldn't visit them.

Q: So the policy was in terms of vetoes.

Admiral Bieri: I never did receive from anyone a statement of our policy in connection with any government in the Mediterranean or bordering on the Mediterranean. I chose to go to quite a number of places. I decided that the only way to do was to cooperate with the senior State Department official--ambassador, consul, consul general, or whatever he was--and do whatever in his judgment was supposed to be done in the area. We got along very well with that.

In connection with that, a friend of mine in the Navy Department sent me copies of orders that had been issued to all the naval commanders that had gone into the Mediterranean, from the very earliest days of our Navy.

Q: From the pirates of Tripoli days?*

Admiral Bieri: There were very interesting. These orders were issued to these officers in great detail, even to the extent as to where they were to buy their supplies, from whom, how much they could spend, and so forth and so on. More often than not, as to very little instruction as to our political relations and so forth with these people. It was a very interesting file.

I had it in my possession. Barbara Gilmore sent it to me. I don't know if you know her or not. She was over here in the history department; she'd been there for years. I think she probably knows where everything is over in that place.

Demaree Bess came down to visit me one time when I was at Naples. He wanted to write an article about the ships, which he did. It was in The Saturday Evening Post.†
He spent about a week with me and lived with me in the cabin. He visited various ships and so forth. I showed him this file one day. He said, "That's very interesting. If you don't mind, I'd like to take it with me, make a copy of it, and read it. I'll send it back to you." It just so happened that I showed it to him just before he left.

I said, "That's fine." And I gave it to him.

I later had a letter from Bess, in which he thanked me very much for it. He said, "I'm giving these letters of yours to one of the commanding officers of one of the carriers that was over there." He had encountered them at another port, or taken passage on when he left me; I forget which. "I'll ask him to return them to you," he said. I never got them back. I don't know what this fellow did with them, but I never was able to find out what he did with them. I'm sure that if Demaree Bess gave them to him, they were just mislaid.

---

* In 1805 U.S. Navy and Marine Corps forces waged a joint land-sea operation against the Barbary pirates' state of Tripoli in North Africa.
† Demaree Bess wrote two articles that appeared in consecutive issues of the magazine: "Our Big Stick in the Mediterranean," 8 May 1948, pages 15-17, 140-143; "Our Navy in Striped Pants," 15 May 1948, pages 30, 169-172. The articles contain material on Admiral Bieri and also information drawn from the historical files that Bieri supplied to the writer.

They included orders to all the old commanders that ever went into the Mediterranean, including orders to Admiral Bristol.*

Q: In Turkey?

Admiral Bieri: In Turkey. As I said, they were very interesting. At least they told them what consul or officer to deal with and what the relations with some of the local governments were, and the extent of their authority in various places. They were all signed by the Secretary of the Navy.

But all I ever got over there was an order telling me to go over and take charge.

Q: In reviewing all these past orders, was there any consistent policy visible?

Admiral Bieri: Only insofar as to how the business of these ships was to be handled. Of course, Admiral Bristol's orders were very special. I suppose in addition to the order assigning him to there and making him High Commissioner, he undoubtedly had instructions from the State Department and the Navy Department.

Q: I was going to ask if there was any consistent policy visible? Did it in any sense apply to your circumstance, even though you hadn't been given orders of that nature?

Admiral Bieri: None that I could see, no.

Very shortly after we got the people off the beaches in the Mediterranean and put them on board ships, we got other ships. We always had a carrier or two, and eventually we had three landing ships with Marines on board. We had instructions that we were not to establish a base anyplace. As a principal anchorage, we could use the harbor of Naples.

Q: Could you use Malta?

---

* Rear Admiral Mark L. Bristol, USN, as U.S. High Commissioner to Turkey in the early 1920s, was quite successful in establishing diplomatic relations with that nation.

Admiral Bieri: No, we could visit Malta, but we weren't supposed to use Malta. The British were glad to make repairs at that time, and we went to Malta or Gibraltar, either one. We had very good relationships with the British.

I was eventually told, for instance, to make a visit to Turkey. I was given no instructions or information about the political situation in Turkey or anything like that. I presume that they thought that when I got there that I would be taken in tow by the American ambassador, and that he would see that I got everything that I should get. That was all right, except that before I saw the American ambassador, I visited Smyrna. Istanbul was where the ambassador was at that time. I had no difficulties there in Smyrna. Everybody seemed to be very friendly. We had an American consul there whom I made contact with. I found out what the local situation was and met all the local officials. We stayed there quite a time, about a week I guess, and had a very profitable visit.

In Istanbul we had the American Ambassador, Mr. Wilson, whom I'd known.[*] I kept a look around on the situation through our State Department officials and found them all very cooperative, and they were always happy to see us come in and spend time with us. Other than that, we never got mixed up in any the fracases that were going on in Palestine, or the arguments that were going on with the Spaniards. We were kept out of Egypt for quite a while, but eventually permitted to go there.

The reason they gave me for not letting us go to Alexandria in the first place was that they thought we would have trouble with the Egyptians on account of our bluejackets being dressed so much like the British bluejackets. The feelings of the Egyptians were much against the British at that time, to say the least, and they didn't want us to get into any trouble.

The Ambassador, Mr. Patterson, there wrote to them and said that they had no reason to be concerned about that.[†] We went down there and were well-received by the Egyptians. At that time, Farouk was still on the throne.[‡]

---

[*] Edwin C. Wilson, U.S. Ambassador to Turkey.
[†] Richard C. Patterson, U.S. Ambassador to Yugoslavia.
[‡] Farouk I was the King of Egypt from 1936 until his abdication in 1952.

Q: Admiral, why almost this vacuum in terms of specific orders? This is really not characteristic of the Navy, is it?

Admiral Bieri: No, it's not. It shouldn't be characteristic of the Navy. I wrote to Sherman shortly after I got over there and told him what the situation was; that I had no orders or no statement of policy in regard to any of these governments in the Mediterranean; and what our relation with them should be, and so forth and so on.*

He wrote back and told me that the Navy Department and State Department were in the process of developing and getting these things out. I was there a couple of years, and I never got them. It seemed to me a rather odd way to do business. The senior commander going into a place like that, I suppose, was supposed to be well enough informed without being told about things. At that particular time, there wasn't much information.

Q: How could a commander with a fleet be informed about diplomatic developments and so forth when he didn't have access the codes of anything?

Admiral Bieri: No. We were having this thing--facing the Yugoslavs, for instance, across the border with our people sitting on one side with an armed division and the Yugs on the other side with their divisions. There was a possibility of a clash there almost anytime. There should have been some very definite instructions as to what to do. Of course, I just took it for granted that my business was to back up the Army in whatever they had to do. There were never any definite instructions on that thing.

We never had definite instructions what we should do about Albania, for example, except to keep away from the place. Our merchant ships had a great deal of trouble with the Albanians because they had staked out a lot of territory which they said belonged to them. They had mine fields around that they didn't report to anybody. Every once in a while we had a little trouble with them about our merchant ships. Apparently at that time

---

* Vice Admiral Forrest P. Sherman, USN, served as Deputy Chief of Naval Operations (Operations), 1945-48.

the merchant ships had gone off on their own, and they weren't placed under any military control when they came in the Mediterranean. They were supposed to be furnished before they came into the Mediterranean with the latest information on all mine fields and changes in mine fields. If they didn't have them, they were supposed to stop at Gibraltar and get them, but there wasn't any check on them. They didn't even have to report to the senior naval commander in the Mediterranean that they were coming into the Mediterranean. We had several instances where these fellows came in and ran into mine fields; then we had to take steps to get them out.

Q: Could you offer an explanation perhaps for our lack of specifics, or lack of policy in terms of postwar disorganization? We had made such a mighty effort during the war itself, I suppose it's only too human that there's a relaxation in this.

Admiral Bieri: I don't know. For instance, when I arrived in Italy, Italy had been an ally of ours for a very considerable length of time. She came over to our side. We still had a lot of administrative troops and military bases in Italy, including General Lee's headquarters in Rome and Caeserta and a large Army supply base.* Lee was operating a private train. We were in there with these people who were apparently allies of ours. You'd think an ally would be your equal, and you'd treat him as an equal.

One of the first contacts that I made when I went to Naples was the British. I talked to the British naval commander, and I said, "What are your relations with the Italians and the Italian Navy?" They just didn't have any relations with the Italian Navy, except that the Italian Navy, as far as they were concerned, was still subservient to them. For instance, if an Italian flag officer came aboard a British ship, he got no honors. There was practically no mention of him. I said to myself, "That's a stupid thing to do."

Very shortly after I got there, I had a call by my staff officer made on the local naval commander. I found out that the senior commander there was an Italian rear admiral, and

---

* Major General John C. Lee, USA, Commanding General, Mediterranean Theater of Operations, January 1946 to September 1947.

that he had headquarters and so forth. He said that he would like to call on me. I said that would be very nice, and I set up time for him to call.

When he came on board, we gave him the regular honors which you always give a foreign flag officer. We paraded the guard and band and fired a salute, and had the colors up, and all the customary courtesies. It took him very much aback, because the British did nothing. They wouldn't even pipe him over the side.

Q: Of course, they had fought more closely against the Italian Navy than we had.

Admiral Bieri: Yes, but after all the war was over. We were supposed to be over there making friends with these people.

Q: Doesn't this all say that there was indeed a crying need for NATO?

Admiral Bieri: There was a crying need for somebody to set up a policy amongst these people, I must say that my treatment of this Italian naval officer paid great dividends. The rest of the time that I was in the Mediterranean, we had nothing but the finest relations and cooperation with the Italians. They'd do anything for us that we wanted them to. We also developed some very good friends amongst them.

Our naval relations with the other countries were pretty well established. There wasn't much trouble there any place.

I had very good relations with the British at Malta, with Admiral Willis.[*] We became very good personal friends, and I still see him occasionally when I go to Europe.

My French opposite in Algiers was Admiral Ronarc'h.[†] We had very good relations, and I visited there quite frequently. I knew him up until the time he died. I used to have quite a correspondence with him. In fact, his daughter visited us here a couple of weeks ago.

---

[*] Admiral Algernon U. Willis, RN, was appointed Commander in Chief Mediterranean Station on 23 April 1946.
[†] Rear Admiral Pierre Ronarc'h.

Q: Oh, yes, you told me.

There's a question still hanging in my mind about something you said earlier and it hasn't been resolved. In talking about getting the men off the beaches and the disposing of the material, you said that your greatest problem was with motor torpedo boats. You didn't actually tell me why.

Admiral Bieri: In the first place, the Navy Department didn't want to dispose of these motor torpedo boats to individuals.

Q: For non-military purposes?

Admiral Bieri: For non-military purposes. Apparently there had been smugglers that would like to have gotten a hold of them.

Q: Because they were speedy?

Admiral Bieri: They were fast, easy to handle, and didn't take much of a crew. We could have sold them off individually undoubtedly to various people around.

What we were trying to do was to sell them in groups to different countries around there in the Mediterranean or to some firms that would want to salvage them and get the engines out of them. A great many of them were not in good condition. I forget how many we had tied up there, but it must have been well over 100 of them. Of course, they were very difficult to take care of. The Italians are great pilferers. We had them in an enclosure at docks, but they were still being picked to pieces.

The paymaster of my staff was given the job of selling. He finally got rid of them. I think the Greeks took some, the Turks took some, the Italians took some. Then there were some salvage firms that took them on agreement that they would break them up. It took us quite a few months to get rid of those.

Q: In the case of the Turks, the Greeks, and the others who did take them, what use would they find for them in peacetime?

Admiral Bieri: They used them for training purposes, I suppose. They weren't building any of their own small craft. They wanted some ships to train their sailors and that sort of thing. The Army used quite a few of them around Italy for ferrying purposes from one island to another, especially to Capri.

Q: That must have been really a kind of pleasant assignment, without any specific objectives to accomplish.

Admiral Bieri: It was. We got a new set of ships every three months. In other words, they would send over two new cruisers, sometimes three--one for my flagship and the other one or two under the flag officer to be part of the fleet. They'd send over a new squadron of destroyers, and the old destroyers would go back. The tender we kept for a very considerable period. I think we kept the tenders about six months. The carriers only stayed three months. So, it was a constant shift of personnel.

Q: And why this rotating system?

Admiral Bieri: Because we had no repair facilities over there, except this one destroyer tender.

Q: Except what the British might offer.

Admiral Bieri: We had no source of supplies over there, except the supply ships that were sent over from the United States and the oilers the same way. They would send over a supply ship occasionally, and we'd practice or shift supplies while we were under way at sea. Target practice ammunition--we did the same thing. We carried out target practices while the ships were over there, as designated by the fleet commander whose ships we were getting from the Atlantic Fleet area.

It was a very interesting job. I thoroughly enjoyed it. At that time, the housing situation was very bad, especially in Italy where we hung out most of the time. The transportation situation wasn't good, because it hadn't been reestablished yet in the Mediterranean. The result was the Navy Department decided the only families that could come over at that time were the families of myself and the staff who had to stay over there continually. In the ships that rotated, they didn't bring their families over.

Of course, down there in Naples a lot of the hotels had been bombed out, and they weren't fixed up yet. So there wasn't anyplace for families to stay. The military, when they occupied Naples, had commandeered a great number of quarters still there; they had nice houses and so forth.

The British are very adept at that sort of thing. They always have a lot of world travelers in their armed forces. They know where all the good places are to live and to eat and so forth. When they go into a place, they know just which ones to pick out.

When I arrived in Naples, the British were not only billeted pretty well all over the town in excellent buildings, but we also had excellent billets. For instance, the billet that was assigned to me was the Villa Emma, which was the home of Emma Hamilton.[*] Before I got there and before James got there, it was occupied by the British admiral. It was occupied from the time they first went in. It was a beautiful villa. It was right up on the bluffs overlooking the Bay of Naples, and Vesuvius, Sorrento, and Capri. It had a wonderful building, a marvelous place, and beautiful gardens.

When the British pulled the admiral out of there, Sir John Cunningham, he said they wanted him to turn it over to the Army.[†] He said, no, that wasn't in the cards. It was a naval house.

---

[*] Emma Hamilton was the mistress of Lord Horatio Nelson, Britain's great naval hero of the late 18th century and early 19th. Hamilton was the mother of Nelson's daughter Horatia, born in 1801.
[†] Admiral Sir John Cunningham, RN, was appointed Commander in Chief Mediterranean Station in October 1943.

Q: Lady Hamilton belongs with the navy.

Admiral Bieri: So, it was turned over to the U.S. Navy. I think James got a lot of use out of it, because he never went to sea on his flagship.

I took it over from James in June, and I kept it until about October. Then we finally gave up all the houses we had. The Navy had at least two dozen fine houses and quarters.

Q: Did Mrs. Bieri come over to occupy Lady Hamilton's house?

Admiral Bieri: She was there with me for a couple of months. Also George Dyer and Adaline Dyer were with us during one of his tours over there with his position.[*] Ed Burrough and his wife were there with us.[†] It was a beautiful place and we enjoyed it very much. I didn't spend too much time there, Mrs. Bieri did.

We had joined the Army, and I had supposed that I'd go over there and find all the Army living in tents like General Grant and General Lee did during their time. I found out that that isn't the way they operate these days. They go into a city, pick out the best places in the town to live, and that's where they live.

Q: That is not peculiar to this time either. If you read history, you discover that to the conquerors belong the spoils.

Admiral Bieri: It's always been that way in Europe. I don't think it was that way in our country so much in the Civil War, because our people were not able to sit down that long in one place.

Q: And so many of the areas where they were were so completely devastated, that there wasn't anything to claim.

---

[*] Rear Admiral George C. Dyer, USN, took command of Cruiser Division Ten in December 1946, and it sailed almost immediately for the Mediterranean.
[†] Rear Admiral Edmund W. Burrough, USN.

Admiral Bieri: When we went into Algiers, for instance, they had a billeting officer. I forget what his title was, a quartermaster of some sort in the British Army. He was billeting officer from headquarters. He had houses all picked out before you got there. I didn't pick one out, I was going to stay in the Old St. George, where they had our headquarters. He told me that I couldn't.

So I finally moved out in the senior officer bachelors' quarters, which they had set up in a house. They took me around there to show it to me. They were just in the process of moving a French family out of this house. It was a rather sad affair to me, to see these people just picked up bag and baggage and thrown out of the house.

Q: Their reaction, in most cases, was probably not very good either.

Admiral Bieri: No. People on the continent get used to that sort of thing, I guess.

Down in Naples, for instance--this house that we occupied down there was left quite well furnished. The paintings were left there, the library was left there, and the furniture was left there. Most of the houses in those places, the minute the people know that the enemy is going to move in, there's not much left in the house when the enemy gets there. It's been taken out and stored some place in the back country, in a cave, or someplace and it stays there.

I remember one house which was occupied by Goering.*

Q: There's good reason for taking everything out.

Admiral Bieri: This house was completely furnished when I saw it with furniture that was made by the Germans and brought in by them. It was built to the size of Mr. Goering. That, of course, was about five feet deep.

---

* Field Marshal Hermann Goering was head of the German Air Force during World War II.

Bernhard H. Bieri #5 - 218

After I'd been there for some time, the Italian people who owned this place took it back over. We were invited around there to a tea or something. They had refurnished it with their own stuff that they had brought in from the country--beautiful paintings, beautiful furniture, beautiful rugs. Everything was most artistic. I asked the lady, "Where did you get this stuff?"

She said, "We just took it out in the country and hid it. We took it back in the country as soon as we knew the Germans were coming here."

Q: By all means, they wouldn't leave art works where Goering was going to be.

Bernhard H. Bieri #6 - 219

Interview Number 6 with Vice Admiral Bernhard H. Bieri, U.S. Navy (Retired)

Place: Bethesda, Maryland

Date: Thursday, 19 October 1969

Interviewer: John T. Mason, Jr.

Q: Admiral, at the beginning of this sixth interview, I wonder if it wouldn't be a good idea to summarize the accomplishments of your command in the Mediterranean in the year 1946.

Admiral Bieri: My first project in the Mediterranean was to get rid of the remaining shore bases and stations that were still extant after the end of the war fighting. This we accomplished by October of that year.

Q: I don't think I asked you previously--were there any legal technicalities involved in the liquidation of some of these bases?

Admiral Bieri: No, there were no legal problems.

Q: There wasn't a matter of leases or anything of the sort?

Admiral Bieri: No. These were just places that had been set up by the military forces in the course of carrying out operations during the war. They had just more or less dwindled down but kept in existence by retaining certain officers and certain material in those places.

The first problem was to get rid of the Navy material which we had over there, which we accomplished quite easily and quickly, with the exception of the disposing of a considerable number of PT boats that were based in northern Sicily at Palermo. This took a considerable length of time on the part of the supply officer in command. He eventually got rid of all of them by sales to various civilian organizations and turning certain numbers of them over to other allies in the Mediterranean. In the meantime, this work of disposing of materials was being supervised by Captain Fitzgerald, my chief of staff.

A little difficulty arose up around Trieste, where we had a division of troops under General Bryant Moore. I went up there with my flagship and several destroyers to look out for the situation which turned out to be not much of an affair. We had to establish relations with Moore's outfit up there and made certain agreements with him about the ships we would keep there and what billets we needed for him to call on us in case he wanted help.

Q: What had the problem seemed to be?

Admiral Bieri: It was merely the fact that he was facing the Yugoslav forces across the border. There was considerable feeling in that area, and they didn't know whether it might break out into some fighting of some sort.

Q: That certainly was the tradition of Trieste, wasn't it?

Admiral Bieri: Yes. I, myself, stayed up there two or three months.

In the meantime, we began to receive ships to increase the size of the Mediterranean force. We received two cruisers under Rear Admiral Burrough and several destroyers.[*] Later on, in the next six months or so, we received another cruiser and two aircraft carriers and some additional destroyers. This continued to be the size of the force until about the later part of 1947, when it was increased by three transports.

Q: When did it come to be known as the Sixth Fleet?[†]

Admiral Bieri: That was following my departure.

---

[*] Rear Admiral Edmund W. Burrough, USN, served as Commander Cruiser Division 12, 1946-48.

[†] On 1 October 1946 a new command was established, U.S. Naval Forces Mediterranean. In June 1948 the command was redesignated as the Sixth Task Fleet and in February 1950 as the Sixth Fleet.

Q: It was just known as the Mediterranean?

Admiral Bieri: We were known as Naval Forces Mediterranean.

During the time that I remained there, from '46 to February '48, we did considerable cruising in the Mediterranean--visiting various ports and carrying out target practice. Each three months we received a new assignment of ships and sent the ones we had back to the Atlantic Fleet--ship for ship.

We made the first visits to these ports after the war was ended, with the exception of the visit which Admiral Hewitt had made to Istanbul to return the body of the Turkish ambassador who died in the United States.*

We visited Athens, Izmir, Istanbul and Beirut; also the French ports of Algiers and Bone in the north coast of Africa, also Tunisia. On several occasions, we visited French quarters at Villefranche, Marseilles; and the Italian ports of Genoa, their naval station at Sardinia, Gulf of Taranto, and Augusta. We also made frequent visits to Malta. All the ships stopped in and out at Gibraltar. We also visited Athens, Piraeus, Souda Bay, Herakleion.

Q: Did you by chance visit the Balearics?

Admiral Bieri: No. I visited Tangiers. I also visited Casablanca by air, flying to the air station that we had near Casablanca at that time.

We were not allowed to visit Palestine, and for a considerable length of time we didn't go to Egypt. We didn't visit any of the Spanish ports. We were having arguments with the people of Spain at that time. The British still maintained their mandate in Palestine.

---

* In the spring of 1946, with Admiral H. Kent Hewitt, USN, Commander U.S. Naval Forces Europe, embarked, the battleship <u>Missouri</u> (BB-63) visited Istanbul, Piraeus, Naples, and Algiers. On 5 April, the ship delivered the body of Mehmet Munir Ertegun to Istanbul. He had died in 1944 while serving as U.S. ambassador to the United States.

Our people in Washington were a little leery about letting us go to Alexandria, because the British had had some trouble there with their naval personnel. They went into that place, and weren't very well received.

However, when we eventually went to Alexandria we were quite well received. We were received and had a very successful visit.

Q: What was accomplished on these various visits? What was your purpose?

Admiral Bieri: I had no particular instructions about any of these visits. My idea was that showing the fleet, or whatever ships we had over there, would strengthen the hand and the prestige of the diplomatic representatives. We would also establish friendlier relations with naval personnel. In all these places where we went, where there was a head of government, we had short conferences with the heads of government.

Q: What kind of preparation was made in advance of a visit to a certain port?

Admiral Bieri: If there was an American diplomatic representative there, we would take the matter up with him as to a proper convenient date. Then we submitted a proposed schedule of the ships, every three months in advance to the Navy Department via Commander 12th Fleet in London, and got their approval of it.

We were always very careful, too, to indoctrinate our personnel as to the conditions that existed in these various ports and the conduct that was expected of them. We had no difficulty on that score.

Q: Were stores necessary, the purchase of supplies and fuel?

Admiral Bieri: No, we did not purchase too many supplies in those places. We were supplied by our own supply ships that passed through the Mediterranean. We did take fuel from the shore in Beirut.

One of the places we also visited was the French naval base in Tunisia at Bizerte. I think we had an ambassador there at that time. He arranged a conference with the Tunisian Bey.

I frequently visited Rome by car when we were in Naples. On one occasion, Mrs. Bieri and I were received by the Pope in person in his private quarters.

Q: This was Pius XII?

Admiral Bieri: Pius XII, yes; very impressive, very charming, and a very delightful person who spoke excellent English.*

Q: What was the topic of your conversation?

Admiral Bieri: We discussed quite a few things about what we were attempting to do in the Mediterranean. We discussed a lot of personal matters. Neither Mrs. Bieri or I were Catholic. He discussed our family with us; that was our general conversation.

Q: Was she required to dress in black with a veil?

Admiral Bieri: She wore a black dress and a little black covering over her head. We had a private audience with the Pope in his own office. Following that, he came out and had audiences with various smaller groups, and eventually a larger group which was waiting for him outside.

Q: Lap back a moment and tell me about your visit with the Bey of Tunis.

Admiral Bieri: He was a very pleasant gentleman, who professed to speak no English, but I was quite sure that he understood English. I had an interpreter and we had a very

---

* Pius XII was Pope 1939 to 1958.

interesting conversation. I went in by myself; there were no Frenchmen with me. He expressed his admiration for our country and what we were doing. He was happy that the American ships were in that area. He was a very fine looking elderly gentleman, immaculately dressed in the European costume. He was sitting in a chair on a sort of a dais at the end of a large room as I came in.

This interpreter, or secretary, who spoke English, brought me in. I proceeded to a position up in front of him and bowed and expressed my pleasure in being there. Then he had me sit down next to him in a chair that he had alongside of him. We carried on this conversation for some time, his French and my English being interpreted. After I'd been there some minutes, he actually began talking English to me. He was a very fine looking man, immaculately dressed, and very pleasant.

At Tangier we had an ambassador there; it was more or less being run at that time by the ambassadors from the United States, England, and France. But they were preparing to turn the government back over to the Arabs. I think they had a shah; I was received by him one afternoon. We had tea. He spoke a great deal of English and we had quite a conversation about various things.

Q: It wasn't a republic then--the Republic of Lebanon at that time?

Admiral Bieri: No, this was not Beirut, but Tangiers.

In Beirut, I met all the high government officials, including the President, and dined with him and his family. We were very lavishly entertained for several days.

In Athens, I met the King, who on the occasion of my first visit was George. I had lunch with him in his palace with Mr. MacVeagh, the ambassador, and his brother Paul and his wife.* On the occasion of my second visit, I again had lunch at the palace. George, at the time of my first visit, presented me with the Grand Order of the Phoenin, a Grecian medal. He was a very talented fellow, spoke English well, and was quite entertaining. Also his sister, Princess Sophia, was present.

---

* Lincoln MacVeagh, U.S. Ambassador to Greece.

On the occasion of my second visit, I had lunch with Paul who had them become the King and his Queen Frederika.* Others present included Sophia and an uncle of the King named George, who was married to the Duchess of Kent. The latter old fellow was a very interesting and entertaining chap. Lunch was very pleasant, and the conversation was pleasant.

Before I left, the King, Frederika, and Sophia came out to dinner on the ship one evening. They stayed until sometime after midnight.

Q: They must have enjoyed themselves.

Admiral Bieri: They enjoyed themselves very much. The final thing that wanted to see was the ice cream fountain for the men. We opened up, and we all went down to see the ice cream fountain and sat on the benches and had some ice cream before they went home.

Q: Were you impressed with Frederika, who apparently is quite a person?

Admiral Bieri: I was very much impressed by her. She impressed me as being a most intelligent person and a very pleasant person.

At the other places, I met the senior officials and the prefects in Bone and Algiers. In Algiers, I got to know Rear Admiral Ronarc'h quite well. His daughter was here about two or three weeks ago, Genevieve. He and I became very good friends while I was in the Mediterranean and later when we came back.

I saw him twice on subsequent visits to Europe after I retired, but he has since passed away. He was a Breton, very jovial and a very friendly fellow. He had a very delightful wife who had undergone some very terrible experiences during the war when the Germans occupied her home and used her more or less as a personal servant, which resulted in rather bad health for her. She also passed away a few years after we were retired.

---

* On 1 April 1947 King George II died suddenly of a heart attack and was succeeded by his brother, who became King Paul I.

I had very pleasant relations with the Italians. The admiral in command at the Naples station was Admiral Balsamo, with whom we had very pleasant social relations that continued after the war. About two years ago when we went to Europe, we visited them once or twice at their home in Sittignano above Florence.

Three years ago when we visited Europe, we had a most urgent invitation form his widow to visit her in her old home in northern Italy. So we dropped down and spent a very pleasant two days with her.

The Balsamos had had a rather hard experience during the war, as he was caught in Japan as the Italian naval attaché. When Italy came into the war with us after the defeat of Italy, the Japanese made them prisoners and they were rather roughly handled.

Q: He was naval attaché in Japan?

Admiral Bieri: In Japan.

Of course our relations with Admiral Willis at Malta were most cordial and helpful. He visited me in Naples on one occasion, and we made one or two visits to Malta. We maintained our friendship after the war, and have seen him several times in England when we've been over there.

The senior naval officers at Gibraltar were always most cooperative and did a great deal for us in the way of minor repairs on the ships that came through there.

The only time that we had any call for what you might call naval support or naval assistance was in the early part of my tenure when we went up to Trieste and kept ships up there for several months, in close touch with General Moore's force.

We also, at one time, were sent over to southern Greece. The Communists were getting pretty active over there, and they thought that the presence of the ships might lend a little support to the Greeks. The Greeks, at that time, would very much have liked our country to put a division of American troops in there to help them solve their problems; but they had plenty of personnel. Mr. Truman wound up by sending over a military mission headed by General Van Fleet, who did an excellent job in organizing the Greeks and getting them into the field to do something about keeping the Communists from getting down into Greece.* They eventually cleared the place up.

On several occasions I visited Souda Bay in Crete, which was an excellent anchorage. On the occasion of my first visit, it created quite a lot of enthusiasm. We were not only received by all the local officials, but by officials from all over the island. They came to call on me, and various organizations came to call on me.

Q: What was the reason for this?

Admiral Bieri: Just the pleasure of having the American fleet come into the place. They had been pretty badly mauled up during the war.

Q: Were there any political implications in this? Weren't the leaders in Crete anxious for independence from Greece?

Admiral Bieri: No, they weren't. They didn't express that to me while I was over there.

A great many of these Greeks know a lot about the United States. One very interesting group that came to see me was a group of about a dozen members of the First World War veterans, the American Legion Post in Candia. They came out not only to make a courtesy call, but also to let me know that they knew all about the Communists on the island and anytime I wanted some information to let them know and they'd help me out.

These visits were rather interesting. The Mayor of Candia was a little Greek who spoke no English, but spoke a little French. He had a peculiarity of speech which was very interesting. He'd say a few words, and then he'd whistle. Apparently, he had a stammer. We got on quite well together. He was very kind in showing me around the island, but we were always accompanied by a military escort. They insisted that there was still a lot of the Communist elements around there getting ready to take a pot shot at us if they got a good chance.

---

* Lieutenant General James A. Van Fleet, USA, Director, Joint Military Aid Group to Greece, 1948-50.

While I was in Souda Bay, our force at that time had gotten up to a considerable size. We had two carriers, three cruisers, and a squadron of destroyers.

The officials gave a formal dinner for us, which was very interesting. It included the Governor of the island, the Patriarch, the Mayor, and all the prominent citizens. This banquet was given in the Mayor's palace. The dinner was served by Cretan ladies in native costume.

There were the usual speeches. The Patriarch sat on my right and the Governor on my left. We had a young Greek whom I knew who was the interpreter. But I hardly stopped to give him a chance to interpret my first idea. He had gotten part way through it, when there was considerable confusion amongst the audience insisting that he wasn't interpreting it right. This went on through the entire speech, so it was not only amusing but made one wonder if they knew what I did say. They didn't appear to disagree much on the speeches made by the Mayor and the Governor. The Patriarch's sole purpose seemed to be to keep my wine glass filled with resinato.

Q: It's a white wine?

Admiral Bieri: Red and white. It's cured in casks and has a taste of resin. It's not the most delightful wine that I've had.

The Patriarch could speak some German, so I could pass a few words with him.

Those were the most interesting people we encountered. These ships became quite familiar in the different ports.

We had no Bureau of Personnel difficulties. A different group of ships came over each three months, so it never became monotonous for the crews and officers to visit the various ports.

I was finally relieved in February of 1948 by Vice Admiral Forrest Sherman, who had been Assistant Chief of Naval Operations.

Q: As a footnote, Admiral, would you comment on this rotation system employed with the ships in the Mediterranean? What is the purpose of that, and how effective is it when you maintain a command?

Admiral Bieri: It wasn't too effective as far as maintaining and influencing a command. The purpose, of course, was to have the ships away from the main Atlantic Fleet the minimum length of time and not get into a position where they had to have any major overhaul work or to be out of the big fleet for too long a time.

After the first two or three changes, then they began to repeat their visits. We managed quite well. The admirals that came over with the cruisers were Admiral Burrough and Admiral Dyer. I think both of them had two trips over there.

The carriers changed; I never got the same bunch of captains back on the carriers. We had no difficulty, of course.

The maneuvers with a small force were rather simple, We worked at sea at usual tactical maneuvers and target practices. We did considerable antiaircraft firing at towed targets and robots, which were flown from the ships. The carriers had plenty of opportunity to do their flying.

The carriers were very effective when we made these visits to the various ports. There would usually be launchings before we entered the port and then recovered again before we got in. Right after we left, we would launch them, and they would make flights over these various places and return to us at sea.

Q: Kind of a farewell salute.

Admiral Bieri: This was a farewell salute to these people.

As I said, I was detached in February of 1948 and relieved by Admiral Sherman. I returned to the United States on the destroyer tender USS Grand Canyon, which was in the command of Captain E. R. Sperry.[*]

---

[*] Captain Edward R. Sperry, USN.

We landed in Boston in rather cold February. We brought back a number of Italian wives which had been accumulated by sailors and enlisted men in the fleet at various times while they were over there.

At the end of the month--I had a month's delay--I reported to the Chief of Naval Operations for assignment.

It was my understanding when I came back that I was to relieve Admiral Hewitt at the United Nations in New York as the Representative as the Naval Member of the Joint Chiefs of Staff on the Military Staff Committee. However, Hewitt chose not to retire at that time. So I was given a choice of a couple of jobs. I chose to go to San Diego as Commandant of the 11th Naval District, at which time I reverted to the rank of rear admiral.

Q: Did that mean a demotion in pay?

Admiral Bieri: Yes. This was a very interesting assignment to me. The organization of the fleet had been very largely changed since the end of the war. There were a large number of commands in the San Diego area, over which I had no military command but I was the senior officer on shore. I supervised the establishments on shore that supported these various forces. I also carried out the usual duties in connection with the relations with the local officials and affairs that concerned them. In addition to San Diego, there was a very considerable demand from various other places for the commandant to visit for one reason or another. This extended all the way from San Luis Obispo to Las Vegas, and the capital of Arizona, Phoenix.

Q: What were these appearances?

Admiral Bieri: Usually ceremonial visits in connection with establishing or disestablishing some naval activities. We were establishing at that time a large number of Naval Reserve training centers in various places. There were visits in connection with Navy Day. There were requests from chambers of commerce and other civic organizations to speak.

We had a very busy time in San Diego. We lived on North Island, had quarters under the landing circle of the air station. We entertained local and visiting officials. We coordinated some of the requirements of some of the activities of the fleet. Also, we were in the process of cutting down in the Navy under Mr. Johnson.[*] The time at San Diego passed very quickly. It was very pleasant with one or two exceptions.

Our relations with the local civil establishment was very good.

Q: What were the exceptions that were not so good?

Admiral Bieri: There was in San Diego at that time an editor of one of the local papers whose name was Kennedy.[†] Kennedy was not a local man; he had come there after the war. During the war, he had served in some capacity in the Secretary of the Navy's office. He seemed to go to considerable pains to try to stir up and find out something that he could chastise the Navy about. One thing that he finally brought up was that venereal disease in San Diego and vicinity would never be cleared up unless the Navy stopped letting its personnel cross the border into Mexico. Of course, I didn't agree with him. We maintained a proper prophylactic station on our side of the border. The men had their instructions from their ships and stations. There were also other military personnel there over whom I had no control in the matter of keeping them out of Mexico. Such as a big Marine establishment up the coast, and several Army establishments, and Coast Guard establishments. None of those considered it necessary to restrict their experienced personnel. They could visit Mexico with their families if they wanted to or otherwise.

Near the end of my tenure out there, this man Kennedy, who came from West Virginia, had a senator friend of his out as a personal guest. I called on the senator and made arrangements for him to see and visit the various parts of the naval establishment. He was not on the naval committee or anything of that sort.

---

[*] Louis Johnson served as Secretary of Defense from 28 March 1949 to 19 September 1950.
[†] John A. Kennedy, a captain in the Naval Reserve, was president of the company that published the San Diego Journal. He had a background as an investigative journalist.

Q: Who was he?

Admiral Bieri: I'll think of his name, and put it in.

This thing was getting pretty hot. So I told the press that it was not in my province to stop these men from crossing the border into Mexico, and that the only ones I controlled were Navy personnel. The venereal rate in the Navy was very low and well controlled. Furthermore, most of these naval personnel would within weeks or months be detached from San Diego and go into the fleets and go to foreign ports or have to visit places that were as bad or worse than Mexico. I was sure that if the young men had been properly brought up at home and properly instructed in the Navy and military forces, their families wouldn't have to worry about them.

About this time, I got orders detaching me. This man Kennedy came out with the statement in the paper that I was being detached because I failed to prevent the military personnel crossing the border. He gave the impression that this was done at the request of the senator.

Some of the young reporters on this paper came to see my press officer, a Navy captain. They asked about this. "How about the admiral being retired? How about the senator having the admiral removed from command?"

This young fellow got mad about this thing and he said, "That's a darn lie. As a matter of fact, neither the senator or the editor of the newspaper are fit to shine the shoes of the admiral."

Q: That got in the paper too?

Admiral Bieri: That, of course, got in the paper and stirred up a ruckus in the Navy Department. Fortunately, by that time, I was halfway across the continent on my way to my new assignment in New York. I did have to stop off and see the Chief of Naval Operations, who at that time was Forrest Sherman, who had come back from Europe.* I explained the situation to him and the Secretary and heard nothing more about it.

I went to the United Nations as the Senior Naval Member of the Military and Naval Staff Committee, representing the Joint Chiefs of Staff of the various countries. We worked with the Russians, French, English, Chinese, and ourselves.

I relieved Admiral Hewitt. At the time of my arrival, the only project they were working on was a matter of setting up a military force for the use of the United Nations in the event of difficulty between members or other countries.

Q: Constabulary force?

Admiral Bieri: This problem had been worked on right from the beginning, first by Admiral Turner as our representative and by Hewitt and passed along to me.† At first, the Russians apparently went along with it to a certain extent. As it went further and further along, they would have nothing to do with it, so it died a natural death. Then we were called in for certain advice in regard to other military matters occasionally by the chief of the mission.

Q: Where were you stationed?

Admiral Bieri: We had offices with the United States Mission on east 33rd Street, in a large office building there.

Q: The United Nations at that point was in Flushing Meadow?

---

* Admiral Forrest P. Sherman, USN, served as Chief of Naval Operations from 2 November 1949 to 22 July 1951.
† Admiral Richmond Kelly Turner, USN, served as U.S. naval respresentative to the United Nations from December 1945 to July 1947.

Admiral Bieri: The United Nations was in New York in Flushing Meadow. That's where they held their meetings. All of the countries had offices in New York City. Whenever there was a meeting at Flushing Meadow, all the interested people would drive out there.

By that time I left, only one of the permanent buildings was finished. That was a small building which was being used by the small countries. We were assigned space for our committee meetings in that building.

Q: This was over on the east side?

Admiral Bieri: On the east side of New York.

The work, as far as I was concerned, was completely frustrating, and we accomplished nothing. We would meet once a week. The Russians usually would file in after they were sure that all the rest of us were present. Each month a different senior member of one of the countries would chair the meeting. The business usually consisted of the mention of the fact that the committee met, read the minutes of the last meeting, and adjourned until the following week.

It became, to me, so perfectly useless to have all these military people around doing nothing. They were getting nowhere. I recommended to the Chief of Naval Operations that we abolish the job and give the duties of the representative to the commandant of the naval sea frontier or the naval district as additional duty. This they did sometime after I left.

Q: They did do that?

Admiral Bieri: Yes. I was finally detached from that duty in May 1951.

Q: Tell me, sir, there was a lot of social activity connected with that.

Admiral Bieri: An enormous amount of social activity. It was really very demanding and wearing on not only myself, but Mrs. Bieri. There were luncheons, dinners, cocktail parties, and all sorts of things--every day of the year.

Q: Were you supplied with an apartment in New York?

Admiral Bieri: Incidentally, I was re-promoted to the rank of vice admiral, with my previous date of commission, when I took this job over. My predecessors had been admirals, but the Naval Committee of the Congress said they wouldn't make any more admirals.* They would make me a vice admiral and give me the pay of an admiral. So I received the pay of an admiral.

Q: That was technicality, wasn't it?

Admiral Bieri: The interesting thing about that was when I discovered that my two American associates, who were lieutenant generals, were also obtaining a certain allowance which was given to military officers for some vague sort of business. I don't remember whether it was maintaining a horse or what it was. It occurred to me, if these fellows were getting that kind of pay for doing nothing, I might take a crack at it myself. So I wrote to the Navy Department and they referred it to the Comptroller General, and he said I was entitled to it. So I got another $1,000 a year and was getting more pay as vice admiral than as an admiral.

Q: But there were so many expenses attached to your entertaining, dress, and all, the rest.

Admiral Bieri: Yes. We were given quarters in the old Naval Hospital, which was known as Quarters R. These quarters were a delightful old Victorian house which was built about 1848 by the Livingston family who owned all that land in that area.

---

* After the creation of the Defense Department in 1947, the old Naval Affairs Committees of the House and Senate were merged into the new Armed Services Committees.

Q: Where is that?

Admiral Bieri: This was the only house right next to the Navy Yard.

Q: In Brooklyn?

Admiral Bieri: In Brooklyn. This house had been lived in for years by the commanding officer of the naval hospital. The naval hospital, during the war, was moved out in Long Island, and the commanding officer had quarters and lived out there. The Navy reassigned the house then to the head of our mission. It was a perfectly delightful house--I thought one of the nicest houses that the Navy had anywhere. We were given a staff of servants, and that part of it was very well taken care of.

Q: You entertained there at the house?

Admiral Bieri: The house was large enough so that we could entertain a very large group of people at any time. It's really a very interesting house. It had large rooms with high ceilings. Throwing what furniture we had in with what was already there, it was quite livable, and very well adaptable to having large receptions and good sized dinners and luncheons. We enjoyed it very much.

Q: Were the Nimitzes there at that time?

Admiral Bieri: No, he had retired. When he retired, Forrest Sherman came to the Mediterranean and relieved me.

Q: He had a United Nations assignment for two years.

Admiral Bieri: Oh, yes. Admiral Nimitz came to the United Nations. They brought him there with the hope that he would be able to settle the dispute between Pakistan and India. He never accomplished much on this proposition.

He and Mrs. Nimitz were only in Washington intermittently, sometimes for a very considerable lengthy period. They chose to live out on Long Island and had quarters out there.

Q: They lived out on Sands Point.

Admiral Bieri: Yes.

Q: Did you see much of them?

Admiral Bieri: No, I didn't see much of them. We would meet occasionally at social functions. His work was entirely outside of what we were trying to do.

I stayed there until May 1951, when I was retired physically.

Q: And since then you have lived in Bethesda all that time?

Admiral Bieri: No. Since then, we came back to Washington. I was undergoing observation and treatment out at the naval hospital and finally fully retired.

I was asked by the head of the CIA, General Bedell Smith, to come down and see him.[*] He asked me to serve on the National Board of Estimates of the CIA.

Q: What does that entail?

---

[*] Lieutenant General Walter Bedell Smith, USA, was Director of the Central Intelligence Agency, 1950-53.

Admiral Bieri: I told Smith that I was physically retired and I didn't know whether I was up to the job or not. But he assured me that it would require very little of my time, probably four hours or so a day.

This committee was composed of a retired State Department ambassador, a retired Army general, a retired Navy admiral, and a number of people who were political scientists. One member was Dr. Raymond Sontag, who had been the head of the history department at the University of California. He had done quite a considerable amount of work for the government during and after the war. We had Dr. Hoover of Duke University, who I believe was an economist.* We had two other economists and civilian lawyers. I think that was about it. Dr. Sontag chaired the committee. We had a fairly good size staff of young professors, political scientists, and so forth.

We would get intelligence reports from the Army, Navy, Air Force, Treasury Department, State Department and the CIA. From the various reports, we would draw up a total estimate on whatever the subject was. That went to the National Defense group.

A great part of our work developed then into what they called making crash estimates on something that happened. They would want the opinion of the estimate board. We would call together all the different representatives of the different intelligence activities, interview them, discuss the subject, and draw up our estimate and then present it.

This was a rather cumbersome process, because after we drew up this estimate there was still another meeting attended by the Chief of Naval Intelligence, the Chief of Army Intelligence, the Chief of Air Intelligence, and the State Department representative, the Chief of the CIA, Smith, and one or two others. They would sit down and go over this report which we had drawn up, and argue it over again. Which usually took a considerable length of time, sometimes a day or two. They would make changes in it.

Q: Based on their knowledge?

---

* Dr. Calvin B. Hoover, an economist, was dean of Duke University's graduate school.

Admiral Bieri: Yes, and take exceptions to certain parts, put in an order, and all that sort of stuff. So it was a very laborious process of getting these intelligence reports to the top committee--the National Defense Committee. However, the crash estimates were usually not subjected to this type of process. They went through a little quicker.

I had a very good Army officer friend who served on the big committee of which the President is supposed to be the head. He said, "The estimates were very good, but as a general rule he had read most of it in The New York Times before ours got to him."

I stayed there for a little over two years.

Q: Did it actually mean giving four hours a day to it?

Admiral Bieri: No. It started off with a full day's work, from 8:00 o'clock in the morning until 4:30 in the afternoon. Usually it was supposed to be five days of the week, but quite frequently we had these crash estimates and worked seven days a week. Often times we worked late into the evenings. It got rather strenuous, as far as I was concerned.

I decided when Bedell Smith was relieved by Allen Dulles, I would resign.* I was only hired as a consultant. In other words, if I was hired in any other manner, I would lose my retired pay. At that time, there was no provision for hiring me in any other way than as a consultant.

As a consultant, the Comptroller General had ruled that we could be used only four days in any week. Although we worked all this extra time, we were only paid as a consultant for four days a week. The rate of pay for a consultant at that time was $50.00 a day. My pay for this was $800.00 a month. It didn't add any to my Social Security status or to my retired pay status. Regardless of that, I figured at the end of two years and a half that I was working a little bit too hard at my age, and I stopped.

Q: Tell me, with the professors who were members of this committee, they simply had to give up their teaching activities?

---

* Allen W. Dulles served as Deputy Director of the CIA, 1950-53, and as Director, 1953-61.

Admiral Bieri: They had to have leave from their school. For instance, Raymond Sontag from California was a very good friend of mine. He, at that time, was head of the history department and he was on leave. He was there for somewhat longer than I was. I think he must have been there for about four years. Then we went back and he choose to teach in the graduate school.

Q: Resuming his departmental job?

Admiral Bieri: Yes. He's still out there as president emeritus of the history department. He still teaches graduate students. He usually comes back here about twice every year to attend some meetings. I see him when he comes back.

After I'd been there about a year or so, Dr. Hoover developed a heart condition and it made it necessary for him to leave. After some months, he went back to teaching at Duke University. He's still there, although I don't think he's teaching anymore.

Q: What was your estimate of the effectiveness of this system actually?

Admiral Bieri: I think that it was good in that it furnished support and eliminated a lot of differences of opinion and controversy between the different services. It, unfortunately, was an entirely too slow system. It should have been possible for this board to make up an estimate and furnish it directly to the Defense Committee, without hashing it over further. I really don't recall any real great differences in what came out after it went in the final committee, than the report that we put in.

Q: So it was just one more step that could have been eliminated.

Admiral Bieri: It could have been eliminated and speeded up.

Whether they are following the same procedure now or not, I don't know. I know they still have the same setup down there. They have a National Estimates Board. I think it has five retired people: an ambassador, four military men, and quite a number of civilians.

A number of these young men who were our assistants at that time, who did the research work for us--two or three of them are now on the committee itself. I noticed the other day in the press that one of them had just gotten a big job with the State Department. They were a group of bright young men and very dedicated to their work. They helped to draw up some very good papers.

We lived in Chevy Chase during that time; we rented a house over there. Then, after I retired, we gave up the house. We traveled for about a year in Europe. Then came back and we lived in Chevy Chase.

We've done quite a lot of traveling. We've made quite a number of trips to Europe and a great many trips around the country to see our children. They live all the way from Texas to New York.

Q: Traveling is one of your great interests?

Admiral Bieri: Yes. In the coming year, if all goes well, me might make another trip to Europe.

Q: Very good. I thank you, sir.

Interview Number 7 with Vice Admiral Bernhard H. Bieri, U.S. Navy (Retired)

Place: Bethesda, Maryland

Date: Unknown

Subject: Fleet Admiral Ernest J. King, USN

Interviewer: John T. Mason, Jr.

Q: Admiral you served for so long on the staff and served in an intimate fashion with Fleet Admiral King, would you tell me about some of your experiences with him?

The idea being that some day perhaps the material I gather on King will be used by a biographer, to give him his rightful place as one our great naval commanders.

Admiral Bieri: I had never served with Admiral King up until the time he became Commander in Chief of the fleet.

It so happened, at that time, that I had been ordered to the Office of Naval Operations as an assistant to Rear Admiral R. K. Turner. As such I went with him to the meetings of what they called the joint planners at that time, the Army planners and the Navy planners. When Admiral King took over, he took Turner on his staff as planning officer.

Q: Admiral King had been serving on the General Board, had he not?

Admiral Bieri: No, he was the Commander in Chief of the Atlantic Fleet. He was on the General Board before that.

He came there and started setting up his staff. Turner moved over on his staff as planning officer, and I was his assistant. We attended the various early meetings of the Joint and Combined Chiefs of Staff in Washington.

Turner left very shortly and was relieved by C. M. Cooke. From then on, I remained as Cooke's assistant.

Q: How did King go about taking over his tremendous duties, this tremendous job that had been given to him?

Admiral Bieri: He apparently had it planned out in his own mind. He was a good organizer. He picked out able men to fill his top places. Then, after telling them what the wanted done, he left it up to them to do it.

Q: Were they largely men who had served with him in one capacity or another?

Admiral Bieri: Yes, I'm quite sure that he knew them. If they hadn't served directly with him, he knew them by reputation. They'd all been in the service at one time.

For instance, Admiral Horne was designated as Vice Chief of Naval Operations under King.* Horne's job was principally material and personnel. He had a big organization. He had to pick out his own juniors and go ahead and set up his organization under King.

King took Russell Wilson as his chief of staff. He had C. M. Cooke as his assistant chief of staff for plans. They set up their own organizations.

Then he set up the antisubmarine organization, which he kept command of himself. He appointed younger men to do the actual work, like George Dyer for example.

Q: Why did he keep command himself of the antisubmarine work?

Admiral Bieri: That was a very important and immediate problem at the time he took over in the Atlantic. We were short of escort vessels. We had to set up convoys and patrols. We were losing an awful lot of merchant ships, because the merchant ships hadn't been organized for the purpose of being taken care of. The sea frontiers had to be jacked up to do their share of the work.

---

* Admiral Frederick J. Horne, USN, served as Vice Chief of Naval Operations from 26 March 1942 to 10 October 1945.

At that time, too, the Army Air Forces was campaigning to take over the protection of all the coastal areas with aircraft. As a matter of fact, they set up an antisubmarine organization which was overlapping.

Q: Without consulting the Navy?

Admiral Bieri: Yes. That, of course, created quite a problem which had to be settled on very high level with the President and General Marshall. King was about the only man that could do that. I think that's one reason why he hung on to the command of the antisubmarine forces.

Q: Why wasn't the criterion to be the most effective way of combating the enemy rather than empire building?

Admiral Bieri: Don't ask me, because it had always been taken for granted more or less that the Navy was the service to control the antisubmarine warfare. But they were having a lot of trouble.

The Army Air Forces people saw an opportunity to move into this area, so they decided they'd move in there. There had been a struggle for years between the Navy and the Air people about the jurisdiction that each one of them would have. The Army Air Forces, at times, were for restricting the Navy to operations that were purely from the ships and none from the shore, the distances they could fly, and that sort of thing. It was a long problem that started way back before the war.

Q: It started with the beginning of aviation, probably, didn't it?

Admiral Bieri: Yes. The Army, during the war, still had a lot of these ideas that nobody should have anything to do with air except the Army Air Forces.

For instance, just before the Battle of Midway, they wanted to have complete control of all heavy bombing from Hawaii. The only reason they didn't get it, I think, was because they made such a botch of tracking the Japanese transports that were bound for Midway that they were told by the President to let the Navy have all the long-range aircraft they wanted and to run it the way they wanted to. So that thing was settled.

Coming back to King and my relations with him. I had very little direct contact with King. Cooke, of course, was quite a confidant of King's. He lived with him on the ship. Cooke was a very able man, and had a lot of excellent ideas. He was a very forceful man. He dealt directly with King, and I dealt with Cooke.

I did see Admiral King several times a week at the meetings at the Joint and Combined Staffs, when the planners would all be present. I never had a meeting with him in his office.

I would occasionally walk back from the meetings of the Combined Staffs. Sometimes we'd discuss something and sometimes we'd walk back the two blocks from the Navy Department without saying anything.

Q: Would he welcome it, if you introduced a subject?

Admiral Bieri: Oh, yes. As long as I worked under Cooke for him and went to these meetings, he never took issue with any proposition that I put up to them.

I was the senior one of the Joint Staff planners all the time I was there. So it fell to my lot to present to the Joint Chiefs any of the problems that they were considering.

Q: And he never once took issue with what you presented? This is probably a commentary on your care in preparing these proposals.

Admiral Bieri: He seemed to be satisfied with what I did.

I was kept in close touch with the situation. Cooke kept me very well informed. Later on, I had very close relations with Admiral Edwards, who relieved Wilson as chief of staff. He kept me informed on a great many things. I often went in to see him in his office, when I had problems that involved him and Cooke wasn't around.

I didn't go to any of the big conferences. Cooke usually went to the big conferences. Except that both of us went to the Cairo conference. They took along all the planners to the Cairo conference.

I had several sessions there with Admiral King discussing various subjects. Just before the conference was over, he sent for me and told me that the conference was to adjourn at noon. We were meeting at the Mena House. He said we might need to stay there that afternoon and discuss with the British planner, Charles Lamb, a very able English officer, the matter of sending British ships to the Pacific. My instructions from King were, "You know my ideas." And that was it. Which were that he didn't want any British ships out there until they could support themselves, and were able to look out for themselves logistically. The British were in no position to do that. They wanted to get some combat ships out there and have us look out for them.

There wasn't too much I could do for my good friend, Lamb. We sat and talked about it all afternoon. I left the next day for home.

Q: Tell me, I'm thinking in the terms of a biography, about the human side of Admiral King. He seems such a cold and distant figure to most people. You said that he lived on board a yacht in the Potomac. Was that Sequoia?

Admiral Bieri: No, the Dauntless.* He and Cooke lived on the Dauntless. He had a couple of their secretaries, chief yeomen, who were always available, and a few staff officers, flag lieutenants and that sort of thing. But the rest of the staff lived on shore at their homes.

Q: What was the reason for living on board ship?

---

* The USS Dauntless (PG-61) had been built as a civilian yacht in 1921. She was acquired by the Navy on 21 January 1942 and commissioned 11 May 1942. On 16 June 1942 she relieved the USS Vixen (PG-53) as flagship for Commander in Chief U.S. Fleet. She was based at the Washington Navy Yard during World War II and remained there until decommissioned 11 May 1946.

Admiral Bieri: I think he wanted a place where he could go and not be bothered by anybody and have direct communication at all times with his headquarters. He also had a suite of living quarters right in his headquarters, but as far as I know he never used them. They were built for him there.

He had this flagship down there.

Q: What was she, a converted yacht?

Admiral Bieri: A converted yacht. She was his flagship, and the staff were all attached to the Dauntless. We were all, nominally, on sea duty.

Q: I see, to meet the requirements of Navy Regs.

Was Dauntless anchored there? Did he cruise on the river ever?

Admiral Bieri: At the Washington Navy Yard. No, he never cruised on the river. She was moored at the Washington Navy Yard.

When he left his office in the evening from the Navy Department, he would motor down to the Dauntless. In the morning, he would motor back. Apparently his idea was that he was available all the time, and I think he was.

You never heard of King being involved in any social affairs during the war. As a matter of fact, you never heard of General Marshall being either.

There were few parties given by service men, Britishers and other officers. I attended, and King would come in for a short time and leave.

He was a very abstemious fellow. I never say him drink anything but a glass of sherry.

Q: This is contrary to what one has heard about him.

Admiral Bieri: When he was away from his duty or something like that, but I can't imagine that there were times that he was like that. Every time that I was with him where there was any liquor served or the possibility of having liquor, his limit was a dry sherry.

One night Arnold of the Air Force gave a big party over at the Bolling Field.[*] He had all the British high ranking officers down through their planning staffs there. He had the Army people from General Marshall down, at least through [unclear]. Duncan was there. Admiral King was there and all the staff.

Q: The top brass was there.

Admiral Bieri: Yes. I didn't see King drink a thing that night, except to get a glass of sherry. I know at Cairo it was the same way, and traveling on the plane it was the same way.

Q: And yet, he was supposed to be a fair drinker at times, wasn't he?

Admiral Bieri: Yes. He was very abstemious as far as I know during the war.

He was a man, I think, who didn't go out of his way to make friends with people, or to take personal interest in his people. Maybe he did with people with whom he had served and had known before the war.

As far as myself and other young fellows who served with him there at headquarters, we had no personal relations with him other than the fact that he maintained a noon mess at the Navy Department, and we all messed with him.

Q: As a matter of fact, you were commanded to do so, were you not?

---

[*] Bolling Field was an Army Air Forces base in Anacostia, D.C., across the Anacostia River from Washington.

Admiral Bieri: Yes. I was a little bit on the heavy side, at that time, and I was trying to avoid eating lunch. So when they came around to me to come down to the mess, I said, "I don't eat lunch. I prefer not to join the mess."

They said, "Admiral King wants everybody there." So I joined the mess.

Q: Was there any social chitchat at the mess?

Admiral Bieri: A little bit, yes, there was some. There wasn't any shop talk. There was social talk, personal talk about various things.

Q: And he entered into that?

Admiral Bieri: Oh, yes. If somebody had a good joke or something like that, he'd enjoy it. Quite frequently, most of the time, he would have a guest of some sort down there --a British naval officer or Army officer, or some of our people who were in town. Then there would be quite a lot of conversation with him at the table. Otherwise, the conversation was more or less restricted to the chaps you sat with around the table.

Q: How many men participated in this then?

Admiral Bieri: About 25 or 30 of us.

Q: This was a daily affair?

Admiral Bieri: A daily affair, yes. There was Edwards, Cooke, myself, and the admiral. I think Duncan was there later on. George Dyer and Russell, or whoever happened to be the secretary, was there.[*] Then there was Admiral Horne and Farber, who was Horne's chief of staff, and Delany, and several other people from Horne's outfit.[†]

---

[*] Captain George L. Russell, USN.
[†] Vice Admiral Walter S. Delany, USN.

I say generally there were about two dozen people there. It did give a chance, for instance, for the people on King's operational staff to see the outfit that was with Horne's staff down below. We exchanged ideas.

Q: Kind of cross-fertilization of ideas them.

Admiral Bieri: Yes. We had ideas for interchange and that sort of thing.

Q: Admiral King, eventually, took over the duties of CNO, didn't he?

Admiral Bieri: He was CNO, he was Commander-in-Chief and Chief of Naval Operations from the beginning. The actual work of Chief of Naval Operations, in the way of providing the material and planning for it and the personnel and so forth, was done by Horne and his outfit. Getting all the material together, the mechanics of getting shipping together, getting ships built, and so forth.

King's immediate staff was practically an operational and planning staff. We would make out our plans, for instance, all of it of course with the assistance of the people down below. We'd determine the number of ships, of a certain type, that we wanted for the amphibious force which we had to build up. Once we got this approved and started, Horne's outfit took over and produced the ships.

Q: Why did King take over both jobs?

Admiral Bieri: I think it was so that he would have a better control of the whole thing, particularly over the bureaus.

The bureaus, under the old Navy Department organization, were directly under the Secretary. The Chief of Naval Operations, in those days, was just as the name said; he was the operations manager. King wanted to get a better grasp on the bureaus. He knew that if he was going to command the fleet, he would still have to have his organization that dealt with the bureaus, and he wanted to control it.

Q: This wasn't entirely approved by the rest of the Navy, was it?

Admiral Bieri: I don't know whether it was or not. But I thought it was a very good arrangement myself.

Q: How did he function vis-a-vis Admiral Nimitz out in the Pacific?

Admiral Bieri: King, to my mind, was a very excellent commander. He was a man who picked his subordinates and told them what to do, and then the rest of it was up to them--how, when, and where. He never interfered with the subordinate. If the subordinate didn't live up to his job, he got a new one.

Q: Right off.

Admiral Bieri: Yes.

Q: He wasn't very kind about that, was he?

Admiral Bieri: No, he was cold-blooded. You either did your job, or you got out.
 I think his relations with Nimitz were excellent. I think they had perfect understanding of how things were to go.
 I think his relations with Royal Ingersoll were good, of the Atlantic Fleet. Another man under him was Stark. He was a very good commander in that respect.
 The only thing he wouldn't stand for was when somebody was given a job, for somebody to tell them how to do it. That would finish him in a minute.

Q: You mean to listen to somebody else . . .

Admiral Bieri: If you are a commander of any sort of a unit or an organization and you were given a job to do, he didn't want to have to tell this commander how to do the job. If a commander parceled out his job amongst people, he didn't want a commander that had to tell the other fellows how to do the job. That's the way the show was run.

Q: Did he give people to understand this at the outset?

Admiral Bieri: Oh, yes. Everybody understood that, right from the top down. And it worked.

Q: I heard of one instance of a man on his staff was summarily dismissed, and George Dyer was told to relieve him. George was only a commander. The man was to be out of the Department by 4:30 that afternoon. He didn't want to see him again. That's pretty severe.*

Admiral Bieri: I wasn't in on that. I heard talk of it. And I knew George came in to do the job.

I think that probably came from the same thing. That he gave this man a job, and instead of going ahead and doing the job he came to King and asked how he was to do it. That's probably why he got rid of him.

As far as personal relations with Admiral King, when I was finally detached from his command and was going to leave Washington, I went into his office to pay my respects and say good-bye. We talked about various things. Then he said to me, "Are you married?"

I said, "Oh yes, Admiral, I'm very much married. I have five sons; they're all in the services."

He said, "I never knew that."

Q: After four years.

---

* This incident is discussed in the Naval Institute oral history of Vice Admiral George C. Dyer, USN (Ret.).

Admiral Bieri: I was there from '42 to almost '46.

Q: This speaks volumes, as a story. This says an awful lot about Admiral King, in his personal relationships.

How did he manage family connections? The family lived in Washington.

Admiral Bieri: I never knew the King family. There was always a lot of talk about them. I don't know anything about them. I know that socially, Admiral and Mrs. King didn't mingle much--neither together nor separately in social affairs.

He had a lot of daughters and one son. I think the son is still in the service.

Q: He retired as a commander.[*]

Admiral Bieri: He had several attractive daughters. They all are married and doing quite well.

I didn't know the family at all.

Q: Since he lived on board a yacht and was on duty 24 hours a day, I wondered how he managed any family relationship since they lived in the same city.

Admiral Bieri: He had a home over in Wesley Heights or Georgetown. I think Mrs. King lived there up until the time she passed away recently.

What his family life was, I don't know.

Like all those things, unless you become involved in them, at least my feeling is that it's none of my business, so I stay out of it.

Q: Was he gracious enough to commend a man when he'd done a good job?

---

[*] Commander Ernest J. King, Jr., USN, retired from active duty 1 March 1968. He was in the Naval Academy class of 1945. The Naval Institute oral history of Admiral Stuart S. Murray, USN (Ret.), discusses the junior King's experiences as a midshipman.

Admiral Bieri: Yes, he was.

When the war started, he was very much opposed to the Army system of handing out a medal every time a fellow turned around, or went from one sea to another, or one job to another.

His idea was that you were expected to do your duty. Most of the things that you did pertained to your duty. It was all right to pass out medals for acts of valor and acts out of the ordinary. But just the fact that you had filled a certain office for a certain length of time was no reason why you should be given a Distinguished Service Medal.

Nimitz and people out in the field finally had to prevail on him that he had to change this thing as far as the men and young officers were concerned. Because all the other services were pinning stars and medals on their people just as fast as they turned around, and our people weren't getting anything.

We had an organization checking up on this business. Our people began to get recognition of that sort. I think he was always very fair. If you did a particularly good job, he'd tell people about it.

Q: Can you tell me, in your own case, where he commended you?

Admiral Bieri: I don't recall any particular case, but I always felt that the fact that he didn't do otherwise was because he thought I was doing a good job.

Q: Just the silence, or the lack of contact.

Admiral Bieri: As far as his own staff was concerned, he never relented on this medal business.

I served on his Joint Planning Committee practically all the time that I was there. I think I had four or five different air officers, and four or five different Army officers that served on the same staff with me. Every time one of these fellows would be detached, the Army would pin a Distinguished Service Medal on him.

Finally when the war was over, or practically over, Cooke and Edwards told me that they had been designated to recommend to the admiral what recognition to give to his staff in the way of decorations.

Cooke said that he recommended me for the Distinguished Service Medal. There were several other people on my level that had been there that length of time.

On the final list he gave out a Distinguished Service Medal to his chief of staff and a Distinguished Service Medal to Cooke. I got a Legion of Merit, with a citation.

Q: Sometimes this worked to the detriment to the service, did it not?

I recall a case of a man who was deciphering on Pearl, whom Nimitz himself said had a major share in the victory at Midway, who was recommended for a Distinguished Service Medal at Com 14 and by Nimitz, and denied this.[*] This had disastrous effects.

Admiral Bieri: Of course it had.

Most of the people on King's staff had an opportunity to rotate between sea duty and staff duty. The minute they got out into the Pacific and got command of a ship, they began to accumulate decorations.

Q: But not when they were with him?

Admiral Bieri: The fellows that had to work back there all the time were out of luck. I never gave it much thought.

I wanted to go back to sea. I'd been there a long time. After both these trips to Europe, I thought they had the organization set up well enough in Washington that I could be permitted to go out and join in the fracas in the Pacific. But I never got there.

These chaps would go out there and take command of a ship, or command of a division, or something like that. When the war was over, they were all promoted according to their citations.

---

[*] This is covered in the Naval Institute oral history of the cryptographer, Captain Joseph J. Rochefort, USN (Ret.).

We fellows that sat back here, we didn't do anything.

Q: George Dyer managed that whole thing rather cleverly, I think, in writing his own ticket, in springing himself loose.

Admiral Bieri: Yes.

I thought I had sprung myself loose after I came back from Europe the second time. I went in to see Edwards. Cooke and King were out talking with Nimitz. I suggested that Edwards let me go out to the Pacific; I was out of a job. He said, "Wait a minute. I'll be talking to the Admiral tonight on the telephone and I'll ask him about it."

When I came in in the morning he laughed and said, "I've got good news for you."

I said, "What's that?"

He said, "I got the admiral last night. I told him that you were ready and anxious to go out to the Pacific. He said, 'Tell him to keep his shirt on. I need a few people around Washington to work myself, and Nimitz's got plenty of them out here.'"

So that's where I stayed.

Q: Do you know anything about King and the gray uniforms that he insisted upon?

Admiral Bieri: No, I don't.

Q: In the Pacific khaki was worn. Nimitz never would permit, he didn't exactly order the men in his command to wear the blue, but he wouldn't permit it really, in denial of King's specific orders.

Admiral Bieri: Didn't we wear khaki around the Navy Department?

Q: It was this dingy colored uniform.

Admiral Bieri: I've got some of them yet, sort of khaki colored. I did have some gray ones too; they were terrible looking things. We couldn't get the cloth, that was the main reason. They couldn't get decent cloth to cut a good uniform, so we got practically work clothes.

Q: I understood that King was absolutely adamant about that. That was what he ordered, and, by golly, everybody was going to wear those uniforms. But they didn't.

Admiral Bieri: No, they didn't. We started off wearing them.

It was a question of procurement of material; we just couldn't get it. We could get this other material because the Army had a lot of it. We wore the blue in the winter time, and in the summer time we wore this khaki.

Doyle probably knew a great deal about King, because I think he served with him at sea.

I never served with Admiral King at sea. I was always in some other fleet than the one he was in.

For a few days, he visited Admiral Richardson when Admiral Richardson had command of the fleet. He messed in the admiral's mess, or the chief of staff's and my mess. I used to have conversations with him upon the bridge during maneuvers. I was the operations officer. Otherwise, I didn't have much contact with him.

Index To

Reminiscences of

Vice Admiral Bernhard Henry Bieri

U.S. Navy (Retired)

Accidents
    The battleship <u>Texas</u> (BB-35) ran aground on Block Island in 1917, 26-28

Alaska
    The destroyers <u>Corry</u> (DD-334) and <u>Hull</u> (DD-330) escorted the transport <u>Henderson</u> (AP-1), with President Warren Harding on board, during a cruise to Alaska in the summer of 1923, 48-50; the <u>Corry</u> and <u>Hull</u> were involved in surveys for a new Alaskan cable in 1924, 56-57; Army aviator Frederick Martin's plane was stranded in the area during an around-the-world flight in 1924, 57-60

Alcohol
    Admiral Ernest J. King abstained from liquor during World War II, 247-248

Algeria
    Allied military personnel set up shop in the port of Algiers following the invasion of North Africa in late 1942, 121; salvage job on damaged merchant ships, 121-123; Algiers was the site of French naval headquarters in North Africa in 1946, 212, 225; housing at Algiers for Allied military personnel following World War II, 217

Algiers, Algeria
    Allied military personnel set up shop in the port following the invasion of North Africa in late 1942, 121; salvage job on damaged merchant ships, 121-123; Algiers was the site of French naval headquarters in North Africa in 1946, 212, 225; housing for Allied military personnel following World War II, 217

Amphibious Warfare
    Joint Army-Navy planning in 1942 for transports and landing craft for upcoming operations, 96-99

Anderson, Colonel Orvil A., USA
    Opinionated Army Air Forces officer who rubbed people the wrong way during dealings in World War II, 95-96

Antisubmarine Warfare
    Jurisdictional questions between the Navy and the Army Air Forces over airborne ASW in World War II, 243-244

Army, U.S.
    Joint planning with the Navy in early 1942 for transports and landing craft needed for upcoming amphibious operations, 94-99; planning for the Allied invasion of Europe, 100-101; interest in postwar unification of U.S. armed services, 186-187; presence in Italy in the immediate aftermath of World War II, 205, 211, 220, 226; presence in Greece shortly after World War II, 226-227

Army Air Forces, U.S.
    Had many inexperienced pilots early in World War II, 106-107, 117-118; planning in late 1943 for the use of B-29 bombers against Japan, 132-134, 148-149; command of

strategic air forces in World War II, 150; interest in postwar unification of U.S. armed services, 186-187; role in antisubmarine warfare during World War II, 244; wanted to control bombing in World War II, 244-245

Army Air Service, U.S.
Had difficulties in Alaska during the course of an around-the-world flight in 1924, 57-61

Atomic Bombs
Tightly held information on the U.S. Manhattan Project late in World War II, 167-169, 171, 173, 179

Augusta, USS (CA-31)
Heavy cruiser that served as flagship for the U.S. portion of the invasion of Normandy in June 1944, 155-156

Australia
Received a visit from U.S. Navy ships in 1941, 86-88

Awards-Naval
Admiral E. J. King gave medals sparingly during World War II, 254-255

B-24 Liberator
Army bomber that was flown by inexperienced pilots during a transport mission in 1942, 117-118

B-29 Superfortress
Planning in late 1943 for the use of this Army Air Forces bomber against Japan, 132-134, 148-149

Bailey, USS (DD-269)
Decommissioned and put into reserve on the West Coast in mid-1922, 43-45

Bennett, Rear Admiral Andrew C., USN (USNA, 1912)
As commander of a portion of the amphibious force for the invasion of North Africa in November 1942, objected to a British plan for the use of U.S. Coast Guard cutters at Oran, Algeria, then complained afterward, 109-116, 123

Bess, Demaree
Writer who in 1948 wrote magazine articles about the U.S. Navy in the Mediterranean Sea, 207-208

Bieri, Vice Admiral Bernhard H., USN (Ret.) (USNA, 1911)
Boyhood in Minnesota around the turn of the century, 1; parents of, 1-5; education of, 1-2, 5; siblings of, 1-4; as a Naval Academy midshipman, 1907-11, 6-11; service in 1911-12 in the battleship Delaware (BB-28), 11-15; served in the gunboat Nashville (PG-7) 1912-13, 15-19; wife of, 15, 19, 23, 40, 61, 216, 223, 235; as a junior officer in

the battleship Virginia (BB-13) from 1913 to 1916, 19-24, 30-40; duty from 1916 to 1919 in the battleship Texas (BB-35), 24-34; as aide to the commandant of the Fifth Naval District, 1919-22, 35-39; decommissioned the destroyer Bailey (DD-269) in mid-1922, 43-45; commanded the destroyer Corry (DD-334) from 1922 to 1925, 45-61; communications duty in the Navy Department, 1925-27, 61-67; children of 61, 74, 252; as navigator of the battleship Utah (BB-31), 1927-28, 67-69; as navigator of the battleship Texas (BB-35), 1928-31, 69-70; service in the Bureau of Navigation, 1931-33, 70-74; duty from 1933 to 1935 as executive officer of the destroyer tender Altair (AD-11), 74-75; as a student and faculty member at the Naval War College, 1935-38, 76-81; served in 1938-39 on the staff of Commander Battleships Battle Force, 80-81; served in 1939-41 on the staff of Commander Battle Force and then Commander in Chief U.S. Fleet, 80-86; commanded the heavy cruiser Chicago (CA-29) in 1941-42, 86-92; duty in early 1942 on the staff of Commander in Chief U.S. Fleet, 92-107; served in the latter part of 1942 as Deputy Chief of Staff, U.S. Atlantic Fleet, in connection with the invasion of North Africa, 108-123; planning duty in 1943 on the U.S. Fleet staff, 123-138; administrative duties as U.S. Fleet assistant chief of staff in early 1944, 139-140; role in support of the Allied invasion of France in June 1944, 140-147, 152-164; role on the fleet staff in the final year of the war, 164-199; as Deputy CNO for Administration, 1945-46, 199-200; commanded the Tenth Fleet in 1946, 201-202; commanded U.S. Naval Forces Mediterranean, 1946-48, 202-229; as commandant of the 11th Naval District at San Diego, 1948-49, 230-233; duty from 1949 to 1951 as JCS representative to the United Nations, 233-237; post-retirement activities, 237-241

Blue, Captain Victor, USN (USNA, 1887)
Was commanding officer of the battleship Texas (BB-35) when she ran aground in 1917, 26-28

Boston Navy Yard
Served as home yard for the battleship Virginia (BB-13) in the mid-1910s, 23-24

Brown, Vice Admiral Wilson, USN (USNA, 1902)
Commanded a task force at sea in the Pacific in the days after the Japanese struck Pearl Harbor in December 1941, 88-90

Buchanan, Captain Allen, USN (USNA, 1899)
As commanding officer of the transport Henderson (AP-1), was involved in a collision with a destroyer and a windjammer near Seattle in 1923, 50-52

Bureau of Navigation
Detailing of enlisted personnel in the early 1930s, 71-73

Burrough, Rear Admiral Edmund W., USN (USNA, 1914)
As a war planner during the Cairo Conference in late 1943, 132; commanded Cruiser Division 12 in the Mediterranean shortly after the end of World War II, 216, 220, 229

Cairo Conference
　　Meeting of top Allied officials in late 1943 to plan war strategy, 123-134, 246; side trip to Teheran, Iran, for a meeting with the Soviet Union's Josef Stalin, 131

Calver, Commander George W., MC, USN
　　Navy doctor who spent a long career serving Congress in the 1920s and 1930s, 73-74

Casablanca, French Morocco
　　Planning for the Allied invasion there in November 1942, 108-113; British Admiral Andrew Cunningham was interested in information on the progress of the landings, 119-120

Central Intelligence Agency
　　Work with the National Board of Estimates in the early 1950s, 237-241

Ceylon
　　Discussion in late 1943 of a plan, which was never executed, to base Army Air Forces B-29 bombers in Ceylon for strikes against Japanese forces in the Dutch East Indies, 133-134, 148-149

Chaumont, USS (AP-4)
　　Navy transport that was in lousy condition in January 1922 as a result of carrying junketing congressman just before Christmas, 40-41; trip from Norfolk to the West Coast in January 1922, 41-43

Chicago, USS (CA-29)
　　Visited Australia and New Zealand in 1941, 86-88; operations at sea in the Pacific in the period around the Japanese attack on Pearl Harbor in late 1941, 88-92

Churchill, Winston
　　British Prime Minister who in World War II pushed forth a number of amateurish schemes in his attempts to advance the war effort, 102-104; met with Allied leaders at the Cairo conference in late 1943 to plan war strategy, 130

Coast Guard, U.S.
　　A Coast Guard cutter provided support to an Army Air Service around-the-world flight in 1924, 57, 60; disastrous use of two cutters in support of the 1942 invasion of Oran, Algeria, 109-116, 123

Codebreaking
　　U.S. Navy cryptography work in the 1920s on Japanese codes, 64-65

Collisions
　　The transport Henderson (AP-1) collided with a destroyer and a windjammer while operating near Seattle in the summer of 1923, 50-52; the destroyer Corry (DD-334) was rammed by another destroyer while at San Francisco in 1923, 53

Combined Chiefs of Staff
    Met at the Cairo conference in late 1943 to plan war strategy, 123-134, 246; meetings in Washington during the course of World War II, 176-178

CominCh (Commander in Chief U.S. Fleet)
    See King, Fleet Admiral Ernest J., USN (USNA, 1901)

Communications
    Development of high-frequency radio transmitters by the Navy in the 1920s, 62-63; U.S. Navy cryptography work in the 1920s on Japanese codes, 64-65; use of facsimile machines in the 1920s, 67

Congress
    Inquiries concerning Navy enlisted personnel assignments in the late 1920s, 72-73

Convoying
    Escort duty performed by U.S. battleships operating in the British Isles in 1918, 30-31

Cooke, Rear Admiral Charles M., Jr., USN (USNA, 1910)
    Brilliant officer who served as assistant chief of staff for plans on the U.S. Fleet staff in World War II, 93-94, 97, 245; attended the Cairo conference in late 1943, 131; involved in the spring of 1944 in the planning for the Allied invasion of France, 141, 143, 159, 246

Coontz, Admiral Robert E., USN (USNA, 1885)
    As Commander in Chief U.S. Fleet in the mid-1920s, had a remarkable ability to remember the names of men with whom he served, 82

Corry, USS (DD-334)
    Initially had a limited operating schedule after being commissioned in 1921, 45; installation in 1922 of a sonic range finder that proved useful thereafter, 46-47, 55; escorted the transport Henderson (AP-1), carrying President Warren Harding, to Alaska and Seattle in 1923, 48-52; provided assistance to a destroyer that was abandoned after colliding with the transport Henderson (AP-1) in 1923, 51-52; rammed by a destroyer at San Francisco, 53; Pacific operations, 53-54; went to Vera Cruz, Mexico, after the cruiser Tacoma (CL-20) grounded there in 1924, 54-55; transported a sick man to Panama in the mid-1920s, 55-56; survey for a new Alaskan cable in 1924, 56-57; support of an around-the-world flight by the Army Air Service in 1924, 57-61

Cradock, Rear Admiral Sir Christopher, RN
    British officer in command of a naval force that was defeated in November 1914 off the coast of Chile, 39-40

Crete
    Received a goodwill visit by U.S. Navy ships shortly after World War II, 227-228

Cunningham, Admiral Andrew, RN
Served as naval commander for the Allied invasion of North Africa in 1942, 117-119, 151-152; interest in progress at Casablanca, 119-120, 152; involvement following the landings, 121-122

Dauntless, USS (PG-61)
Yacht in which Admiral Ernest J. King lived while serving as Commander in Chief U.S. Fleet in World War II, 246-247

Delano, Commander Harvey, USN (USNA, 1906)
Martinet who was executive officer of the battleship Utah (BB-31) in the late 1920s, 68

Delaware, USS (BB-28)
Several of the ship's officers from 1911-12 later achieved flag rank, 11-12; gunnery practice, 12-13; East Coast operations in 1911-12, 13-15

Demobilization
As a result of the rapid demobilization at the end of World War I, ships had to do their own recruiting, 34

Dill, Field Marshal Sir John
British officer who died in Washington in 1944 and was buried in the Arlington National Cemetery, 176-178

Dutch East Indies
Discussion of plans in late 1943 to use Army Air Forces B-29 bombers against Borneo, Java, and Sumatra, 133-134, 148-149

Dyer, Rear Admiral George C., USN (Ret.) (USNA, 1919)
Served as a cruiser division commander in the Mediterranean shortly after World War II, 79, 216, 229; was flag secretary to CinCUS, Admiral J. O. Richardson, at the time Richardson was relieved in 1941, 85; served on Admiral E. J. King's CominCh staff in World War II, 252, 256

Edwards, Admiral Richard S., USN (USNA, 1907)
As Deputy Commander in Chief U.S. Fleet shortly after World War II, was involved in a delay of Bieri's promotion to vice admiral, 115-116; relayed to Bieri in early 1943 or the summer of 1944 Admiral Ernest J. King's message that Bieri would not be going to duty in the Pacific, 123, 166, 256; in 1944 gave Bieri assignments concerning the capture of a German U-boat and the atomic bomb project, 167-169

Egypt
After initial restrictions, U.S. Navy ships in the Mediterranean were permitted to visit Egypt shortly after World War II, 206, 209, 221-222

See also Cairo Conference

Eisenhower, General Dwight D., USA (USMA, 1915)
Headed the planning effort for the invasion of North Africa in November 1942, 108; caught in a dispute over the use of Coast Guard cutters at Oran, Algeria, 110-114; wanted to get information on the progress of the Casablanca landings, 119-120, 152; commanded the invasion of France in the spring of 1944, 141-143, 149, 151, 153-154, 157-160, 163-164

Eleventh Naval District
Bieri's activities as commandant in the late 1940s, 230-233

Ellsberg, Commander Edward, USNR (USNA, 1914)
Did some salvage work on merchant ships at Algiers in late 1942 but had physical problems, 122, 151

Families of Servicemen
In the 1910s Atlantic Fleet ships didn't really have home ports, so it was difficult for married crewmen to spend time with their families, 14, 23, 29; Bieri's family rode the transport Chaumont (AP-5) from Norfolk to the West Coast in January 1922, 41-43

Fargo, USS (CL-106)
Service as Tenth Fleet flagship in the Caribbean and South Atlantic in early 1946, 201-203; operations in the Mediterranean in 1946, 205-206

Fathometer
A sonic range finder, forerunner of the Fathometer, was installed in the destroyer Corry (DD-334) in 1922 and proved useful thereafter, 46-47, 55

Fechteler, Rear Admiral Augustus F., USN (USNA, 1877)
German-born naval officer who was commandant of the Norfolk Navy Yard and Fifth Naval District, 1918-21, 35; died in 1921 following a stroke suffered after a game of tennis, 35-36

Fifth Naval District
Rear Admiral Augustus F. Fechteler served as commandant from 1918 until his death in 1921, 35-36; Rear Admiral Hugh Rodman as commandant thereafter, 36-38, 40-41

Fire Control
Spotting from the tops of the battleship Delaware (BB-28) during gunnery practice in 1911-12, 12-13

Flanigan, Captain Howard A., USN (Ret.) (USNA, 1910)
Able, aggressive officer who served on the staff of Admiral Harold Stark in London during the invasion of France in the spring of 1944, 153-154

Fog
    The transport Henderson (AP-1) collided with a destroyer while operating in the fog near Seattle in the summer of 1923, 50-51

Foster, Captain Paul F., USNR (USNA, 1911)
    Naval Academy classmate of Bieri, 10; inquisitive while working in the Navy Department in World War II, 171-172

France
    Planning for the Allied invasion of Normandy in June 1944, 141-147, 152-154; execution of the invasion, 155-157; conditions ashore in Normandy in the aftermath, 157-158, 163-164

French Navy
    Algiers was the site of French naval headquarters in North Africa in 1946, 212, 225

George Washington, USS
    Transport that carried President Woodrow Wilson to France shortly after the end of World War I, 32-33

German Navy
    Served as a threat to British convoys in 1918, 30-31; surrender in 1918, 32; ships were stationed off Mexico in 1914 when World War I broke out, 39-40

Goering, Field Marshal Hermann
    German officer who had sumptuous quarters in Naples, Italy, during World War II, 217-218

Great Britain
    Efforts to get the United States involved in an invasion of Europe early in World War II, 102; planning in 1944 for the invasion of France and for the postwar world, 141-147, 152-154, 162

Greece
    Received a goodwill visit by U.S. Navy ships shortly after World War II, 224-225; U.S. troops in the country in the late 1940s, 226-227

Green, Lieutenant (j.g.) Fitzhugh, USN (USNA, 1909)
    Was serving as officer of the deck when the battleship Texas (BB-35) ran aground on Block Island in 1917, 27

Guantanamo Bay, Cuba
    Site of training for the battleship Delaware (BB-28) in 1911-12, 13

Gunnery-Naval
Target practice by the battleship Delaware (BB-28) in 1911-12, 12-13; U.S. concern about inadequate plans for gunfire support of the Allied invasion of France in the spring of 1944, 141-142; during the invasion itself, 155-156

Handy, Major General Thomas, USA
Army planner who worked closely with the Chief of Staff, General George Marshall, during World War II, 131, 141

Harding, President Warren G.
Died while on a trip to Alaska and Seattle in the summer of 1923, 48-52

Heim, Lieutenant Commander Schuyler F., USN (USNA, 1907)
Commanded the destroyer Hull (DD-330) during various operations in the early 1920s, 48, 55-56

Henderson, USS (AP-1)
Transport that carried President Warren Harding on a cruise to Alaska and Seattle in the summer of 1923, 48-52; collided with a destroyer and a windjammer during the cruise, 50-52

Hewitt, Admiral H. Kent, USN (USNA, 1907)
Served as naval commander for the Allied invasion of North Africa in November 1942, 108-109, 119-120, 152; commanded U.S. Naval Forces in Europe shortly after World War II, 202-203, 221; JCS representative at the United Nations in the late 1940s, 230, 233

Hill, Lieutenant Harry W., USN (USNA, 1911)
Was officer of the deck of the battleship Texas (BB-35) when he ran into heavy weather en route to Europe in 1918, 29-30

Hood, Captain John, USN (USNA, 1879)
Capable officer who commanded three battleships early in the 20th century, 12, 25, 29

Hull, USS (DD-330)
In the early 1920s was equipped with a sonic range finder that proved useful in survey work, 47-48, 55; escorted the transport Henderson (AP-1), carrying President Warren Harding, to Alaska and Seattle in 1923, 48-52; went to Vera Cruz, Mexico, after the cruiser Tacoma (CL-20) grounded there in 1924, 54-55; survey for a new Alaskan cable in 1924, 56-57; support of an around-the-world flight by the Army Air Service in 1924, 57-61

Ingram, Lieutenant Commander Jonas H., USN (USNA, 1907)
Requested as aide to the Commandant of the Fifth Naval District in 1921 but unavailable to serve, 36

Intelligence
  The Central Intelligence Agency's work with the National Board of Estimates in the early 1950s, 237-241

Iowa, USS (BB-61)
  Made a voyage to the Mediterranean in late 1943 to deliver President Franklin Roosevelt and his party to the Cairo conference, 123-124, 133

Italian Navy
  Relationship with the U.S. Navy in the Mediterranean shortly after World War II, 211-212, 226

Italy
  In 1946 the Navy shut down a number of shore bases it had established in the country during World War II, 204-205, 219; unrest in 1946 on the Italy-Yugoslavia border, 205, 210, 220; strained relations between the United States and Italy in the wake of World War II, 211-212; housing for U.S. naval personnel who supported the fleet, 215-218

Jackson, Captain Richard H., USN (USNA, 1887)
  Impressive officer who commanded the battleship Virginia (BB-13) in the 1910s, 21

Jacobs, Vice Admiral Randall, USN (USNA, 1907)
  As Chief of Naval Personnel shortly after World War II, was involved in a delay of Bieri's promotion to vice admiral, 115-116; reported that the President wouldn't approve a flag selection board right after World War II because it didn't have reserve officers on it, 193-194

James, Rear Admiral Jules, USN (USNA, 1908)
  Served as Commander U.S. Naval Forces Mediterranean shortly after World War II, 202-203, 206, 216

Japan
  U.S. Navy cryptography work in the 1920s on Japanese codes, 64-65; planning in late 1943 for the use of Army Air Forces B-29 bombers against Japanese-held territory, 132-134, 148-149; disagreement among U.S. planners in 1945 over whether the Allies would have to invade Japan, 165-166

Joint Chiefs of Staff
  Dragged their feet in 1942 on planning for the craft needed for amphibious assaults, 98-99; sometimes put up with amateurish schemes from Churchill and Roosevelt during World War II, 103-105; met with other Allied leaders at the Cairo conference in late 1943 to plan war strategy, 123-134, 246; deference toward General Douglas MacArthur during World War II, 134-138; views in 1945 about the need to invade Japan, 165; meetings during World War II as part of the Combined Chiefs of Staff, 176-178

Kennedy, Captain John A., USNR
Newspaper publisher who printed critical material about the Navy and venereal disease in the <u>San Diego Journal</u> in the late 1940s, 231-233

King, Fleet Admiral Ernest J., USN (USNA, 1901)
Assembling of a staff after taking over as Commander in Chief U.S. Fleet in December 1941, 92-94, 242-243; sent Bieri as a representative to Eisenhower in the planning and execution of the North Africa invasion in 1942, 108-114; in early 1943 or the summer of 1944 denied Bieri's request for duty in the Pacific, 123, 166, 256; at the Cairo planning conference in late 1943, 128-130, 246; was respectful toward General Douglas MacArthur in World War II but declined to give him command over the Pacific Fleet, 134-137; sent Bieri to London in early 1944 in connection with the upcoming invasion of France, 141-145, 162-163; view in 1945 about the need to invade Japan, 165; directive early in World War II about yeomen on the staff, 169-170; visited Admiral J. O. Richardson shortly before he was relieved as CinCUS in 1941, 174-175, 257; personal relationship with Bieri, 175-176, 248-250, 252-253; directed Bieri to make a study on the Navy Department moving to the new Pentagon building, 186-187; involvement in Navy public relations in World War II, 188; concern with ASW at the outset of World War II, 243-244; lived on board the yacht <u>Dauntless</u> (PG-61) at the Washington Navy Yard during World War II, 246-247; abstained from liquor during the war, 247-248; fired subordinates who didn't perform, 251; family of, 253; gave medals sparingly during World War II, 254-255; introduced gray uniforms during World War II, 256-257

Kirk, Rear Admiral Alan G., USN (USNA, 1909)
Commanded the western naval task force for the invasion of Normandy in the spring of 1944, 144, 146, 152, 155

Knox, Frank
As Secretary of the Navy in 1940, made a visit to the fleet that gave him too much confidence about the U.S. Navy's ability to deal with Japan, 84-85

Leonard, Captain John C., USN (USNA, 1882)
Had a poor background for serving as commanding officer of the battleship <u>Virginia</u> (BB-13) in the 1910s, 20-21

<u>**Lexington**</u>**, USS (CV-2)**
Operations at sea in the Pacific in the period around the Japanese attack on Pearl Harbor in December 1941, 88-90

Littlefield, Captain William L., USN (USNA, 1896)
Martinet who was commanding officer of the battleship <u>Utah</u> (BB-31) in the late 1920s, 68

Logistics
Support for U.S. Navy ships operating in the Mediterranean in the immediate post-World War II period, 214-215

MacArthur, General Douglas, USA (USMA, 1903)
Unsuccessful in getting his proposal for the invasion of Rabaul approved at the Cairo planning conference in late 1943, 125-127; stayed in power during World War II because he had considerable clout, 134-138; didn't receive the naval support he wanted during the fall of the Philippines in 1942, 137; command arrangements in his Southwest Pacific theater in World War II, 147-148; view in 1945 about the need to invade Japan, 165

Manhattan Project
Information on the development of atomic bombs was tightly held during World War II, 167-169, 171, 173, 179

Mare Island Navy Yard, Vallejo, California
Installed sonic range finders in the destroyers Corry (DD-334) and Hull (DD-330) in the early 1920s, 46, 48

Marshall, General George C., USA
Involvement in 1942 in the planning for transports and landing craft needed for upcoming amphibious operations, 98-99

Martin, Lieutenant Commander Frank C., USN (USNA, 1902)
Was serving as navigator of the battleship Texas (BB-35) when she ran aground on Block Island in 1917, 26-28; stationed in Hawaii in the years just before World War II, 60-61

Martin, Major General Frederick L., USA
As a major, was involved in an Army Air Service around-the-world flight in 1924, 57

Matthews, Francis P.
As Secretary of the Navy around 1950 had questions about a particular flag selection board, 196

McDonald, Captain John D., USN (USNA, 1884)
Capable officer who commanded the battleship Virginia (BB-13) from 1911 to 1913, 20

Mediterranean Sea
In 1945-46 the U.S. Navy shut down many of the support bases it had established in the Mediterranean area during World War II, 203-204, 219; fleet operations by U.S. Navy ships in the Med in 1946-47, 205-211, 214-215, 220-229; history of U.S. Navy operations in the Med, going back to the 19th century, 206-208; U.S. disposal of PT boats to Mediterranean nations, 213-214

Merchant Ships
During the early part of World War I, the battleship Texas (BB-35) was in the York River and Chesapeake Bay to train gun crews for merchant ships, 25-26; use of in

Europe in 1918, 30; conversion of to use as amphibious transports during World War II, 97-98; use of the fast British Cunard liners as troop transports in World War II, 100; the port of Algiers, Algeria, was filled with damaged merchant ships after the Allied landings there in late 1942, 121-122

Merring, Midshipman Harry L., USN (USNA, 1911)
Took part in sail training at the Naval Academy in 1907, 7-8

Mexico
The battleship Virginia (BB-13) operated off Tampico and Vera Cruz during a period of government unrest in 1913-14, 22-23; landing at Vera Cruz in April 1914, 23-24; the cruiser Tacoma (CL-20) grounded at Vera Cruz in January 1924, 54-55; accusation in the late 1940s about Navy men catching venereal disease in Mexico, 231-232

Moore, Major General Bryant E., USA
Stationed with troops near the Italy-Yugoslavia border shortly after World War II, 205, 220, 226

Morocco
Planning for the Allied invasion at Casablanca in November 1942, 108-113; British Admiral Andrew Cunningham was interested in information on the progress of the landings, 119-120

Mountbatten, Admiral Louis, RN
Presented the strategic concerns of the Southeast Asia Theater at the Cairo Conference in late 1943, 125-127

Naples, Italy
In 1946 the U.S. Navy closed down its shore base in the area, 204-205; housing for U.S. naval personnel who supported the fleet, 215-218

Nashville, USS (PG-7)
Small complement of officers in 1912, 15-16; represented U.S. interests in Santo Domingo, 16-19

Naval Academy, Annapolis, Maryland
Instruction in swimming in 1907, 6; academics, 6-7; sail training in the square rigger Severn, 7-8; summer training cruises, 8; members of the class of 1911 who made flag rank, 9-11

Naval Reserve
President Harry Truman wouldn't approve a flag selection board right after World War II because it didn't have reserve officers on it, 193-194

Naval War College, Newport, Rhode Island
Program of study in the mid-1930s, 76-77; future leaders of World War II were there at the time, 76-78

News Media
   The San Diego Journal published critical material about the Navy and venereal disease in the late 1940s, 231-233

Newton, Rear Admiral John H., USN (USNA, 1905)
   As a cruiser division commander, was on board the USS Chicago (CA-29) for a trip to Australia and New Zealand in 1941, 86-88; cruiser operations at sea around the time the Japanese attacked Pearl Harbor in December 1941, 88-90

New York Navy Yard, Brooklyn, New York
   Served as the home yard for the battleship Texas (BB-35) in the late 1910s, including repairs after she grounded in 1917, 26-28, 34; provided quarters for Bieri, 1949-51, when he was serving at the United Nations, 235-236

Nimitz, Fleet Admiral Chester W., USN (USNA, 1905)
   Relationships with Bieri over the years, 189-190, 203-204; highly admired in the fleet, 190-191; had a tour of service at the United Nations from 1949 to 1951, 236-237

Normandy
   Planning for the Allied invasion of France in June 1944, 141-147, 152-154; conduct of the invasion itself, 155-158; conditions ashore in the aftermath, 157-158, 163-164

North Africa
   See Algeria, Morocco, and Tunisia

Oran, Algeria
   Dispute concerning the planned use of Coast Guard cutters during the invasion of Oran in November 1942, 110-113

Patton, Major General George S., Jr., USA (USMA, 1909)
   Role in the Allied invasion of Casablanca, Morocco, in November 1942, 108-109, 119-120, 152

Pearl Harbor
   Development of plans in 1941 to defend the fleet against air attack, 85-86

Pentagon
   Late in World War II, Admiral Ernest J. King directed Bieri to make a study of the Navy Department moving to the Pentagon, 186

Peru
   The United States sent a delegation to Peru in July 1921 to observe that nation's centennial of independence, 36-38; U.S. naval mission to Peru, 38-39

Philippine Islands
General Douglas MacArthur didn't get the support he requested from the Navy as the islands were falling in 1942, 137

Planning
Development of plans in 1941 to defend the fleet at Pearl Harbor against air attack, 85-86; joint Army-Navy work in procuring transports and landing craft for amphibious assaults in World War II, 96-99; for the Allied invasion of Europe, 100-101; the Joint Chiefs of Staff sometimes put up with amateurish schemes from Churchill and Roosevelt during World War II, 103-105; for the North Africa invasion of November 1942, 108-113; top Allied officials met at the Cairo conference in late 1943 to plan war strategy, 123-134; in London in early 1944 for the upcoming invasion of France, 141-147, 152-154; British planning in 1944 for the postwar world, 145, 162; disagreement among U.S. planners in 1945 over whether the Allies would have to invade Japan, 165-166; plans made during World War II for the unification of the U.S. armed services after the war, 186-188

Pope Pius XII
Hosted a visit from Admiral and Mrs. Bieri shortly after World War II, 223-224

Promotion of Officers
After World War II, Bieri was slow in being promoted to vice admiral because of an incorrect perception of actions he had taken at the time of the North Africa invasion in 1942, 115-116; selection boards were reinstated shortly after World War II to pick naval officers for promotion to higher rank, 191-194; after the war, selection boards had to pick more specialists than previously, 194-199

PT Boats
Disposal of surplus U.S. boats to Mediterranean nations in the immediate aftermath of World War II, 213-214, 219-220

Public Relations
During World War II, the Navy had programs to recognize the contributions that defense contractors made to the war effort, 139-140, 188; Bieri's contacts with the public while serving as commandant of the 11th Naval District at San Diego in the late 1940s, 230-231

Rabaul, New Britain
General Douglas MacArthur was unsuccessful in getting his proposal for the invasion of Rabaul approved at the Cairo planning conference in late 1943, 125-127

Radio
Development of high-frequency transmitters by the Navy in the 1920s, 62-63; use of facsimile machines in the 1920s, 67

Ramsay, Admiral Bertram H., RN
Involved in the planning for the Allied invasion of North Africa in November 1942, 106, 110-113; had a stiff personality, 110, 117-119; as Allied naval commander for the invasion of France in the spring of 1944, 141, 143-147, 149, 151-152, 158-161

Recruiting
As a result of the demobilization at the end of World War I, ships had to do their own recruiting, 34

Richardson, Admiral James O., USN (USNA, 1902)
As Commander Battle Force and CinCUS, 1939-41, was a forceful and able officer, 81-83; disagreed with President Franklin Roosevelt about basing the battleships at Pearl Harbor, 83; relieved as CinCUS in 1941, 84-85; had a visit from Admiral Ernest King, probably in early 1941, 174-175, 257

Rodman, Rear Admiral Hugh, USN (USNA, 1880)
Commanded the U.S. battleship division that served with the Royal Navy in World War I, 26, 30; served as Commandant of the Fifth Naval District in the early 1920s, 36-38, 40-41; was part of a U.S. delegation to Peru in July 1921, 36-38

Ronarc'h, Rear Admiral Pierre, French Navy
Commanded the French naval contingent at Algiers, Algeria, shortly after World War II, 212, 225

Roosevelt, President Franklin D.
Was quite interested in the Navy when he took office as President in 1933, 75-76; directed the relief of Admiral J. O. Richardson as CinCUS in 1941, 83; met with Allied leaders at the Cairo conference in late 1943 to plan war strategy, 123-124, 130; agreed at the Yalta Conference in February 1945 to give war materials to the Soviets, 180

Royal Navy
The Texas (BB-35) was among the five American battleships that served as part of Britain's Grand Fleet in 1918, 26, 29-32; Thanksgiving celebration following the Armistice in November 1918, 32-33; ships were stationed off Mexico in 1914 when World War I broke out, 39-40; a British mine layer took a party of staff officers from Gibraltar to Casablanca for a progress report on the invasion there in November 1942, 119-120; efforts at the Cairo planning conference in late 1943 to gain a role in the Pacific, 128-129, 246; command relationships with U.S. warships in World War I, 150; command relationships in World War II, 150-152; service in the Pacific toward the end of World War II, 189; role in the Mediterranean Sea in the immediate post-World War II period, 211-212, 215, 226

Salvage
Refloating of the battleship Texas (BB-35) after she ran aground on Block Island in 1917, 27-28; work on damaged merchant ships at Algiers following the Allied landings there in late 1942, 121-123, 151

Santo Domingo
In 1912-13 the gunboat Nashville (PG-7) was sent to the country to represent U.S. interests, 16-19

Scotland
U.S. battleships were based at Scapa Flow and the Firth of Forth in 1918 while supporting the British Grand Fleet in World War I, 30-32

Security
Information on the development of atomic bombs was tightly held during World War II, 167-169, 171, 173; people were granted access to information during the war only if they needed it, 171-174

Selection Boards
Reinstated shortly after World War II to pick naval officers for promotion to higher rank, 191-194; after the war, selection boards had to pick more specialists than previously, 194-199

Severn, USS
Square-rigger used for sail training at the Naval Academy in 1907, 7-8

Sherman, Vice Admiral Forrest P., USN (USNA, 1918)
As DCNO (Operations) shortly after World War II worked with the State Department to coordinate U.S. policy in the Mediterranean, 210; took command of U.S. naval forces in the Mediterranean in 1948, 228-229; as Chief of Naval Operations in the late 1940s, 233

Shore Bombardment
U.S. concern about inadequate plans for gunfire support of the Allied invasion of France in the spring of 1944, 141-142; during the invasion itself, 155-156

Smith, General Walter Bedell, USA
Service as General Dwight Eisenhower's chief of staff during World War II, 142, 146-147, 158-161; as director of the Central Intelligence Agency in the early 1950s, 237-238

Sontag, Dr. Raymond
University of California history professor who took leave to spend time on the National Board of Estimates in the early 1950s, 238, 240

Soviet Union
At the Yalta Conference in February 1945 the United States agreed to furnish ships and equipment to the Soviet Union, 179-180, 182-185

Stark, Admiral Harold R., USN (USNA, 1903)
As Commander U.S. Naval Forces Europe, was involved in the planning for the invasion of North Africa in November 1942, 110-113; involved in the planning for the

invasion of France in the spring of 1944, 152-154, 163; didn't really have much of a substantive role in London, 154-155

Strategy
Top Allied officials met at the Cairo conference in late 1943 to plan war strategy, 123-134

Surveying
The destroyers Corry (DD-334) and Hull (DD-330) did survey work in the 1920s with early models of sonic range finders, 47-48, 55-61

Sutherland, Major General Richard K., USA
As General Douglas MacArthur's chief of staff, in 1943 pushed a plan for the invasion of Rabaul, 125-127

Swimming
Taught at the Naval Academy in 1907, 6

Tacoma, USS (CL-20)
Grounded at Vera Cruz, Mexico, in January 1924, 54-55

Taylor, Dr. A. Hoyt
Work for the Naval Research Laboratory in the 1920s on the development of high-frequency radio transmitters, radar, and sonar, 62-63

Tenth Fleet
Operations in early 1946 in the South Atlantic, 201-203

Texas, USS (BB-35)
During the early part of World War II, was in the York River and Chesapeake Bay to train gun crews for merchant ships, 25-26; ran aground on Block Island in September 1917, 27; salvage and repair, 27-28; ran into heavy weather while en route to Europe, 29-30; served in 1918 with Britain's Grand Fleet, 29-32; Thanksgiving celebration in 1918, 32-33; return to New York in December 1918, 33-34; dismal postwar recruiting, 34; ran aground in the late 1920s, 69; operations in the early 1930s while serving as fleet flagship, 70

Training
Swimming was taught at the Naval Academy in 1907, 6; the square rigger Severn was used for sail training of midshipmen at the Naval Academy in 1907, 7-8; Naval Academy summer cruises around 1910, 8; during the early part of World War I, the battleship Texas (BB-35) was in the York River and Chesapeake Bay to train gun crews for merchant ships, 25-26

Troubridge, Rear Admiral Thomas, RN
 Commanded a task force for the Allied landing at Oran, Algeria, in November 1942, 113; present at the Cairo conference of late 1943 in connection with plans for Southeast Asia, 126-127

Tunisia
 Received a goodwill visit by U.S. Navy ships shortly after World War II, 223-224

Turkey
 Visited shortly after World War II by the small U.S. naval presence in the Mediterranean, 209, 221

Turner, Rear Admiral Richmond K., USN (USNA, 1908)
 Served on the faculty of the Naval War College in the late 1930s, 77-78; arranged for Bieri to join the U.S. Fleet staff in early 1942, 93; was involved in some joint planning work with the Army before going to sea in mid-1942, 94-96, 100-101, 242

Unification
 Plans made during World War II for the merging of the services after the war, 186-188

Uniforms-Naval
 Admiral E. J. King introduced gray uniforms during World War II, 256-257

United Nations
 Bieri's role from 1949 to 1951 as Joint Chiefs of Staff representative, 233-237

Utah, USS (BB-31)
 Unhappy ship in the late 1920s with poor officers and martinets as skipper and exec, 68-69

Vardaman, Commodore James K., Jr., USNR
 As naval aide to the President shortly after World War II, was involved in a delay of Bieri's promotion to vice admiral, 115-116

Venereal Disease
 The San Diego Journal published critical material about the Navy and venereal disease in the late 1940s, 231-233

Vera Cruz, Mexico
 The battleship Virginia (BB-13) operated off Tampico and Vera Cruz during a period of government unrest in 1913-14, 22-23; landing at Vera Cruz in April 1914, 23-24; the cruiser Tacoma (CL-20) grounded at Vera Cruz in January 1924, 54-55

Virginia, USS (BB-13)
 Had an unusual arrangement of gun turrets, 8-inch on top of 12-inch, 19-20; discussion of commanding officers, 1913-16, 20-21; operated off Tampico and Vera Cruz,

Mexico, in 1913-14, 22-23, 39-40; support of the U.S. landing at Vera Cruz in 1914, 23-24; based at the Boston Navy Yard, 23-24; placed in reserve in 1916, 24

Von Heimburg, Lieutenant Ernest H., USN (USNA, 1919)
Was executive officer and navigator of the destroyer Corry (DD-334) during a difficult cruise to Alaska in 1924, 58-59

Weather
The battleship Texas (BB-35) ran into heavy seas while en route to Europe for service with the British Grand Fleet in 1918, 29-30; the transport Henderson (AP-1) collided with a destroyer while operating in the fog near Seattle in the summer of 1923, 50-51

Wedemeyer, Colonel Albert C., USA (USMA, 1919)
In early 1942 put forth an overly optimistic plan for the Allied invasion of Europe, 100-101

Women
Use of WAVES in the CominCh headquarters in Washington in World War II, 169-170

World War I
During the early part of the war, the battleship Texas (BB-35) was in the York River and Chesapeake Bay to train gun crews for merchant ships, 25-26; the Texas served in 1918 with Britain's Grand Fleet, 29-32; as a result of the rapid demobilization at the end of the war, ships had to do their own recruiting, 34; German and British ships were stationed off Mexico in 1914 when the war broke out, 39-40; command arrangements with the British during the war, 150

Yalta Conference
Held in the Crimea in February 1945, it dictated, among other things, that the U.S. Navy had to turn over ships and other war materials to the Soviets, 179-180, 182-185

Yugoslavia
Unrest in 1946 on the Italy-Yugoslavia border, 205, 210, 220

www.ingramcontent.com/pod-product-compliance
Lightning Source LLC
Chambersburg PA
CBHW080616170426
43209CB00007B/1443